from Babette
love, Xmas 1586

Russian
Journal

Andrea Lee

Russian
Journal

Vintage Books
A Division of Random House
New York

First Vintage Books Edition, February 1984
Copyright © 1979, 1980, 1981, by Andrea Lee
All rights reserved under International and Pan-American
Copyright Conventions. Published in the United States by
Random House, Inc., New York, and simultaneously
in Canada by Random House of Canada Limited, Toronto.
Originally published by Random House, Inc. in 1981

Selections from this work previously appeared in
The Boston Phoenix, The New York Times Magazine,
and *The New Yorker.*

Library of Congress Cataloging in Publication Data
Lee, Andrea, 1953–
Russian journal.
1. Soviet Union—Social life and customs—1970–
2. Soviet Union—Social conditions—1970–
I. Title.
[DK276.L37 1984]   947.085′3   82-40035
ISBN 0-394-71127-0 (pbk.)

Manufactured in the United States of America

For Edith, Lloyd and Alan,
and especially
for Tom

Foreword

Half of the entries in this journal were written during my ten months of life in Russia, in 1978–79, and half were composed later, in America, from notes and fragments jotted down at the time. As I look over the book now, I see that it does not begin to reflect the scope of the experience I lived through in that complex, beautiful, and troubling country. In collection, the entries are like a set of photographs taken by an amateur who is drawn to his subjects by instinct and capricious inclination: I wrote about only what pleased and excited me, leaving many important subjects unexplored. I have to beg the forgiveness of the reader for this, as well as for any factual errors, or naïveté of observation.

I came to Russia with my husband, Tom—then a Harvard doctoral candidate in Russian history—as part of a government-sponsored exchange of scholars. At the time I was also a graduate student at Harvard, in English. Neither Tom nor I had in our backgrounds any link with Russia, but for almost all of our lives, both of us had felt an irresistible attraction to that country. Throughout a childhood filled with books, I explored Russian folklore and literature, and the characters I encountered there—whether the hag Baba Yaga or Anna Arkadeyevna Karenina—remained with me as few others have done. When we arrived in Moscow, Tom already spoke near-native Russian, as the result of years of study and a previous summer in Leningrad; I had to rely on a far slighter knowledge of Russian strengthened only by a good ear for language—a combination that allowed me to carry on conversations from the beginning of our stay, and to gain quick fluency.

The fact that we both spoke Russian and were allowed to live among Russian students—for eight months in Moscow State University and two months at Leningrad State—made it easy for us to make a number of Russian friends from outside the restricted circles normally accessible to foreigners. Since we lived on rubles, stood in queues, and rode the metro with ordinary Russians, we got a view of life in Moscow and Leningrad that was very different from that of the diplomats and journalists we knew, who drove cars, lived in isolated foreign "ghettoes," and shopped in well-equipped foreign-currency stores. The fact that we were young (we were both twenty-five) made meeting people still easier: most young Russians, even the politically orthodox, have a devouring curiosity about Westerners their age. For reasons that are obvious, I have changed the names, and in some cases, the appearances, of the Russians I describe here, with the exception of the journalist Victor Louis and the composer Tikhon Khrennikov.

I wrote many of these pages sitting in the musty chill of a reading room in the Lenin Library of Moscow, as Soviet and foreign academicians studied texts all around me. Very often I would stare out the window at the domes of the Kremlin cathedrals and then glance at the research in progress at other desks, thinking how comical it was that I, a foreigner who had never studied the Soviet Union, should sit here in a forest of scholars and write descriptions of shops and apartments and the person I'd drunk tea with the day before. Frequently, the journal seemed to me to be trivial busywork. But now, returned to life in another dimension, in a country on the other side of the looking-glass, I find that many of these modest sketches speak the truth of our Russian experience in the kind of small, accurate voice that too often grows blurred or grandiose if preserved in memory alone. I don't pretend—nor did I ever expect—that this journal might explain the character of a political system, or a people. Each entry presents a small piece of Russian reality as seen by an American whose vision, if not refined by study, was at least not much distorted by prejudice for or against Communism. If, as sometimes happens, the separate parts of *Russian Journal* combine in the imagination of the reader to give an impression of a broader scene, it is important to realize that this is still largely a personal landscape—my own and my husband's. The Russia of other sojourners might be quite different.

Russian
Journal

Arrival

The tower in which we will live for most of the next ten months is one of the landmarks of Moscow, an absurd thirty-two-story wedding cake of gray and red granite, set above the city in the Lenin Hills. This titanic building, the main dormitory of Moscow State University, is a monument of the pompous and energetic style of architecture nicknamed "Stalin Gothic." Seen from a distance, it suggests a Disney version of a ziggurat; its central spire, like the Kremlin towers, holds a blinking red star. Inside, as in a medieval fortress, there is everything necessary to sustain life in case of siege: bakeries, dairy store, a fruit and vegetable store, a pharmacy, a post office, magazine kiosks, a watch-repair stand—all this in addition to classrooms, and student rooms, and cafeterias. On the outside, it bristles with a daft excess of decoration that is a strange twentieth-century mixture of Babylonian, Corinthian, and Slavic: there are outsized bronze flags and statues, faïence curlicues, wrought-iron sconces—even a vast reflecting pool decorated with metal water lilies the size of small cabbages. As I climb the endless stairs and negotiate the labyrinth of fusty-smelling hallways, I feel dwarfed and apprehensive, a human being lost in a palace scaled for giants.

I came to this odd new home with my husband on a summer evening two days ago, when exhaustion from long-distance travel gave every new sight the mysterious simplicity and resonance of a dream. I had my first glimpse of the Soviet Union as we broke through a cloud barrier near Sheremetyevo Airport, and found ourselves flying low over a forest of birch and evergreen, dotted with countless small ponds. There was an almost magical lushness and secrecy about this flattish northern landscape that I found powerfully attractive; suddenly I remembered that my earliest visions of Russia were of an infinite forest, dark as any forest that stretches through a child's imagination, and peopled by swan maidens, hunter princes, fabulous bears, and witches who lived in huts set on chicken legs. Tied to Russia by no claims of blood or tradition, I still felt, while very young, an obscure attraction to this country that I knew only from its violent, highly colored folklore; its music, through which ran a similar vein of extravagance; and the dark political comments of adults. It seemed to me to be a mysterious counterweight to the known world of America—a country, like the land at the back of the north wind, in which life ran backward and the fantastic was commonplace.

Our disembarkment and passage through customs at Sheremetyevo were standard chaos, involving a long, dazed wait in a crowded room traversed from time to time by hot breezes smelling sweetly of cut grass. Only one memory remains with me from those hours: the sight of a Pioneer * excursion group of twenty small girls who seemed, by their Asiatic faces and straight black hair, to be Siberian. They all wore the blue shorts, white shirts, and red neckerchiefs that I had seen in pictures, as well as ornately curled hair bows that gave them a queer geisha look, and as I studied them with the dreamy precision of fatigue, all twenty stared back at me with an avid, unadorned curiosity. Standing beyond the customs barrier was a young man who introduced himself in English as Grigorii, a journalism student sent to meet us by the university's office of foreign affairs. Grigorii was a dark-haired young man in his twenties, with very small eyes behind enormous round glasses and a pinched, rather gnomish body in a large, baggy suit; the impression he gave was that he had melted down slightly inside his clothing. He led us outside to a black Volga, a Soviet car that looks like a cross between a Rambler and a Plymouth. A short-legged driver, wearing a checked cap pulled down very far over his

*The Communist Party organization for children.

ears, stowed our bags, and soon we were speeding down a road with the vaguely horrifying sense of freedom one feels only when going through absolutely strange territory in a strange car. It was dark by now, and the smell of fields and forest rushed in through the windows Grigorii had discovered that we both spoke Russian, and had grown garrulous. "So you are a student of Russian history?" he was saying to Tom. "I myself am extremely interested in American history—especially in your Civil War. Two years ago I even wrote a paper on the Great Barbecue."

"The what?" asked Tom.

"The Great Barbecue—the turning point of the Reconstruction period. Don't tell me you haven't heard of it!" (Grigorii pronounced the word "barbecue" with the gleeful relish of a Frenchman saying "Marlboro.")

"I haven't," said Tom, and as the car slid through the darkness, Grigorii illuminated for us this lost part of American history, mentioning feudal remnants, the industrial bourgeoisie, and the struggle of the working class. Listening to his small, dry, pedantic voice mention names and places I'd never heard of, I wondered what Marxist looking-glass we'd stepped through. Where on earth were we? Was he talking about the same America we had just left?

When the monstrous silhouette of the university tower appeared on the skyline, Grigorii paused to point it out proudly. "Impressive, isn't it?" he said. "It's the most luxurious dormitory in the Soviet Union—every year hundreds of tourists come to visit it. It's a city block in circumference; some other time I will give you the figures on its height and number of windows. I'm sorry that we won't be passing the reflecting pool tonight, but there is a very handsome giant barometer that I will show you. I feel very lucky to live there. We'll be neighbors, so to speak!"

"Hurrah!" I whispered to Tom, and he dug his elbow into my ribs. Then we sat silently as the black tower grew larger against the sky.

Our arrival meant passing through a gatehouse, climbing a great many stairs, crossing a chilly marble hall, and threading through a maze of corridors on a path that led at last to a long ride in an elevator, and some kind of fuss with an old woman over a key. Although it was only about nine o'clock in the evening, a charmed stillness seemed to reign in the dormitory; we saw very few students. Instead, there seemed to be inordinate numbers of *babushki* —old women—in semi-official posts, knitting and nodding in dark corners like watchful beldames out of a Grimms tale. The *babushka* of the keys, a tiny creature with a fierce squint under a cowled white shawl, watched us struggle with the door to our room and then turned to whisper portentously to a still smaller companion, "*Ischo Amerikantsy.*"—More Americans.

When Grigorii left us, we flicked a switch, and in the sudden bright light, faced our living quarters for the year. They were what Russians call a *blok*—a minute suite consisting of two rooms about six feet by ten feet each, a tiny entryway, and a pair of cubicles containing, between them, a toilet, a shower and washstand, and several large, indolent cockroaches. The two main rooms were painted the dispiriting beige and green of institutional rooms around the world, and furnished, rather nicely, with varnished chairs, tables, bookcases, and two single beds. (I've since discovered that our rooms represent great luxury, since Russian students in the same building often live four and six to such quarters.) Each room held a radio that tuned in to only one station—Radio Moscow—and at this particular moment, news was being broadcast by a woman with an excited, throaty voice. "Today," she said, "the Party Government delegation of the Democratic Republic of Vietnam, led by Comrades Le Duan and Pham Van Dong visited the Kirovsky factory in Leningrad . . . In front of the monument to V. I. Lenin in Factory Square, there took place a meeting of Soviet-Vietnamese friendship . . . The Leningraders arrived at the meeting with flowers, red flags, and signs in honor of the unbreakable friendship . . . The people gathering together greeted the emissaries of the heroic Vietnamese people with warm applause . . ."

The news went off, and on came a medley of Komsomol songs delivered stalwartly by what sounded like an entire nation of ruddy-cheeked young patriots. "You can't turn this thing off," said

Tom, fiddling with the radio knob. Indeed, like one of Orwell's telescreens, our official radios could be turned down to inaudible, but never turned off. I began to giggle hysterically, and to calm myself, walked over to the window, from which I could see, illuminated by a spotlight on one of the pediments of the building, a gigantic bronze flag.

A bit later, in one of the fits of witless energy that sometimes replace exhaustion, we decided to take the metro into Red Square. Everyone describes the Moscow subway system, so I won't, except to say that it is as clean and efficient as they write, and that it is awesome, for an American, to see the veins of a city lined with marble, gilt, and mosaic instead of filth and graffiti. It was in the subway that night that I first endured the unblinking stare of the Russian populace, a stare already described to me by Tom and by friends who had been in the Soviet Union before. "You will never not be stared at," they told me, advising me to stare back coolly and steadily, especially at the shoes of my tormentors, since the average Soviet shoe is an embarrassment of cracked imitation leather. When we got on at the University metro stop, the scant group of passengers included two minute, humpbacked *babushki*; a pretty fresh-faced girl of eighteen or nineteen, who opened her mouth to yawn and revealed two aluminum teeth; a fat young mother in a minidress and platform shoes, who held a baby tightly swaddled in a ribbon-bound blanket; a group of stylish young men dressed in greasy American jeans and vinyl snap-front jackets. They all looked us up and down with undisguised fascination and whispered comments to their neighbors. Although we were dressed in what we thought was a neutral, inconspicuous fashion, the clothes we had on—cotton pants and shirts—now seemed infinitely newer, crisper, better cut than anything anyone else had on; my sandals, also, seemed to fascinate everyone. So we sat, practically riddled with stares, in the dim light of the rocking subway car, breathing an atmosphere heavy with odors of sharp tobacco, sausage, and perspiring human flesh. Tom drew a deep, happy breath. "It still smells like Russia," he said.

We got off at the Lenin Library stop, and walked up the street to Red Square. My first view of that expanse of architectural marvels—the rolling red brick walls of the Kremlin, with the angular mass of Lenin's tomb directly beneath them; the Victorian birdcage that is GUM, Moscow's largest department store; and, at the far end, St. Basil's, the preposterous, sublime fantasy in cartoon color and buoyant plaster—made me reflect a bit enviously that whatever deficiencies there may have been in freedom and economic well-being throughout Russian and Soviet history, the people have always had compelling symbols. I have often found in myself a surprising, childish hunger for patriotic pageantry. How easy it would be, I thought, to summon up a blind surge of chauvinism if one could draw upon this vision—the sacred enclosure of Red Square, where Lenin lies preserved like a Pharaoh. Except, perhaps, for the Statue of Liberty against the steep rise of lower Manhattan, there is no emblematic scene in America with comparable drama. Facing the Kremlin, I realized for the first time how unfailingly chaste and low-key are America's national icons; it is at once our weakness and our great strength to be bad at symbols. Our emblems seem designed for the measured response of rationality, while Russian monuments—like the Stalinist monstrosity where I am to live—evoke raw emotion.

It was a warm, humid night, and small groups of Soviet and foreign tourists were roaming the square. When we stopped to see the goose-stepping soldiers change the guard in front of Lenin's tomb, we found that we were standing in the midst of a group of men from Soviet Uzbekistan. Brown-faced, wearing embroidered skullcaps and long quilted coats, they stared in mild amazement at this spectacle that must have seemed as alien to them as it did to us. Behind us, *babushki* in black dresses and shawls were sweeping up cigarette butts from the cobblestones.

Later we walked over to have a glass of *gaserevenaya vada*, carbonated water flavored with fruit syrup, from one of the dispensers that apparently take the place of drinking fountains in Moscow. For two kopecks, a glass is filled with the fizzy drink; one swallows it, and then replaces the glass, to be washed by a cold spray of water for the next drinker's use. (Hearing the amount of coughing around me even in August made me decide already that I wouldn't make a habit of this.) We didn't have the two kopecks for the machine, so we asked a passer-by, a tall, mournful-looking man wearing creased dark pants and a bright nylon shirt. He gave us a whole handful of change, and refused our ruble. "You're Americans, aren't you?" he asked us in a low voice, tugging glumly at the ends of a dandyish mustache. "Then keep the ruble. I can't do anything with it. It's not money. They tell me it's money, but look in our stores and tell me what I can buy with it. Nothing!" He spat on the ground and vanished up the street.

We took the metro back to the University stop, then walked up toward the dormitory along an avenue lined with apple trees. We passed through the tiny gatehouse in which the old woman who was supposed to check our identification was sleeping, her face a puckered mass of wrinkles, her feet resting on a rag rug where an equally ancient dog slumbered. In the courtyard was a clump of trees, and from this small grove came strains of guitar music and laughter. A girl's voice sang snatches of "Makhno," the poignant song from the Russian Civil War that I had heard once back in America; in her thin, tipsy soprano, however, the song sounded merry rather than sad, the voice of any student when there are still some drinks left and some time left in the evening and in the summer. Outside the grove, in the stone courtyard itself, a teenage boy and girl were chasing each other around and around, in and out of the light of the big iron lamps. They were clearly Russian, but both were dressed in jeans. When the boy neared the girl, he would try to grab her, but she dodged him each time with a shriek of laughter, her long braid streaming behind her. Their voices and footsteps echoed, faint but definite, against the walls of that monstrous folly of a building, as if they were light-heartedly defying a hostile authority. Watching them, I felt disarmed and curiously moved; I realized as well that nothing this year would be predictable or easy to fathom. In a few minutes we were climbing the steps to our own small space, and our first night in the tower.

Grigorii

We've overcome our initial confusion by indulging the stodgy Protestant tendency to form a routine under the most chaotic circumstances. It's amazing how many surprises, risks, and adventures one can undergo with a noble serenity of spirit as long as one knows one will sleep and eat at regular times. We get up around seven each morning to the sound of the exercise program on Radio Moscow: a stentorian female voice saying "Raise your arms! Bend over! Straighten! Now march! One! Two! Three! Four!" while piano music thumps in the background. The weather on these mornings is warm and sunny, with limpid blue skies brushed with a few cirrus and the air filled with the fresh smell of the woods around the university. I know from experience that by noon the sky will cloud up and sprinkle us with fitful thundershowers all afternoon until six or so, when it blooms suddenly into sunset. Leaning precariously out of my window, I can just see the university track, where male students are jogging in flimsy blue sweatsuits. (The fall semester hasn't yet begun, but the dormitory is still nearly full of students who have returned early, or who are participating in an interim course.) Later, around eight o'clock, the grass near the track will be filled with girls, in the same types of sweatsuits, who are attending a mandatory exercise class. All plump, their faces still flushed and creased with sleepiness, they giggle helplessly with their friends about the impossibility of curl-ups and leg lifts demonstrated by an impatient man with a frostbite-scarred face, who shouts, "Now, girls! Attention!" Tom, jogging before breakfast, saw another type of exercise: each girl had to pretend to pull out a pin with her teeth and lob a dummy grenade over the green field near the university orchard.

In spite of all this exertion, the average Russian is fatter than I would have believed possible, with a dense, compact heftiness made for asserting itself in subway crowds. The reason for this is clear when we descend to the cafeteria, a high-ceilinged room of a dismal apricot color, filled with spotted black Formica tables and dozens of sleepy students. The breakfast menu (it never changes) reads: *kasha* (meaning any kind of stewed grain; this is a sort of cream of wheat) with butter. *Kefir* (a fermented milk drink) with or without sugar. Beef with potatoes. Chopped beef with potatoes. Ground beef with fried egg and potatoes. Bread. Tea with sugar. The menu is printed on a blurry sheet posted outside two little wooden cashiers' booths; one stands in line to pay the cashier, and then takes one's slip to the serving line where a horde of students clutching greasy trays wait to be served by six or seven irritable, slatternly women wearing stained aprons and white gauze turbans. Elsewhere in the cafeteria are small "buffets" which sell breakfast alternatives: dried-out sandwiches of sausage, cheese, or fish; jellied meat; hard-boiled eggs; lethal-looking cookies with a dollop of ancient whipped cream on top. After an initial revolt, our stomachs have become ironclad, and we can down any of this with nonchalance.

At breakfast we often see Grigorii, the journalism student who initially met us at the airport; he's becoming part of our routine. By now it's clear that he is a *stukach* (an official stool pigeon), in this case, an orthodox student with KGB affiliations who is encouraged to associate with and report on foreign students. It is perfectly possible to be friendly with Grigorii, if we assume he will report anything we say. (It's an assumption I'm learning to make with many of the Russians I meet.) He greets us warmly these mornings, and the three of us sit and chat while we struggle to cut our gristly meat with the aluminum forks and spoons provided. (Here, and in other Moscow cafeterias, no knives are provided, as if customers might try to use them in some kind of prison break.) Now that I've gotten to know him, I find that Grigorii is my idea of the perfect young Communist. Physically, he is one of those young men in whom youth seems an aberration: he projects a stiffness and pomposity that make his thin young body and his occasional giggles seem terribly inappropriate. At fifty he will be flawless, when his body has slowed and stiffened to match his mind. He does not make the mistake of dressing in the expensive black-market jeans many of his classmates favor; this would give him the damning brand of "unserious" in the eyes of his professors and Komsomol superiors. Instead he wears the unofficial uniform of the most zealously orthodox students: dark turtleneck, dark pants, dark jacket. Every few mornings he makes the same dull joke as he watches the university sportsmen lined up in the cafeteria: "I must admit that I prefer to exercise my mind!"

Grigorii is a young man who is obviously going to succeed in the Soviet system. The fact that he has been assigned to associate with capitalist foreigners is proof of his high esteem in official eyes. He is the ultimate volunteer, a waver of flags in the October Revolution and May Day parades; where other Moscow State students we know invented medical excuses to avoid the tedious month-long student potato harvest last fall, Grigorii not only volunteered to go, but headed a work brigade. At the unusually early age of twenty-five, he is already a Party *kandidat*, that is, a provisional member of the Communist Party. Being with him is a bit like being with a professional Boy Scout; one has only to look at his heavily underlined copy of the Party rulebook to understand the way his mind works.

We've spent a number of evenings visiting Grigorii in his room, which is in the "Soviet" wing of the dormitory, where the rooms are more densely populated and in poorer condition than those allotted to capitalist foreigners. Oddly enough, the walls of his small green cubicle (half of a *blok*) are decorated, almost papered, with liquor and automobile advertisements cut carefully from the American magazines Grigorii has received as presents from other foreign acquaintances. These cutouts show another side of Grigorii, the side that holds a minor fascination with the capitalist West. This fascination stems, I think, from a timid sensuality that manifests itself in the way Grigorii narrows his black eyes and smacks his lips over food, and over the underwear ads in my copies of Vogue. His deep interest in material things comes out in his loving descriptions of his family's new Soviet Fiat—his father, a distinguished chemist, is privileged enough to have access to the scarce luxury of a car—and the elegant new stove-refrigerator-sink set his parents bought for their apartment in the suburbs. But it is capitalism which sends a scandalized thrill through Grigorii, capitalism with its wickedly shiny automobiles, its sleek bottles of Scotch, its naked and bejeweled women. Grigorii owns a tape player, and his pride and joy is an incredibly grainy third-hand recording of Donna Summer's "Love to Love You, Baby." He plays it constantly, to the delighted horror of his friends, who appear to see Donna Summer's protracted orgasms as the symbol of alluring Western vice.

The Donna Summer tape was playing last night as we sat around Grigorii's desk, which he had covered with a piece of flowered oilcloth and laid with a teapot, a bottle of vodka, and an enormous sticky cake from the bakery downstairs. Things have gotten livelier since the night we arrived: on this warm evening nearly all the windows in the tower seemed to be open. From the first floor drifted a snatch of Spanish singing from a gathering of Cubans; a few stories up, some young men were hoarsely bellowing the English words to a disco song: "Dancing queen . . ." Every five or ten minutes there was a smash of glass as students tossed empty bottles out the window. Alcohol is illegal in the dormitory; the bulletin boards in the hallways are filled with notices describing the dire fate of students like "Tatiana M.," expelled in "the battle against drunkenness." However, everybody, even Grigorii, drinks all the time, throwing the vodka and beer bottles out the window to destroy the evidence. At dawn every morning the university sends out two or three babushki to sweep up the mounds of broken glass.

There were four of us sitting around in Grigorii's room: Grigorii himself; Nina, his sister; Tom and me. Grigorii's sister is a tall, flat-chested young woman of thirty, with a faded face and the sweet, resigned smile of an old-fashioned provincial maiden destined never to marry; she teaches English at an obscure *institut*. Grigorii treats her with a devotion that is the most touching thing about him, escorting her to plays and concerts, addressing her as "Sister" as they chatter in the stilted British English they both learned at school. He once showed us a tiny wooden plaque she gave him as a keepsake on his birthday; it depicts a nightingale, and on the back Nina had written in English: "To Brother Dearest very truly from His Loving Nina."

Tom and I talked with Grigorii about the school of journalism, which is one of the most prestigious faculties at the university, accessible only to students who have shown unusual promise both scholastically and in Komsomol activity, or who have unusually good connections. Grigorii's schedule last year included a standard course in Leninist theory, as well as a course that examined the "bourgeois press." "We're studying American yellow journalism, propaganda, and how your government controls newspapers like the *New York Times* and the *Washington Post*," he told us earnestly, his small eyes glistening from the vodka and an unusual flush on his cheeks. The Donna Summer tape ended as he spoke, and he interrupted our conversation to put on a tape of "We Shall Overcome." It was, he informed us, sung by the great American rock star Dean Reed.

Neither Tom nor I had heard of Dean Reed before we left the States. But for Grigorii and other strait-laced young Komsomol members, Reed, a young American Communist with a voice like Pat Boone's and an unctuous, toothy grin, is a star and folk hero. Reed lives in East Germany, and spends a lot of time in the Soviet Union or singing in protest rallies in the United States. Most sophisticated young Russians we've met take him as a joke, but Grigorii admires him as a soldier against capitalist injustice.

Donna Summer and Dean Reed are the two faces of Grigorii's view of the West: the sensual, corrupt siren call and the righteous wrath that paves the way for the class struggle. Grigorii firmly believes, as he has told us, that capitalism is doomed, but he can't help being fascinated by certain aspects of it. "Which is faster," he asked us last night, "a Cadillac or a Corvette?" Before he strayed too far, however, his orthodoxy caught him up. He straightened his shoulders, blinked, and said, "Very nice, but what about the racism and unemployment in the United States?" It always floors him that Tom and I agree freely with much of his criticism of America. He never admits that there are any problems in Soviet life. "There's no racism here," he told me once, studiously ignoring the fact that we'd just heard a Russian woman cursing a "filthy" African on a crowded bus. On another occasion, he maintained with admirably cool dogmatism that there was absolutely no censorship in the Soviet press. "Anyone can write what he wants here—even complaints about government policy. If such articles don't appear, it's because people are contented with Soviet life."

This bedrock of blind loyalty will probably net Grigorii great rewards. To be a successful Soviet journalist demands absolute orthodoxy of thought, and the higher levels of journalism are among the most prestigious of Soviet professions. Editors and important writers for most Soviet papers and news services have access to large apartments, luxurious dachas, foreign travel, and the special "closed" stores that sell imported goods and the best domestic products. It is toward this status that Grigorii is headed, has been headed, in fact, since his bustling officiousness made him head of his Pioneer troop at the age of ten. His ambitions are clearly mapped out: graduation from Moscow State, a training period on a paper in Siberia or some other part of the country, a return to Moscow, and a job with *Pravda* or *Izvestia*. "He is the perfect candidate for success," our Russian friend Borya, a fellow student and a cynic, said of Grigorii. "There is nothing original in him, nothing alive, nothing dangerous. Even his little lapses toward the West are minor. He's the perfect Communist for this regime, cut out with a cookie-cutter."

At about midnight, having moved from vodka to cake and tea with spoonfuls of Siberian blueberry jam, the party broke up. Nina had to catch a late metro back home, and Grigorii was to walk her to the station, so the four of us caught the elevator together and parted in the hall downstairs. "Good night, my friends," said Grigorii warmly, and I looked hard at him as he stood there, a slight figure with a dark cropped head, and shoulders held very straight inside his baggy jacket with the red Komsomol insignia on the lapel. Even slightly drunk and jovial, he seemed somehow insubstantial, not quite a person, and I could not for the life of me discern the expression in the eyes behind the comically large glasses. After we had left him, I said, "Friends?" and Tom chuckled. "He's all right to eat breakfast with," he said.

The Rynok

Today we took a trolley to visit a *rynok*—a peasant market—in southwest Moscow. We asked a passer-by at the University metro stop for directions—a middle-aged woman with gray hair and a hard, pleasant face. She was surprised and pleased to meet Russian-speaking Americans, and answered us with a friendly shout that was almost military in its forcefulness: "Go to the corner! Yes, that corner! Then take any trolley! Yes, any will get you there! Excellent! Very good! Good luck to you!" This brisk openness and almost violent enthusiasm set the mood for the afternoon. On the trolley, Tom told me a little about the peasant markets. They are an indirect result of Stalin's program of forced collectivization in the late twenties and early thirties. Peasants expressed vehement opposition to the program, in some cases slaughtering their livestock and resisting armed brigades from the cities. Faced with such resistance, and the dire shortages that followed, Stalin was forced to compromise: collective-farm workers were granted the right to farm small plots of their own and sell the produce for a profit. Most of the trading that takes place in this private sector of the economy is conducted in government-owned *rynok* buildings, but citizens do sell their produce elsewhere. During the short time we have been in Moscow, I have often seen old women carefully spreading out a few cups of berries in a tiny display by a subway entrance.

After a ten-minute ride, we stepped off in front of the market, a long, low building that looked like a field house at a Midwestern American university. In the street, a queue stretched back from a yellow cylinder that resembled more than anything else a child's toy locomotive enlarged; this was a *kvas* wagon, from which cups and pails were being filled with the foamy semi-alcoholic drink made from rye bread. We had always wanted to photograph a *kvas* line, with its workmen, teenagers, mothers, and *babushki*, but had heard from local photographer friends about hostility to such picture-taking. We thought up a ploy: spotting a cute puppy in the line, we asked its teenage owner if we could photograph her pet. She and her companion, wearing bright miniskirts and platform shoes, at first dissolved in giggles and then explained—with the pert gravity that makes Russian girls seem so prim and provocative at the same time—that it was impossible, that they had a friend whose dog had died after being photographed. Picture-taking was a clear danger for a young puppy. The entire *kvas* line had turned to look at us, and we backed away before the unassailable strength of this superstition. I thought how often the primitive roots of this society broke the surface, and remembered how last week a sophisticated graduate student from a highly connected, well-to-do family, a young man versed in Western slang and current events, had confided to me his fear for the future moral character of his unborn child, conceived when he was drunk from vodka.

We walked toward the entrance of the market, which was ringed with *babushki* and *dyedushki* selling flowers—old women and old men thrusting stalks of red and white gladiolus into the afternoon sun. Russians of all ages and professions were happily inspecting and buying flowers; like the Scandinavians and other victims of especially harsh and prolonged winters, Russians seem to appreciate the ephemeral products of summer—fruits and flowers—with almost ravenous intensity. Inside the market, the scarcity and preciousness of such products were confirmed as we looked at the outrageous prices of vegetables. Three rubles a kilo for carrots, five for apples—and this in summer in a city where an average worker makes about a hundred and fifty rubles a month. The market was a bustling big room filled with tables and with the smell of fruits, meats, and cheeses, like farmers' markets in the United States.

Meat and dairy counters lined the walls, and in the center of the room fruits and vegetables were set out in small, careful arrangements. I was amazed at the quality and the variety of the produce: peaches, eggplant, lettuce, and squash, as well as the Moscow summer staples of tomatoes, cucumbers, and cabbage.

Behind the counters were not Muscovites, but farmers from the Caucasus and Black Sea regions: Armenians, Georgians, Moldavian women wearing copper earrings and brilliant scarves, Uzbek men in embroidered skullcaps. In the manner of vendors all over the world, they were vocal and dramatic, posturing, cajoling at the top of their lungs. "Expensive, you say! Just take a look around—no price is better! Did you come to look or to buy?" "Taste this pear, just taste it—sugar and honey!" For all their village dress, the farmers looked sleeker than many Muscovites. Tom explained to me the double source of their prosperity. They come up from the Mediterranean climate of the south carrying fruits and vegetables, which they sell for immense profits; with some of the profits they buy luxuries unattainable in their regions—shoes, fashionable clothes, records—and resell the goods for inflated prices at home. Russian humor is full of jokes about wealthy Georgians—who buy entire rivers or have gigantic hidden warehouses stockpiled with goods—but these vendors are no such Soviet Texans. Their wealth means small-time provincial ease, and the week they spend in the capital, which for many comes only once or twice a year, is a time filled with the unimaginable excitements of the big city. Unlike blasé Muscovites, they greet foreigners with enthusiasm. "Where are you from?" demanded an Armenian woman selling her pears. "From America?" She caught her breath on the second syllable, as if her astonishment were too great to contain. A small furor sprang up in our corner of the market as vendors craned their necks to gawk at us or urged us to buy. An old Moldavian woman in black, framed by a rack from which hung strings of dried mushrooms, beckoned to us and asked, "Is it really better there?" When we began an equivocating answer, she waved us away. America had to exist as a promised land of big cars and cheap jeans; it was an attitude we had found before.

Now we were caught in a tourist's quandary: longing to take pictures but afraid of offending. We asked an old Azerbaijani woman at a flower stand if we might take her picture. She blushed like a young girl and shrank back among her flowers. "She's shy about her face," said her equally aged but more aggressive sister, who had gold teeth and an insinuating smile, and who immediately agreed to a picture. The first sister had a large wart on her cheek, and both sisters looked more than a little like Baba Yaga, the Russian witch I used to hear stories about as a little girl. The second, bold sister posed with a broad smile and with a bunch of flowers held up like a torch, and at the last minute the shy sister, with a timid grin, darted into the shot.

A few minutes later we took a second picture—of an Armenian girl selling apples and beeswax candles. She was in her late teens, with hennaed hair, modish clothes, and an incongruous, wide, yearning smile. She also said "America" with that breathless catch of excitement on the second syllable. Her companion, another villainous Baba Yaga, in a paisley shawl, pinched the material of my denim skirt, muttering, "Jeansi, jeansi—how much did you pay for this?" Tom told the girl about Armenians in California, and she begged us to visit her in a small village outside Yerevan, gazing at us all the while with a smile of astonishment and longing. It was a heady and unhealthy feeling to be looked at like that; I understood all at once why even the most level-headed Americans abroad sometimes succumb to the urge to act like traveling princes.

Later we stood and looked around the room. The pace of the market was picking up as the afternoon wore on. Fruit vendors wheedled and babbled; dairy women slapped huge cream cheeses into shape; from across the room came a dull thudding as a butcher beat a carcass with the blunt end of an ax. Customers stuffed paper horns of peaches and tomatoes into net bags while the farmers complacently counted their money. In the air was an intense, almost palpable feeling of private satisfaction. These vendors were hustling for themselves, and the result was a nearly complete absence of the shrugging, languid atmosphere that pervades so many state enterprises, where there is no sense of personal gain. I thought of the state *gastronomi* and vegetable stores where I shop. They are usually dimly lit places whose products lie in functional heaps and where there is a universal, disheartening smell of dry rot. The long lines of customers creep forward, and one often has the baffled, angry feeling of having just missed out on whatever is good. Compared with those stores, the *rynok*, with its huge choice, its bright displays, and its lack of lines, seemed to my Western eyes a real paradise. My Russian friends complain about the high prices of the peasant markets, but admit that these are the only places where you can find fresh vegetables in winter. So the little islands of capitalism continue to thrive throughout Moscow, serving Russians who can afford their prices.

Our musings were interrupted by one of the vendors nearby, a tall Georgian woman with a disdainful face and with a headkerchief tied up in two points, like cat's ears. "What is the matter with you two?" she called out. "You walk all around, and all you do is look. Then you stand in a corner and talk and talk. Why did you come to the market? Look, my eggplants are good. Come over here and buy them!"

Black Market

We're rich in this country, richer than I ever would have dreamed possible. I realized this first at the peasant market, but now it is knowledge I live with every minute. We have what everyone wants: American dollars; clothes, especially jeans; books; records; cosmetics; appliances. Wherever I go, people eye my ordinary outfits with rapacious interest and try to buy things off my back. One woman recently drew me aside in a bus line and asked me in a low voice what I would take for my sweater. "Why do you want it?" I asked. "It's not pretty."

"It's wool," she said. "We used to have wool, but it's *defisitnii* now."

Defisitnii is one of the most important words I've learned since my arrival in Moscow: it means "in short supply," and is commonly used to describe the constant shortages of food and material goods which are accepted here as part of daily life. I don't pretend to understand the Byzantine intertwinings of the Soviet economy, but I am well aware of the meaning of *defisitnii* when I have to scour all corners of Moscow in search of something as simple as a comb, or when I visit a dairy store for five days in a row, only to discover, as I did last week, that eggs and milk have temporarily disappeared from the open market. In such cases, Tom and I can resort to paying the extravagant prices at the peasant markets, or we can delve into our small collection of coupons to shop in the hidden, well-stocked stores that the Russians provide for the diplomatic community. Ordinary Russians, with less money and no connections, must simply do without.

The barrenness of the open market has spawned a large and thriving black market that is integral to the lives of all the Russians we've met. As foreigners, we draw black marketeers the way ripe fruit attracts wasps. Yesterday, when I was alone in the room, someone knocked at the door. I opened it to find a Russian woman named Olga whom I had met once through American friends. These friends had described her as a *fartsovchitsa*, a big-time merchant of contraband, dealing mainly in jeans—the money crop of the Soviet black market—and in currency. With the dollars she changes for rubles (the black-market rate is about seven rubles to a dollar) she buys furs, shoes, jewelry, and radios in *beriozki*—the foreign-currency stores intended for tourists and diplomats—and sells them to Russians at an enormous profit. She deals as well in the illegal sale of antiques like icons and samovars, and, rarely, in hashish from Central Asia. Olga is a short young woman in her late twenties, with the angelically round, slightly gamin face of a young Edith Piaf. There is something disturbing, however, about her mouth, which she habitually compresses as if under the influence of some intense hidden anger, and about her large green eyes, which hold the deceptive mildness I have seen in the eyes of some dope dealers I know back in the States. The second time I met her, I watched her buy two pairs of blue jeans from an English student: she ran an experienced eye swiftly over the two garments, opened her imported leather handbag to expose a wad of notes, and peeled off three hundred rubles. She folded the jeans rapidly, and they disappeared into the plastic *beriozka* bag she always carries.

The world of a Soviet *fartsovchik* is a strange, shady one, involving necessary contact with foreigners. Since most illegal luxuries—dollars, records, jeans—come from abroad, business *na lyevo* —literally, "on the left," or outside the State economy—must continually link East and West. Some *fartsovchiki* hang out near hotels for foreigners; others, like Olga, have regular friends and contacts within the foreign community. To be a *fartsovchik* is a risky business, but Olga seems to enjoy a special immunity to arrest or detention because she is a Party brat, the daughter of a very high official in the Urals. (I sometimes wonder if this immunity might really come from KGB affiliations, but as far as I know, she hasn't double-crossed anyone.) Her tight mouth relaxes into the naughty grin of an *enfant terrible* when she tells of her childhood in the Urals, where her father had a chauffeured car, a spacious apartment and dacha, and access to special Party stores. She once gigglingly told a story of getting picked up by the police in Soviet Georgia for selling jeans. "They took me to jail and I spent the night there. They kept asking me my name, and I said, 'If you really want to know, I'll tell you my dad's name. When you hear it you'll let me go, I guarantee.'

"These cops were Georgians—you know, they're like your Italians. They understand . . . connections. These guys got terrified. They finally let me go without ever finding out my name."

This immunity is all that remains to Olga of her childhood privileges. Disgusted with her activities, her father has for two years refused to see her or to send her funds. She lives on her wits, sharing an apartment with her boyfriend, another dealer, and haunting Intourist bars and hotels. Rumor has it that she is on the lookout for a foreign husband.

The morning that Olga came to my room, she was wearing a handsome leather coat and the kind of leather boots that are sold only in Party and diplomatic clothing stores. (It's almost impossible to get leather boots on the open market.) Under the coat, she had on a Wrangler denim dress—the height of Soviet fashion —that was a bit too tightly strained over her plump bosom; she smelled of Arpège. As I invited her in, she took in the clothes I was wearing with one quick, sharp glance of her long-lashed eyes. It was the first time she'd been in the room, and she made no effort to conceal the fact that she was inspecting everything: our jackets hanging up, my cosmetics in the bathroom, the tape player, the books. After we had drunk a cup of tea, she asked me if she could look through my closet.

"If it's interesting to you," I said.

She gave a rather harsh laugh. "It's much, much more than interesting," she said, looking at me with eyes that had suddenly darkened and gained intensity. "I have friends who would sell themselves for a chance to go through the closet of an American."

I led her into the bedroom, feeling the meekness one often experiences when faced with incomprehensible passions in others. Within a few minutes Olga was running her small white hands with their pink polished nails over my jeans and dresses, checking seams and the quality of the material, and offering a running commentary which taught me more than I ever wanted to know about the black market.

"*Ochen krasiva*—very pretty," she said, holding up a denim blazer. "You could get two hundred for this, maybe two-fifty, when the season is right."

"There's a season for jeans?" I asked. Both of us were speaking in low voices, almost in whispers; all Russians I know are convinced that these university rooms are bugged. Olga fussily replaced the blazer on its hanger, and gave me her broad, greedy grin. "Oh yes," she said. "Prices go up and down. In the summer, when people are going down to Yalta or Sochi *na kanikuli*, on vacation, they naturally want some new jeans clothing to wear, to display. You can get the best prices for something fancy like this. And it's Wrangler—the best."

She opened a drawer. "What are these—underpants? My dear, you could get twenty or thirty apiece for these. Russian girls are desperate for pretty underwear. And if you're interested in selling your eyeglass frames or that nice little umbrella . . ."

Everything in the closet appealed to her except for two scarves printed in a naïve fashion. "Who would want to wear those?" she said, raising her plucked eyebrows. "People might think you were a peasant!"

We went through Tom's closet, through my cosmetics, through our books and records. Everything had its inflated price (records were from fifty to seventy-five rubles), and everything quite obviously awakened in Olga a kind of lust that went far beyond a businesslike interest. As I stood close beside her, breathing in her delicate scent of perfume and watching her busy hands and glittering eyes, I experienced a complicated mixture of feelings; annoyance at having allowed myself to be victimized, a guilty pride at being so rich, and an intense repulsion at the obsessive materialism I saw in Olga. How ironic, I thought, that the Soviet system creates monsters of capitalism.

Olga was disappointed that I didn't want to sell anything just then; she promised to come by in a few days with some icons and antique lacquer work that I'd be glad to pay in denim for. She suggested as well that I could buy things in the hard-currency stores—books, clothing, appliances, cigarettes—that she would pay me for in rubles at double the official exchange rate. "You'd be rich," she said. By this time we were standing by the door as she pulled on her leather coat. Weak spirit that I am, I had given her a blouse and a bottle of nail polish; these had already disappeared into her ever-present *beriozka* bag.

"What on earth would I do with so many rubles?" I said.

She gave me a cold, condescending smile. "So—now you know what it's like," she said. "We can have any number of rubles and still have nothing—nothing—nothing!" She gave the word "nothing" —*nichevo*—a hissing emphasis, and at that moment all the scornful hostility she felt for the rich Westerners she preyed on seemed to gather on her pretty round face, giving her the look of a vicious little animal. In an instant she collected herself, and kissed me graciously enough, her face regaining its customary pure contours, her eyes their mild and caressing light. "I'll see you soon," she said in English, with her engagingly tip-tilted pronunciation. "Yes, soon," I said, knowing that if I didn't see Olga, there would be others like her.

Sasha

Today I visited Sasha the photographer. He is a recent friend—a stocky, round-faced man with gray eyes. He has a strange trick of avoiding the gaze of the person he is talking to and staring off into some mysterious middle distance; I thought at first that this was because he was shy, but it turned out to be because he is a fanatic and sees only one vision. Tom and I met him in his little rat's nest of a studio when he took our pictures for university ID cards. The place is in the basement of an apartment house near the Lenin Hills—a small, damp room full of broken furniture and tattered draperies, ruled by a despotic *babushka* who thinks Sasha is a goof-off and a nut. The first time we went there, we found her scolding him, ranting in her shrill, aged voice about reading and drinking on the job. Sasha came forward to meet us, on his face the guilty, good-natured look of a comic-strip character always destined to be the victim of women—a bumbling Dagwood. He answered our Russian greetings in English. "Welcome, my friends!" he cried. "I am very glad to meet Americans. I have studied your language for many years! I find it very stimulating to speak English." His voice was loud and hoarse, with a peculiarly irritating, insistent edge to it. I had never heard such an accent and intonation: a haphazard mixture of American and British pronunciation, bound together by a heavy, monotonous stress on every syllable, which after a few sentences began to strike my ears like the thud of a boot.

While Sasha's profession is photography, his obsession is the English language. His dream is to speak perfect, idiomatic American English. Unlike our Russian student friends, who have picked up elegant British and American accents from their university teachers, Sasha is entirely self-taught, studying during free moments in a career that has included factory work, forestry, and now photography. He is thirty-six. His interest in English dates from twenty years ago, when he began listening to American jazz programs on shortwave radio. Over the years, his love for jazz became transmuted into a passion for English, and he began to read whatever textbooks and literature he could get his hands on. Strangely, his love of the language is not accompanied by a fascination with American culture. He is deeply, outspokenly patriotic, and finds our cars too gaudy, our women not "simple" enough. He likes twentieth-century American literature the best; his favorite writers at the moment are Saul Bellow and Ralph Ellison, although he thinks there are too many sex scenes in Bellow's work.

I've spent a couple of afternoons drinking beer and talking with him in the studio. It's a queer place, with dusty hangings and dim pink walls lined with ancient, soupy shots of girls with beehive hairdos. Customers drift in and out, and the *babushka* scowls at us as she knits behind a desk. Sasha knows two topics of conversation: himself, and English language and literature. When I offer him any information about myself, he gives me an opaque glance and continues in his bulldozing voice. Often he uses me as a kind of reference work, to supply him with the meaning of expressions he has come across in his reading: "By the way, Andrea, what does this mean—'a tisket, a tasket'?" Or "Can you tell me what is a 'chinkapin woods'? Mr. Ellison has a phrase, 'I was chased out of a chinkapin woods . . .' What is it, please?"

There is a quaint flavor to his English, which took me a long time to figure out. Once, when I mentioned Halloween, his face lit up and he said, "Ah, yes, like Hogmanay!" It fascinated me that a Russian photographer would know the name of an obscure Scottish holiday. When I questioned him, I found that although he is fond of English and American literature, his greatest love is not a novel or a poem, but *Webster's New Collegiate Dictionary*. He reached into a drawer and brought out a battered copy given to him years ago by another American friend. I jokingly began to test him on obscure words, and the game quickly became serious: he looked straight ahead with his bulging pale eyes and gave me correct definitions for "kerf," "grommet," "stirrup cup," and "bogie." In the next twenty minutes he missed only one word—"spud," which he thought had to do with the breeding of animals. I found out that for twelve years Sasha has read and memorized *Webster's New Collegiate* the way some old Baptists I know read and memorize the Bible—with the same rapt, undiscriminating attention. "It is hard to obtain books," said Sasha, passing a fond hand over the dictionary. "This is the best."

His love of English often antagonizes those around him. His neighbors speak of him as "that nut of a photographer who can't take a decent picture." The *babushka* raves when he takes out his dictionary in the studio. And his wife and his mother-in-law despise his hobby and do all they can to thwart it. Both of them call Sasha's English studies moon-gazing and a waste of time; instead of studying, they think, he should take a second job to augment his salary and move them all to a larger apartment. Recently, Sasha's wife threatened to smash his shortwave radio and burn his precious books. He speaks of her in Websterian terms, with a kind of gloomy relish. Today he said, "My wife—she is not encouraging to my studies. In fact, she is a hellcat, a termagant! And her mother is the same. In harmony they sing!" Standing by the studio door, with his rusty-black suit and abstracted gaze, he looked more than ever like a comic bumbler. He glanced at his watch, gave me a rueful smile, and said, "Now I am late to be home for dinner. And when I reach home I will hear a 'curtain lecture.' Do you know what a 'curtain lecture' is? It is a lecture given by a shrewish wife to a wayward husband." He sighed. "She is a true virago."

Poor Sasha, I thought. I said goodbye and left. As I closed the door, I saw him carefully putting away the worn dictionary. The *babushka* had stopped knitting and was talking loudly and angrily about some negatives he had neglected to print that afternoon. And Sasha, forced to abandon English, was nodding his big head confusedly and saying, "*Da. Da. Da.*"

The Banya

Early this morning we met our friends Zhenya and Svetlana near the Sandunovsky Baths. I had begged to visit these baths, drawn by tales of their prerevolutionary luxury. Zhenya and Svetlana seemed amused and bored by the request; they are a well-to-do young husband and wife, and they made it clear that they could wash at home. I'd seen this attitude before. Americans are thrilled by Russian steam baths, which we regard as a luxury; for many members of the Russian intelligentsia, however, the *banya* is a reminder of a peasant heritage they'd rather forget.

We turned a corner and got a whiff of herbal steam. Along a short street, a row of old men sat selling small green bunches of birch and oak twigs, which were piled up on nearby crates. The baths were low buildings with the yellow plaster walls that give an odd tropical air to so many nineteenth-century Moscow neighborhoods. Lines were already forming in the street—men and women with sober expressions, all clutching loofahs and towels. In Russian style, we established our place in line by waiting there for five minutes; then we left to meet Yura and Igor, two student friends, outside a beer store. We bought beer and retired to a vacant lot nearby, where we sat on crates and drank. All around us in the cool early morning, little groups were doing the same thing: everyone was waiting for a turn in the baths. There was a long line at the beer store now, and a scuffle broke out when one man tried to cut in front of another. An alcoholic woman came up and begged us tearfully for vodka; when we offered her beer, she tightened her scarf around her red face and set off grimly down the street.

Zhenya, Yura, and Igor were eating breakfast: black bread, and raw eggs sucked through a hole in the shell. A heavy, back-slapping kind of affection existed among these three young men, who had grown up together in a small industrial town outside Moscow. They kidded each other and used old nicknames.

"We have been rivals all our lives," said Zhenya, leaning over to pat Igor on the shoulder. Igor, a burly young medical student with dark hair and a vulpine jaw, looked at him and grinned.

"Rivals for women?" I asked.

They burst out laughing. "Women, yes, yes!"

Three drunks had installed themselves on crates in the bushes behind us. They were eating salt fish and teasing a black terrier who stood snapping up morsels. One man leaned over and thrust a purplish face against the muzzle of the dog. The dog snarled at him, and he snarled back affectionately. "Oh, dog, dog!" he said. "Oh, my dear friend! You'd like to bite me, wouldn't you? You'd like to eat me! You'd like to gobble me up like a sandwich!"

I left for the women's bath with Svetlana. When we paid our rubles and stepped into the dressing room, I was stunned. I had expected remnants of opulence, but nothing like this—an upholstered turn-of-the-century interior, with soft colors, curving wood, and lace-shaded lamps. (Perhaps the lamps made the difference. Modern Soviet elegance does not include any subtlety in lighting; most restaurants in Moscow are lit by a fierce overhead glare.) Rows of mahogany benches upholstered in white filled the room; oval mirrors were set at intervals above the seats. A flowered carpet covered the floor, and friezes of plaster cupids lined the pink walls. I was struck, as I had been before, by the lavish decoration of public buildings in the Soviet Union—theatres, churches, metro stations. Much of this public decoration dates from before the Revolution, some is modern, but all of it contrasts greatly with the bleakness of the homes I have seen.

The dressing room was full of naked women. For a second the combination of bare flesh and lamplight gave me the jumpy feeling that this was a vicious place—a seraglio or a Victorian brothel.

Then my vision cleared; I saw here a peculiar wholesomeness that is characteristically Russian. On closer inspection, the room had a homely shabbiness, the feeling of human use that is typical of any Soviet apartment or office. The carpet was neatly darned at worn spots; the plaster cupids were chipped; the *babushka* in charge sat knitting comfortably behind a table where a large gray cat slept. The nude women here were the women I had seen carrying string bags on the metro. Minus their flimsy flowered dresses and cheap shoes, they were as I might have imagined them: mainly stocky, often bulging grotesquely, but so unpretentious and unself-conscious that they had a powerful appeal. Many had magnificent braids of hair. Old and young, they chatted, strolled idly around, put on makeup, drank beer. I tried, and failed, to imagine American women of all ages in such a setting.

In the steam and scrubbing rooms, mountainously fat mothers lay on marble slabs while their small daughters scrubbed and massaged every inch of their flesh. In the hottest part of the steam room *babushki* sat clutching their withered breasts, while beside them adolescent girls narcissistically searched their hips for bulges, slapping the skin to increase circulation. No birch beating was allowed in this particular bath. When I asked Svetlana about it, she made a face and said that the women who used birch twigs were "hicks," not born Muscovites, and very uncultured. Like other sophisticated Russians I've met, Zhenya and Svetlana have an outspoken contempt for *krestyanye*—peasants.

I made a face back at Svetlana. I like her. She is a small-boned, attractive girl who has an urchin haircut and a tough grin. She has the mixture of demureness and teasing flirtatiousness I see in so many Russian girls, and the queer blend of romanticism and ruthless practicality. Naked, her slight figure shows a thickening at the waist: she is three months pregnant, and her grin softens when she talks about the baby.

The two of us went from the steam room to the small pool, where we began to splash and play. The water around us was full of women playing tag, shrieking and ducking each other, paddling awkwardly across the pool. The pool itself was elegant, tiled in a mosaic design of garlands. In a niche at one end stood a gold statue of two cherubs, one attempting a half nelson on the other. With their bulging naked bodies and homemade knitted bathing caps, the splashing women looked a little incongruous in this setting of neoclassical elegance. There was a magical feeling of freedom in the air: the unhindered freedom of women in a place from which men are excluded. I have felt this intoxicating sense of liberty in similar situations at home in America, but for Russian women the feeling must be even more intense. It is fairly well known, I suppose, that most Russian women with families have two jobs: an official, often physically exhausting one, and the exceedingly difficult one of keeping a family groomed and fed—a task that few Russian husbands lend a hand with. I have been impressed during my time here by a certain feeling of constraint that occurs in social situations when the sexes are mixed. This constraint disappears in the segregated world of the *banya*, and with it goes the puritanical veneer that leads Russian women in mixed company to squeal and blush at the slightest mention of sex. I saw this clearly a little earlier in the scrubbing room, when a man tried to peek at the women through an air vent. Instead of screams, the air was filled with loud laughter and raunchy comments. Two muscular *babushki* grabbed buckets of hot water and dashed it at the Peeping Tom, who disappeared abruptly. Then everybody—teenagers, matrons, grandmothers, and children—lay back and laughed.

Later Svetlana and I sat on the edge of the pool with our feet in the water. A group of plump pubescent girls jumped into the pool and began bobbing up and down next to an old woman who was quietly paddling back and forth, smiling serenely. In a corner, three matrons were ducking a fourth, who sputtered and shrieked. After a few minutes one of this group clambered out, her large breasts quivering as she adjusted her bathing cap. She giggled and called out to her friends, "*Mui khuligani!*"—We're hooligans! Her smile was pleased and girlish. Back in the dressing room, I saw her again, pulling on a print dress, coiling her heavy braid of hair, gathering loofah and soap into a string bag: a respectable wife of Moscow. In a minute she left, dragging a child behind her, her round face still pink from the steam. She was like any woman I might encounter on the streets. It had been good to see her kick up her heels in the tiny, self-enclosed world of the *banya*.

Freshmen

The nights are cold; the apples are ripe on the trees in the university orchard. Today was the first day of school, and though I slept late and missed the cute and much-photographed primary schoolers (marching in starched pinafores, with flowers for the teachers), Tom and I did catch the opening exercises tonight for freshmen here at Moscow State. We had seen the build-up to the ceremony over the past month, as entrance exams took place around us. Outside the immense glass-and-steel humanities building, crowds of parents stood staring anxiously up at the windows of the examination rooms. The children of many of them had spent the past six months in intensive "prepping" courses for three days of tests. This is an expensive procedure, especially for provincial families, whose children must come to live in Moscow during the half year. The expense is often worthwhile, however, since these all-day examinations really do determine a student's future career. Three papers are posted on the bulletin board outside the building: a description of the exams; a list of appeal procedures for students who fail; and an employment ad from an automobile factory, addressed specifically to candidates whose appeals are turned down. (These young people don't always face a future of factory work. Russian friends have told me that a common tactic after rejection from Moscow State is to try institutes whose prestige is less and which have fewer applications. Determined students can find a place in these humbler schools, as students of, for instance, forest management or soil chemistry.)

The hundreds of students in the auditorium tonight were the

happy winners, survivors of a tough selection system; they seemed like freshmen anywhere. Before the ceremony they straggled into the room, smoking cigarettes, laughing, calling to their friends. A few loners stood gazing at the vast embossed ceiling, obviously overwhelmed by the stupendous size of the building and perhaps as well by the prestige of the institution they were entering. One or two couples strolled in with their arms around each other, but for the most part the sexes stayed in packs, eying each other covertly. By Soviet standards, they were dressed modishly: the girls in bright miniskirts and clumsy platform shoes, the boys in wildly patterned polyester shirts. Among them, a small group stood out in especially naïve clothing: crop-headed boys in tight suits, girls whose tremendous coiled braids were topped with frilly ribbons. These, I guessed, were country kids, in Moscow for the first time. A sophisticated Russian friend had described to me the reaction of these rural students to the university cafeteria: "They all came charging in, wearing these incredible suits—narrow lapels and short trousers. They gawked at everything, and then they started to gobble the food—tough meat and watery soup—as if it was the best thing they'd eaten in their lives." Aside from the provincials, the students made a fairly homogeneous group. I was surprised to find so few representatives of the various Soviet ethnic and racial groups. Most students were clearly Great Russian, the ethnic group that dominates Central European Russia and makes up most of the population of Moscow.

The huge auditorium filled, then quieted, and at seven o'clock the head of the university began to speak. At his first few phrases, I felt stealing irresistibly over me the memory of my own freshman year: the universal confusion; the unexpected liberty; awe; the endlessly proffered, absurd advice, which we ritually ignored. The faraway official, with his plump vest full of medals, was urging the students to uphold the standards of Lenin. He reminded them to follow the principles of the Twenty-fifth Party Congress in their scholarship. He told them that university life itself was an educational experience, that one must be fit in mind as well as body. Two grave, pink-cheeked Komsomol leaders carried in the flag of the Order of Lenin, and the speeches continued. I felt my ears closing, and I guessed that the ears of hundreds of students around me had closed as well. For a few minutes they had all stared up at the platform with the polite forbearance of the young for the pompous old, then the natural life of the crowd took over. Boys elbowed each other and stared at girls; girls put on lipstick and passed notes down the rows to their friends. I could feel the classic freshman sense of universal ogling, and also the question burning in the back of every mind: What will happen tonight? Because what was important was not the ceremony but afterward, when the freshman class had been promised a dance with live music.

The series of long speeches ended with a memorial to the Moscow State University students killed in the Second World War. The freshmen grew quiet as a soldier marched slowly forward with a wreath. I was curious about what they were thinking, these children born in the early sixties, to whom the forlorn hope of crudely armed students in the defense of Moscow could mean little more than an excerpt from a cycle of legends. The young faces around me wore only a strict ceremonial gravity. After a few minutes of silence, a stylishly dressed girl beside me glanced down at her watch and gave a little frown of impatience.

Later Tom and I watched the dance. It was held in the main hall of the dormitory, a dreary marble room whose walls give off a penetrating cold even in the summer. On a small platform in the center, four young men in jeans and suspenders played English and American rock music. Their hair was shoulder-length and their expressions were grim; they pronounced the English words with savage precision. A few girls in miniskirts hovered on the floor below, staring up at the musicians and hurrying to adjust microphones and amplifiers. As the lead singer shook his hair and began to sing "Satisfaction," I had an acute sense of time lag. The music, the setting were those of any small college dance a decade ago in the United States. But there was a naïveté about the crowd which would have been unusual for any group of young Americans. The tiny refreshment stand served only fizzy *limonad*, and we didn't see anyone slip off to drink vodka or beer in a corner. A wall of spectators surrounded the dance floor, where a few shy couples were moving in the strange rhythmless combination of Monkey and Jerk which makes up Russian "pop" dancing. The action, however, was not on the dance floor but among the hovering watchers. Packs of girls and boys approached and fell away from each other, giggling at the near-intersections but never actually meeting. I thought of the formality that seems to govern encounters of sexes in the Soviet Union. Many of my young married Russian friends were introduced by relatives.

So the freshman dance at Moscow State failed as a meeting ground for male and female students. Both sexes listened raptly to the music. Boys roughhoused in corners. Someone upset a tray of *zakuski* (snacks), and the floor was slippery with bologna sandwiches. The band played a slow song, and the few dancers moved heavily and chastely, their heads on the shoulders of their partners. At exactly eleven o'clock a uniformed guard appeared and told the band members to pack up. The dance was over, and in a minute the students had filed obediently away. The freshman class needs its rest, I discovered. Early tomorrow morning they leave on a bus to fulfill another first-year tradition: a month of work in a potato-harvest brigade at a collective farm.

Grigorii (II)

Whether he likes it or not, our strait-laced friend Grigorii is getting an education in capitalism—in its pettier facets, at least. He has developed a positive mania for the game of Monopoly, with which some of us Americans while away the long fall nights. He is a vicious player, hunching over the board, his enormous black glasses sliding down his nose, his insignificant features contorted with glee when his opponents land on the "Go to Jail" space, loading his Atlantic City properties with the green houses and red hotels that mean financial death to the adventurer unlucky enough to land there. He insists on being banker, handling the orange five hundreds and yellow hundreds with brisk efficiency (I am always tempted to make comparison with Soviet money); his tongue curls delightedly around such mysterious phrases as "trust fund," "charity ball," "inheritance tax."

Last night Grigorii had another lesson in capitalism. He was sitting in our room, poring over *Newsweek* (each of our new issues attracts a dozen Russian readers), when I saw his face light up. "See this advertisement?" he said, holding up the magazine. "It says that you can buy ten records for three dollars!" Grigorii, who loves music, was very excited. Like jeans, records from the West are normally available for outrageous prices on the black market; even the conservative Grigorii couldn't resist this bargain. He went on to suggest that he could pay us the equivalent of three dollars, and that we could send away to the record company for him. He stopped short when he noticed us smiling and shaking our heads. "I'm sorry—is there a problem?" he asked us, looking crestfallen.

"It would be a fine idea if the records really only cost three dollars," Tom said. "But you see, very often companies like this . . ." And both of us went on to explain the meaning of "fine print" and a few key features of our national trait of skepticism toward advertisers. I felt strangely guilty as we did it; it was like squelching the illusions of a very small child. Grigorii looked more and more disappointed; even his glasses seemed to droop further than usual. Finally he said, "Yes, I understand, of course," and left soon afterward. We felt terrible. Today I recounted this story to my Russian friend Rima, who laughed and said, "That little prig was just disappointed that he didn't get his records. The straight Komsomol types are dying for foreign goods like anybody else. Besides, he's no stranger to lies in print. You Americans have your advertisements, and we have *Pravda*."

Seryozha

I should write this down while it is still fresh. We have just come back home, tired. It's not weariness brought on by physical exertion, it's the gutless exhaustion that follows shock. Early this morning—a beautiful, hazy autumn morning—we set off for the apartment of our friend Seryozha. We three planned to visit the monastery at Zagorsk, a town about forty-five miles outside Moscow, and make a day of it. Tom was carrying a bottle of cognac and six *pirozhki* (meat dumplings), still warm in their paper wrappings. Now, barely two hours later, we're back, and we don't know when we can see Seryozha again. When we left his apartment, he told us that after everything was over he would send us a letter giving only a date and a time for a meeting. The place we would already know; it would be a metro station where we had met before. After Seryozha said this he told us to run, not walk, away from his apartment, avoiding anyone we might see. The danger, of course, was to him, not to us, but I still felt panicky. We dashed down the stairs and out of the place, the bag of food banging absurdly against Tom's legs, and then walked rapidly until we reached a bus stop around a corner. There we stood, catching our breath. Both of us felt a little sick.

We had known very little about Seryozha's troubles at first. American friends had introduced us. He is a thin young man with the mobile face and the expressive body of an actor or a mime. He has curly blond hair, which he wears long, and hazel eyes, which reveal a lively and ironic wit. Seryozha works as a chemical researcher, but like so many Russians, he is in a profession that has little to do with his real interests: art, literature, music, and anything concerning the West. (Strange that so many scientists we've met here are passionately devoted to the arts. In the past month I've met three or four young poets and novelists whose nominal calling is chemistry or physics.)

The first time we visited Seryozha, he met us at a metro stop near Arbat Street, and we took a trolley to his apartment. He was with his friend Anya, an attractive dark-haired young art student. Tom and I were both struck by their stylish Western clothes: Seryozha wore jeans and an English tweed cap; Anya, a subtly striped sweater dress and heavy silver bracelets. In Moscow, such clothing is a mark of high status, of black-market connections, or of a devotion to taste and quality extreme enough to sustain days and weeks of combing the barren stores. In any case, it is a statement of nonconformity. I was also impressed by Seryozha's apartment. It was closer than anything else I have seen in the Soviet Union to the apartment of a student or a young professional in the United States. Most of the apartments I've visited here combine sheer bleakness with depressingly gaudy attempts at modishness; this one was not only spacious and comfortable but tastefully, even imaginatively, furnished. The kitchen, where we spent most of our time, was a snug place decorated with English and American photographs and posters; there were plants, an old brass lamp, and an elegant china tea set. The bathroom, in true student fashion, was lined with metal signs stolen from construction sites. In Seryozha's bedroom, a wall of books faced a wall covered with photographs of poets and other writers.

That night we drank tea and then vodka with lemon peel steeped in it. The four of us talked in Russian and English about mutual friends and American railroads and the Rolling Stones. Seryozha loves the Stones, and his face grew wistful as we spoke about their recent album *Some Girls*. He played a tape of "Let It Bleed" over and over, until we could translate some difficult phrases for him; after that he came out with the phrases at intervals during the evening, in a pretty decent imitation of Jagger's

British snarl. He was an adroit and oddly formal host, inconspicuously filling our teacups and politely urging us to eat bread and cheese and chocolate. While he talked to us, he teased Anya, calling her "Piglet," and she shook back her bangs and glowered at him. It was clear that theirs was a fiery relationship. After a while we talked about ourselves. Anya told us about painting and printmaking, and about how hard it was to buy supplies in Moscow. There had been something angry in her dark face since the beginning of the evening; I thought at first that it meant she didn't like Americans, but now I realized that it was constant, barely suppressed rage at her own situation. Imagine being a painter, she said, and having only four colors of acrylics to choose from, and being unable to buy canvas. A little later I mentioned the Louvre. Anya gave a sardonic smile. "Oh, Paris!" she said, and her voice was full of bitter humor.

She left the room for a moment, and Seryozha told us that her deepest desire was to travel. "She's ready to do anything," he said. "But it's no good—she won't be allowed." He explained that Anya's father, a Pole living in Moscow, had been sent to a labor camp in the late fifties. The sentence had left a mark on the entire family, and it was unlikely that Anya would ever get to Paris.

"And what about you?" Tom asked.

Seryozha said, "I have some problems of my own." He put his slim hands on the table, looked down, and then hesitated. "I'll tell you about them later," he said. "Not now—the next time."

He took us into his bedroom to see his collection of photographs; heads of Pasternak and Mandelstam; Akhmatova leaning backward in black draperies. Among these was a small sepia portrait of several children in identical sailor suits sitting under a tree. We asked who they were.

"This is my grandmother, sitting with her brothers and sisters," said Seryozha, pointing to a girl with a long blond braid. "And this is their village," he added, pointing to another old picture. From his intonation, and from the look of the children, it was clear that this was not a village that they inhabited, but one that they owned.

Seryozha explained to us that his family had for generations been noble landowners in the Volga region. He told us his mother's maiden name and we recognized it. The family has a long tradition of literary and artistic achievement. One ancestor of Seryozha's was a distinguished minor poet of the eighteen-twenties, and his maternal grandfather is well known as a man of letters, a friend of Pasternak and other writers. Seryozha showed us two daguerreotypes—one a portrait of a beautiful young woman in a riding habit and the other a formal shot of an officer with sharply pointed mustaches. "Two of my great-grandparents," he said. The family, he told us, was listed in the *General Armorial of Noble Families of the Russian Empire*, Imperial Russia's oldest and most distinguished book of heraldry.

Seryozha had given us all this information in a flat, half-mocking voice. Now he flashed his wrist at us and gave the same sardonic smile Anya had given. "We say in Russian, 'blue, blue blood,' " he said.

"But how in the world did your family manage to survive the Revolution?" I asked.

Seryozha shrugged. "They managed." A little later he explained that his grandparents on both sides had quietly decided to go along with the new regime. His father joined the Party in the early thirties and has remained active in it ever since. This membership eventually placed the once-noble family in a position of privilege under Soviet rule. But Seryozha hates the Party, and feels that his father's devotion to Communism springs from willful blindness. "My grandfather—my father's own father—was shot down in the street during the purges," he said. "And my father pretends that it was an accident—that his dear Party could not have deliberately killed an innocent man. The rest of my family think differently." Seryozha's refusal to be active in the Komsomol has become a focal point of tension between father and son, in much the same way that draft resistance did in American families ten years ago. In fact, listening to Seryozha talk about his father made me think of endless conversations I'd heard in the late sixties. "We can go for a drive together and not agree on one single thing," he said. "My father hates the Rolling Stones, my books, my foreign friends, my long hair." Seryozha prefers his grandparents, who carry on the genteel family tradition of literary and artistic involvement. Often he talks to his grandmothers for hours about their life before the Revolution. It's interesting to me that one way in which the minor sixties-type rebellion taking place in Russia manifests itself is in a devotion to all things prerevolutionary. Many of my student friends pointedly call Leningrad St. Petersburg or "Piter."

Seryozha doesn't entirely condemn his father, however. "In the thirties the family had no money, and my grandmother was sick," he said. The entire family was starving in the big old town house they'd been allowed to retain. (The place, torn down in the early sixties, was a crumbling wooden mansion like many that still cluster in the formerly aristocratic neighborhood around Arbat Street. Seryozha was born in the house. He remembers it as a series of big, dark rooms full of old people and enormous stoves.) Seryozha showed us a picture of his father, a dour-faced man in his late fifties. He glanced at the picture himself, and began to whistle through his teeth; the tune was the Stones' "Ruby Tuesday." He was leaning against the bookcase, looking very slim in his jeans and sweater. "My father had to do it, I know," he said. "But he started to believe in it, and that was his great mistake."

On the metro going home, I said to Tom, "I think it shows."

"What shows?" said Tom.

"The blue, blue blood."

Tom laughed, and said that I was in love with anything that had to do with fallen fortunes. "If you hadn't heard that story, you would think he was an ordinary Russian," he said.

I disagreed. I thought I recognized in Seryozha a courtesy so ingrained that it operated by reflex, an instinctive delicacy of wit. There was something else, too—a peculiar frailty. I think that most Russians are tougher, physically and spiritually, than anything we can imagine in America. But Seryozha was not tough. I thought of this as the train crossed the Moskva River and we looked out at Moscow. The huge city was well lit in the cold fall night; with the gigantic Stalin Gothic towers poking up at intervals, it looked a little like a sinister Oz. In this context, the apartment we had just left seemed like a refuge, a shelter for a very fragile way of life. I wished suddenly and intensely that Seryozha lived in any other city in the world.

The following Sunday we visited Seryozha again, arriving half an hour later than we had agreed. (The end of a visit with Russian friends is always occupied with elaborate arrangements for the next meeting—time, place. No one likes to use the phone in Moscow.) After we knocked, we heard quiet footsteps coming toward the door. They stopped and there was a long pause. We knocked again. There was another pause, and finally two heavy bolts were shot back. Seryozha's face appeared through a crack in the door. "Come in, come in," he said rapidly. Once we were inside, he berated us for being late. "You see, when you come to visit me you have to be on time," he said. "Exactly. I will unlock my door for you and only you."

This was our first glimpse of what we took to be Seryozha's paranoia. We learned that there was a reason for it after he made us tea and sandwiches. He put on a Rod Stewart tape, and then sat down and looked at us gravely. There was a pause, which I could not help thinking was a little stagy; like many of my Russian friends, Seryozha has an exaggerated sense of the moment, the grand gesture. "I'll tell you my story now," he said in his stilted English. Then he laughed. "I sound like a novel. But it's a very dirty story."

It was a very dirty story, and one that unfortunately seems not at all out of the ordinary in this country. Here it is, briefly: Seryozha is married, and he and his wife are separated. Like many of our friends here, he married very young; Masha, the wife he chose, was a young Siberian woman. She didn't share his high education or his cultural interests; her parents, Party members in Irkutsk, were conservative, and thought their aristocratic son-in-law a bad bargain, with his interest in literature and Western music, and his disdain for the Party. After a few years Seryozha and Masha separated amicably, leading independent lives in a way that seems common in this country. (Many young Russians we know seem to have a shadowy spouse, even a child, off somewhere—perhaps in another province, perhaps across town.) All fine. But Masha's family, as families will, intervened, pressing their daughter to get a divorce, until she finally agreed. They also wanted to make trouble for Seryozha; the most effective method of accomplishing this was to denounce him to the KGB. (Strange, incidentally, to hear these letters whispered against rock music in a kitchen. The power of their mere sound to awaken nervousness in Russians is incredible. Tom once casually mentioned the KGB as he sat with a Russian friend in a remote corner of a park. She shivered, and stopped him from saying the name again. "It makes me very nervous to hear that," she said.) Seryozha's small desk, which he kept locked, was broken into and searched—he described this to us with a peculiar wincing delicacy, as if he were talking about the loss of a limb. Inside were copies of *The Gulag Archipelago* and Mikhail Bulgakov's *The Master and Margarita*, a modern classic novel disapproved of by the government. There was also a picture of Tsar Nicholas II. ("I used to light candles to it," Seryozha said ironically.) These possessions, along with his aristocratic background, a reputation for associating with foreigners, and his dislike of the Party, were enough to compromise him thoroughly.

What was behind this ugly action was the most commonplace of Russian personal motives. From far away in Siberia, Seryozha's parents-in-law had long had their eye on Seryozha's gem of an apartment—and on the alluring possibility of life in the capital. A Moscow *propiska* (residence permit) is extremely difficult to obtain; one major requirement, as they well knew, is the existence of an available apartment. The denunciation of their son-in-law might mean that he must forfeit the apartment to Masha in a divorce settlement. Seryozha sighed as he told us this, and I thought of the nightmarish housing shortage in Moscow. The loss of a good apartment was a very serious thing. But the other consequences of the denunciation were more serious. One of them was that Seryozha would certainly forfeit any chance of fulfilling his dream of travel outside the Soviet Union. Moreover, his father might be demoted from his rather high position in the Party. This was what Seryozha feared most of all. Anonymous letters concerning Seryozha had already been sent to his father's superiors. "Russian families have strong ties," he told us, "but this would create a rift nothing could bridge."

For the next month Tom and I visited Seryozha twice a week. It was à period of limbo for him. The divorce hearing was set for the indefinite future; the outcome of the denunciation was uncertain. Although we thought that meeting with foreigners at this time might compromise him further, he insisted on inviting us over. He acted with a strange mixture of recklessness and paranoia. We spent one amazing afternoon with him and Anya at the sixteenth-century Novo-Devichy Convent. Seryozha showed us how to slip through a wooden reconstruction barricade and climb to the forbidden top of the ramparts. He laughed as hard as any of us as he led us running around the top of the convent walls, ducking to avoid being seen by guards or tourists. In a taxi going home, however, he forbade us to speak any English—too dangerous for him, he said. He often lectured us on our naïveté about the Soviet Union. "You are not critical enough," he said. He told us about hidden cameras and listening devices. Often, as he spoke, he would get up and turn the tape player up louder. He told us about a friend of his who had been reading a forbidden book while riding on the metro and had been spotted by a KGB agent. The agent hustled his friend off the train and threatened to turn him in. But Seryozha's friend had the presence of mind to offer a bribe of forty rubles, and the agent went away after only issuing a warning. "The danger always exists," Seryozha said, drumming his fingers on the table. "But it is not often the kind of danger you envision. For most of us, it is an ugly, petty danger. The long arm ends in greedy little men."

When we saw Seryozha in the middle of last week, he was uneasy. He had heard rumors that his wife's parents were now in Moscow; this meant they were planning some decisive move. But he promised to visit the monastery at Zagorsk with us on Sunday morning —today. When we knocked on the door this morning, we heard the usual footsteps, then silence, then the rattling of the locks. Seryozha finally opened the door and pulled us inside. The apartment was unlit. Seryozha wore jeans and a shrunken black sweater that made his slim body look theatrically thin. He was very pale, and his mouth wore a trembling smile. He hurried us into the kitchen, putting a finger to his lips until he had shut the door. He said, "I'll explain to you very quickly, and then you have to go."

He told us that his wife's family had pulled some strings to advance the date of the hearing, that it was set for noon on Monday, and that until then he was being watched constantly—by his wife's family, by his own family, and by the KGB. His lawyer had told him that the denunciation was uncontestable; it was almost certain that he would lose his apartment and that his father would suffer as well. Our presence there was dangerous to him: if he should be seen with Americans right now, it would make his case far worse. As he told us this, there was a loud knock at the front door. We froze. The knock was repeated. We heard a slight commotion of voices in the hall, and the sound of someone trying the lock. Seryozha crept out of the kitchen to listen through the door, and then returned to us. "They're all there," he said. "My wife's family—the vultures! But they can't come in. I've changed the locks. They'll leave for a while, and when they do you must go quickly. Run down the stairs, don't walk." He said this last in English; then he added, still in English, "It's a very dirty thing. Very dirty."

The knocking and rattling went on for a few minutes while the three of us sat in the dim little kitchen. The knocking disturbed me very much. It was not loud, but it seemed to be breaking through something inside me, a membrane of privacy I hadn't known existed. I saw Seryozha wincing, and I thought of the purges, of Anya's father—times past when a knock on the door meant the breaking apart of lives.

The knocking stopped, and there was silence. The three of us took several deep breaths. Seryozha grabbed our arms and hurried us out of the kitchen. He set his ear against the door. Then he thrust our coats at us. "All right, go, go!" he said. Then: "Wait.

I'll see you sometime when this is over." And he made the arrangement for getting in touch with us which I have described. As he shook our hands and said goodbye, I took a good look at him. I thought that in the States he would have been a student friend of mine: well-mannered, idle, artistic, mildly radical—in short, someone to frequent a coffeehouse in Harvard Square, not to head a list of political victims. Then I thought of the family who had just left his door. He had got entangled in this shabby web of denunciation not through the operation of some gigantic, all-seeing machine, but through the greed and petty vindictiveness of those near to him. Seryozha's life was not shattered—it had only been disrupted in a particularly degrading way. I remembered his story of his friend's encounter with the KGB agent on the metro. This, it seemed to me, showed the same theme, which is one I've run into constantly since I've been in the Soviet Union: that the evil of the system is aided less by a desire to uphold that system than by some of the nastier personal motives that drive human nature. The greedy little men are everywhere.

All this went through my mind in a rush, confused by fear. For a few seconds Tom and I stood in the hall, looking at Seryozha across the barrier that misfortune erects around a friend. There was nothing to say except "Good luck" and "We will think of you." He opened the door and gave us a slight push. "Go, go!" he whispered. I gave him a kiss, and then we bolted down the stairs.

The Blue Bird

A popular Moscow night spot right now for trendy Russian youth is the Sinyaya Ptitsa, a dinner-and-dancing club on Pushkin Street. If you arrive there after seven on any evening, there is a line of denim-jacketed kids in their late teens and early twenties waiting without much hope outside its door, which is locked. We got there around 5 P.M. the other day, and were welcomed inside by the manager, a gray-haired gentleman in a stylish Western suit. He looked sleek and prosperous, and there was about him a touch of something I hadn't seen since I left the United States: the high-bouncing M.C. who loves "the kids" and the money they bring him. We paid a three-ruble cover charge and were seated by another sleek character in a French suit. A waiter brought us "cocktails" that were weak and oversweetened; that didn't matter, because we were busy staring at an amazing phenomenon—a Moscow night club that looked like a night club. The lighting was dim and the walls dark tile, with a bright mural depicting a blue bird—the namesake of the café. The tables were grouped around a small dance floor, which faced—wonder of wonders—a bar with bar stools. The recorded music was loud and good. It mainly featured the Swedish group Abba and the Caribbean group Boney M., two wildly popular bands that play soft disco-type rock with English lyrics. (When Boney M. performed live in Moscow a few weeks ago, young people stood in line for more than twenty hours to buy tickets. Scalpers' prices reached a hundred rubles.)

A friend of mine at the university had told me that the Sinyaya Ptitsa was the main hangout for Moscow's *Zolotaya Molodyozh,*

"Golden Youth"—the popular name for the spoiled offspring of the Communist elite. I looked around and concluded that he was right. The young clientele looked richer and more bored than any Russians I'd ever seen before. At each table a couple or a three-some leaned back in their seats, smoking with the almost ludicrous cigarette-in-the-air gesture that seems to be the mark of the Soviet snob. I could see packs of Marlboros and Gauloises lying on the tables. Every second person was dressed in denim—the girls in fashionable narrow slit skirts, the boys in name-brand American jeans and jackets. (Labels are very important now in denim-conscious Moscow. I have several times been drawn into debates on the merits of Wrangler versus Levis.) It was an expensive gathering. How many thousands of rubles did these yards of blue jeans represent? How many trips abroad? Many of the girls had fluffy Parisian-looking bobs, a real rarity in this land of long braids and coiled chignons. Everyone seemed to know everyone else; no one laughed or appeared to be having a good time. There was a lot of wandering around between tables for cigarette lighting and brief, intense conversations. I went to the ladies' room and found two beautiful, sulky girls improving their faces with French mascara. Part of their conversation went like this:

"Sasha's here tonight."

"I know. He's here with Olya."

"And so?"

A pause while one girl closed and opened her lashes in the mirror. Then: "Well, I won't say hello."

After a while couples got up to dance. They danced well, doing an exaggerated version of the Bump, which was the sexiest thing I'd seen in this city of chaste, energetic dances. (Most dance floors in Moscow are arenas for crowds of hefty drunken couples, who do an oddly innocent kind of bob and lurch.) Girls in tight dresses danced with boys in very tight pants, and over it all swirled a kind of psychedelic show of colored lights. I thought of my friend Elena's tales of dances in Moscow fifteen years ago: they used to call in the police if anyone did anything other than the waltz or the polka. A shout went up from the tables as a song came on that has been a hit in Moscow for the past few months. It is a song about Rasputin, by Boney M., and it gives an informal account of the sexual prowess of the mystic from Siberia. Its chorus goes like this:

> Rah! Rah! Rasputin,
> Russia's greatest love machine!
> It was a shame
> How he carried on!

Everyone was up on the dance floor for this one, still bored-looking, still unsmiling, but singing along. Stomping their Italian leather boots, bumping their blue-jeaned backsides, the spoiled rich kids of Moscow were celebrating this cosmopolitan in-joke: an irreverent song about Russia sung in English by a black group that records in West Germany. I saw the sleek gray-haired manager standing near the dance floor, snapping his fingers and smiling complacently as he watched the dancers. His hair was pouffed and swept, and I bet myself that he owned one of the few blow-dryers in Moscow. I had been seeing big tips change hands, and I could read his thoughts clearly. He was watching the growing success of the only Western-style club in town and thinking: These kids! Right on! Crazy, but I love 'em!

Anna and Volodya

Sunday morning at about eleven o'clock I was standing on the balcony behind Anna and Volodya's apartment, looking out over a small, dilapidated park. Over the trees I could see the rusty domes of an eighteenth-century church, whose air of dark neglect made the fall sky around it seem a brighter blue; this neighborhood holds many old churches, most of them now warehouses or "institutes." In the living room, Frank Sinatra was blaring from Volodya's expensive West German stereo, and I could hear Voloyda shouting to Tom over the music: "Fine sound, eh? You get what you pay for." A few yellow leaves drifted down, and an autumnal smell rose from the bare trodden earth of the park. Two little boys wearing pointed Pioneer caps were crouching in the sparse bushes down there; one said to the other, "Now I'll shoot and you fall dead. Go on!" An old woman with her head tightly wrapped in a challis scarf came out onto a first-floor balcony and muttered something to a white cat asleep among some flowerpots. All the balconies were made of the same crumbling concrete as the one where I stood, and had the same flimsy wood and plastic railings; many, like Anna and Volodya's, held pots and crockery containers of food, which the October air would keep refrigerated.

I was hungry at that particular moment, as I so often am these days. Food requires forethought in the Soviet Union: one must stand in a cafeteria line for it, or prepare it from the absolutely raw ingredients. Except for ice cream and candy, there are few quick snacks in Moscow. Thus Tom and I spend a lot of time meditating on our stomach pangs, and we are never hungrier than on the Sunday mornings when we arrive anticipating a splendid lunch with Anna and Volodya. We met these two friends through a complicated network of American and English friends. Since the government makes it unpleasant for ordinary Russians who openly associate with foreigners, the letters of introduction we carried to Volodya and other friends of friends had to be carefully concealed at the border and sent out surreptitiously in the local mail. When we got an answer a few weeks later, we arranged to meet Volodya near his apartment, and so began the long Sundays we've spent with them every few weeks.

Volodya is a tall balding man in his forties, with the broad-shouldered, slightly flabby body of an athlete who has gone a bit to seed. His protuberant mulberry-colored eyes and pugnacious jawline suggest a forceful, opinionated temperament, but this side of him is restrained in a way that I did not understand until recently. He is an industrial engineer, an occupation that, as he has pointed out, means very little in the Soviet Union, since every other person who is not actually a manual worker seems to be designated "engineer." He acts vague and bored when asked about his daily work, which he says is dull, and which brings him a very small salary; he prefers to discuss the moonlighting job with which he supplements his income *na lyevo*. This job is a typically complicated black-market affair, involving greasing palms and providing services officially unavailable: Volodya visits different elementary schools in Moscow, and by bribing the principals with bottles of Armenian cognac, gets permission to photograph the students in color. (Color photography is extremely rare here, since film is scarce, but Volodya has an underground source of supply from East Germany.) He sells the photographs privately to the parents. "It's a very nice arrangement," he told us with a complacent smile. "The principal gets his cognac, and the parents get pictures of their darlings that are better than that official black-and-white junk. And I, of course, make a profit."

Volodya's official and unofficial earnings, joined to Anna's salary, allow them to lead a pleasant middle-class existence. The three-room apartment they share with Volodya's grandmother is furnished in the kind of mesmerizing bad taste that, in Russian stores, costs very dear. The living room, which is also Anna and Volodya's bedroom, is dominated by a double bed covered with a bright green furry spread set off with a few hot-pink pillows. There is a great deal of the shiny laminated brown shelving which is the most expensive style sold at GUM, and there is an enormous lamp whose base is a shiny metal representation of a stag. On one wall is a lushly colored oil painting of a forest scene, and on the other a reproduction of Repin's lively painting "A Letter to the Sultan"; below this hangs a large medallion with an insignia that Volodya claims is his family crest. The real pride of the family is the West German stereo (purchased through another black-market connection) and Volodya's extensive collection of foreign records. During each of our visits, he sits us down on the green bedspread and blasts us with Frank Sinatra and Ray Charles.

While the music plays, Anna is usually working in the kitchen. Anna is a beauty in her late thirties, with a neatly modeled full body and the exquisite, fine-textured skin that gives some young Russian girls a look of angelic purity. (Unfortunately, most of the faces I see on the metro are prematurely aged, or sallow and blemished by poor diet and the hardness of life in general.) She has evidently been a knockout all her life, and emphasizes it now by dyeing her carefully set hair a brilliant reddish blond and by painting her lips and nails a flat crimson (Russian cosmetics lack subtlety). She projects the same innocent flamboyance as Dolly Parton.

Anna works as a supervisor in a paint factory, but it is clear that her main occupation is making Volodya's home his castle. She keeps the apartment spotless, knits sweaters, scarves, and hats (though the knitting's had to be interrupted—yarn is *defisitnii*), and scours stores and peasant markets for the ingredients of her fabulous meals. On our Sunday visits she gives us a sumptuous lunch and an equally hearty and festive dinner. "Eat, please eat, don't talk so much," she tells us. We sit in the tiny kitchen, its stove and shelves as crowded with well-worn utensils as any good working kitchen should be, and eat, variously: *borscht* and *shchee* (cabbage soup); sorrel soup with kidneys; tomatoes and cucumbers covered with magnificent sour cream; black bread, white bread, black bread studded with caraway seeds, Ukrainian bread; pork, beef, duck in ethereal gravy; *sirniki* (rich fried cakes made from sweetened farmer cheese) with homemade blueberry, raspberry, or plum jam; cream-filled bakery *tortes* (breads and cakes are the best mass-produced Soviet products, genuinely as good as homemade); and potatoes, of course, covered with about a pound of butter a serving. With this we drink Armenian cognac, Georgian wine, or *zubrovka*, a brownish vodka flavored with buffalo grass. (I should say here that this is the first really good Russian food we've had—and excellent food it is. Food here is scarce, and cafeteria food is vile, but the great advantage to Russian raw materials, when one can get hold of them, is that they are always fresh and untampered with. Dairy products are astonishingly rich, and fruits and vegetables, though small and blemished, are full of flavor. It occurred to me recently that Americans have done with vegetables exactly what Russians have done in architecture: gone after size without taste.)

Throughout the meal Volodya keeps our glasses filled, urging us to eat and drink in the bullying manner of Russian hosts. When he can think of nothing else to do, he cuts another slab of butter and throws it on top of our meat and potatoes. It is clear that he adores his role as host, adores Anna and his home life. He brags about Anna's good looks, about her skill as a cook and shopper, about his stereo and other features of his house. "Everything is better at home," he says often. "Moscow stores are crowded, the metro and buses are jungles, restaurants and movies are impossible to get into. At home you can do exactly what you want to, you can relax." His words echo those of other Russians I know, all of whom seem to feel that there is something sacred about home life. It makes sense. In this city where public life is at once so barbarously rude and so dreadfully regimented—where one is corstantly elbowed, shoved aside, and shouted at in crowds, and where the slightest deviation from "normal" behavior is instantly pointed out either by officials or by bossy citizens—home is the only place where there's a semblance of privacy and independence. In what I've seen of Russian culture, there is an almost Oriental separation between public and private life. The perfect symbol of this is the pair of slippers that Russian hosts often give you to slip on in the hallway.when you come to visit; these *tapochki* (Volodya and Anna have three or four extra pairs for guests) are of course practical for preserving floors throughout the slushy winters, but there is a deeper significance to exchanging one's street shoes for slippers. One is exchanging a public for a private personality, officially entering the relaxed world of the hosts' personal domain. "Relaxation" is a very important word for Volodya, for whom it seems to mean the peace of mind one finds at home. "Everyone needs to relax," he remarks constantly, settling back on his chair legs after one of Anna's meals, and glancing complacently around his kingdom.

After lunch on Sunday, Tom, Anna, Volodya, and I sat talking around the table, while the autumn sun blazed through the kitchen window and Anna and Volodya's little dog Chada sat wriggling with excitement at our feet. No description of Anna and Volodya would be complete without a mention of Chada, a very small, clean, glossy yellow dog who is almost literally the child of this childless couple. (Even the name "Chada" is the diminutive of an old Russian word meaning "child.") "We chose not to have children," Volodya told us on one of our first visits. "We knew that we couldn't have a child and at the same time continue to live as well as we do now. It's money and apartment space. And so we chose."

Because of this childlessness, Anna and Volodya must pay a special ten-percent income tax yearly, a measure the Soviet Government adopted to help boost a declining birthrate. Even the tax seems worth paying, to Anna and Volodya. Instead of a child, they have Chada, whom they bathe daily, feed on small portions of their meals, and give inordinate amounts of affection. "She slept all day," said Anna at lunch, bending her curly head tenderly down to Chada, who gazed intelligently back. "She's my darling baby, my sleepy little girl!"

After lunch on these Sunday visits, we usually go out to a movie, if there's one that's not too crowded, or to one of the parks outside Moscow. This Sunday, Anna stayed home, and Volodya, Tom, and I took a short ride on an electric train to Kuskovo, one of the former estates of the Sheremetiev family. Nowadays the house, grounds, and ornamental lake are preserved as a national monument, and hundreds come there to stroll on Sundays. At three o'clock, when we arrived, the sunlight had already paled and cooled; the woods, glowing with yellow leaves, were alive with a powerful, capricious cold wind. Holding our hands in our pockets against the chill, the three of us strolled down the beautiful hedge-lined alleys, past the low, unpretentious main house, the chapel, the stables, and an enormous ruined greenhouse on which red vines fluttered in the wind. Volodya, who was wearing an absurd knitted kepi that made him look a bit like de Gaulle, first gave us a tedious lecture on how we must build up our health for the Russian winter. ("You must eat bacon and butter and sour cream—yes, a great deal. You're both too thin. And eat garlic and don't go outside without your hats. And go to the *banya* often—it's good for the sinuses.") Then, with an air of relief, as if he'd allowed something exerting tremendous pressure inside of him to burst forth, he began talking about politics.

Volodya's political beliefs explain a lot about the life he leads now. Deeply afraid of listening devices, he will talk about his past involvements and current beliefs only on these long strolls. So we've heard his story in installments as we walked over miles of woodland paths in Moscow's parks and prerevolutionary estates. Volodya was born in the thirties to a peasant family in one of the wooden houses with carved trim that still cluster in villages outside Moscow. (Both Volodya and most of the other Russians we know seem deeply ashamed of these houses, which tourists invariably find beautiful. For Russians, this architecture is too full of associations of a primitive rural life only recently left behind.)

As a teenager, Volodya was an idealistic Komsomol member who worked in a construction brigade. "I helped to build the Moscow State tower where you live," he told us, squaring his heavily muscled shoulders. "To me, it was like building a shrine—every stone laid with sweat and strong beliefs." After that, he attended a forestry institute, and was finally assigned to patrol a game preserve several hundred miles north of Moscow. This solitary job was a turning point in Volodya's life. "Until then," he said, "I was a child—loyal to the State, unquestioning. But up there, I spent my days walking or skiing alone through the woods. I slept alone in a hut. My job was just silliness—it didn't exist. It was simply a slot that had been created for me to fill. I wasn't building Communism as I had been taught to believe. What I was doing wasn't any use, and nobody cared whether I lived or died in that forest. So I began to read, which turned me into a rebel."

For Volodya, rebellion meant abandoning his job, moving illegally back to Moscow (without the required *propiska*), and buying a motorcycle. All this was in 1957, a year after Khrushchev's "de-Stalinization" speech to the Twentieth Party Congress, a period in which many Russians, confronted with the toppling of Stalinism, experienced feelings of confusion and alienation. Volodya, with his cycle and his leather jacket and his anti-establishment stance, seems to have been a bit like a Soviet James Dean. He went to dances and created a scandal by dancing the *boogievoogie*; he listened to foreign jazz and attended the famous Benny Goodman concert sponsored by the International Youth Festival. Without a *propiska*, he lived like an outlaw in friends' apartments, spending entire days immersed in Russian literature. This changed him, he says, from a simple discontented worker to an *intelligent*, or proletarian intellectual, a thinker schooled in Dostoyevsky, Tolstoy, and the bitter political satire of Saltykov-Shchedrin. His anger became more specific, directed at the government, which he saw as corrupt, as having failed to set a moral and spiritual example for its citizens. Eventually he went back to work, this time in a forest outside of Moscow, but his awakening had been permanent. A few years later he formed a *kruzhok*, a circle of young men like himself, who pledged themselves to revolution. "We planned to take on the State with arms," Volodya told us, with a rueful smile. "I was slowly providing us with rifles stolen from my forestry job."

The group met for a year, until they were all suddenly arrested. "One of us, damn him, was a planted informer," said Volodya. "They locked us up in Lubyanka for a week, beat us up and interrogated us. They wanted me to denounce my comrades and recant my own beliefs." One day he was brought before a high KGB official, who unexpectedly granted him his freedom. "They struck a bargain with me. I was to give up my former friends and my politics and they would let me alone. 'Lead a simple life,' they told me, 'and if you ever touch politics again, we'll throw you so far into the camps you'll never see the light of day.' And I agreed. They had beaten me on the head in prison, and that did something to me. I didn't even care any more. They let me out, and just as I had promised, I got rid of my old friends and my big ideas. I met Anna and settled down. When you get older, you want different things; you realize you have to survive. I hardly even read any more. Books are dangerous—they disturb you."

In spite of this, Volodya informed us this past Sunday that he is writing a book. As we were walking back through the Kuskovo woods to the train station, he told us that it would be a great work, a devastating satire of the system after the manner of Saltykov-Shchedrin. It was about four-thirty in the afternoon, and only a few rays of sunlight penetrated the chilly gloom of the woods around us. Volodya occasionally interrupted his discourse to point out different types of trees to us: bronze birch, paper birch, yellow birch. Under his silly cap, his face looked pinched with intensity in a way that made him seem oddly younger; I could suddenly see in him the angry, solitary young forester of two decades back. His voice grew louder. "The book will have to be published abroad, of course," he said. "When it makes it way back to Russia by the underground route, it will truly turn things around here. It will be devastating."

"What exactly will the book be about?" I asked, and Volodya's face flushed a dull red. "It will be about the failure of the State to fulfill its responsibility to the citizens," he said. A pair of lovers was coming toward us through the darkening woods, and Volodya lowered his voice. "About the dishonest, useless lives most of us are forced to lead while the big shots blow trumpets about progress."

"What will you focus on?" I persisted. Tom gave me a nudge, and I knew I should have been quiet. The path we were following had emerged from the wood into a damp field waist-high with catkins under a suddenly lowering sky. Volodya tugged irritably on his cap. "What have I just been saying?" he said in an exasperated voice. Volodya doesn't have a very high opinion of feminine intelligence; he glanced at Tom and rolled his eyes meaningfully. After a short silence he said, "You mustn't think I'm condemning my country as a whole. Though I have some dissenting views, I am first and foremost Russian and a Soviet citizen. I believe in Marx and Lenin. I have no desire to live in the West, like the Jews or the disloyal, materialistic Russians who marry foreigners. You Americans are more decadent and spiritually bankrupt than we are, and that's going to destroy you in the end, mark my words. Your President Carter seems to be your country's only hope: he understands the value of morality."

When we arrived back at Volodya's apartment building, it had gotten dark and very cold; the leaves drifted down into a resonant stillness that was almost that of a winter night, and passers-by walked quickly. When we opened the apartment door and stepped into the dim little hallway, the dog Chada came leaping out to greet us, her small glossy body quivering all over with silent joy. A wonderful smell of gravy and cabbage came from the kitchen, where Anna, her handsome face flushed with the heat of the stove, was hurriedly slipping out of the ragged housedress she uses as an apron. "Hello, Chadushka, little girl," said Volodya, stroking the little dog. "She's been an angel all afternoon," said Anna, coming up to kiss Volodya's cheek. "Oy, it must be cold outside! Volodya," she continued, studying his face, "you look strange. Have you been shouting?" She turned to us. "Has he been shouting at you?"

"What a stupid question, Anna. No, I haven't been shouting," said Volodya impatiently, taking off his shoes and picking up a pair of slippers. "Go on, put on your slippers," he said to Tom and me. "Relax! Soon we'll eat supper, and we'll have some five-star Armenian cognac with it—the kind I give to the school principals. That will chase the chill from your bones."

Already his face was changing from the drawn, intense expression he had had in the woods to a rounded, rosy look of complacent well-being. It occurred to me, although I wasn't sure, that the book he had mentioned would probably never be written, that it was, in fact, one of those fantasies that middle-aged men use to conciliate the dreams of their youth. To the angry young man of the fifties, Volodya's present "quiet life"—founded on bourgeois values and petty black-market dealings, and defined, ultimately, by a KGB threat—would be a symbol of what he found rotten in Soviet society. And so for the short space of his Sunday walks in the woods—the surroundings that helped inspire his youthful anger —the forty-year-old Volodya revives a dream of idealism and protest.

Volodya's grandmother emerged from her room to greet us. She is an ancient *babushka*, very deaf, with a merry wrinkled little face like a dried apricot, and a tiny bun of a few thin hairs. Volodya treats her coldly because he is annoyed that she is using an entire room of their apartment; he believes that she should go to live in the country with another branch of the family. If that happened, he and Anna would have the ultimate in Soviet luxury: a three-room apartment for two people. "Did you have a nice stroll?" she asked in her aged, piping voice.

"Yes, a nice stroll," he said indifferently, going past her into the living room. "But it's good to be home," he continued, switching on the big lamp. "Everything's better at home." In a few minutes he had us seated on the green bedspread and was blasting us again with "That's Life," his favorite Sinatra song. Leaning back in his chair with a grin on his broad face as lordly and expansive as that of an old Russian *barin* surveying his fief, Volodya, who knows no English, sang along phonetically with the song: " 'I've been a poet, a pauper, . . . a pawn and a king . . .' " I stared at my reflection in the window glass near the bed, thinking how dismally close winter was, and wondering what was for dinner.

Running

The past week has been a succession of clear, windy days, a relief after the cold rain of September. The Russians call this *babye lyeto* —grandmother summer. I've been running almost every afternoon in the woods around the university; there are nearly four hundred acres, crisscrossed by little paths, and deer roam remoter corners. This afternoon I came out of the main entrance of the dormitory and jogged slowly down the red-clay path past the reflecting pool. Then I stopped and looked back at the dorm. My feelings about it are complicated: sometimes its vulgarity alarms and repels me, and at other times I feel for it the amused affection one might feel for a monstrous shambling pet—maybe a brontosaurus. I remembered one rainy night last month when Tom and I stood looking up at it through a rapidly moving mist. The huge tower, with its dim red light at the top, seemed to rock and bear down on us like a gigantic ship in a storm. Now I turned and ran on toward the Lenin Hills, the steep bluffs that fall down to the river. There's a path I like here along the edge of the woods. It's a path worn by university sportsmen (who pass me occasionally in their blue sweatsuits and their flimsy black sneakers), but I've seen narrow, muddy paths exactly like it in the countryside far outside Moscow, stretching from villages to bus stops or to neighboring hamlets. The woods are birch and maple, and their leaves these past few weeks have turned a pure, clear yellow, unmarked by any touch of red. This is how I think of the Russian autumn— as the simple color *gold*. The sky this week has been a peculiar blue: not vivid like a New Hampshire fall sky, but with a deep, glassy shine to it. Pasternak has described this weather perfectly. "On such days," he writes, "the sky is incredibly high, and through the transparent pillar of air between it and the earth there moves an icy, dark-blue radiance coming from the north." The suggestion of winter in the word "north" is correct: there is an intense, almost perilous feeling to this short northern fall, as if the first snow (which my friends have predicted for the end of this month) were already bearing down. Even now, it's quite cold once you're out of the strong sunlight. Running, I can feel the shadows of the trees on my back.

Today the woods were full of people. There were old women in black coats and gray shawls sifting the fallen leaves with long sticks as they looked for mushrooms. (These accessible woods are usually picked clean.) In the distance was the university orchard, an unkempt clearing full of tall pale grass and stunted fruit trees. Here I saw an old man helping an old woman to climb up; she rattled her stick among the branches, and he gathered the tumbling fruit into a large basket. I passed mothers and fathers whose small children were already extravagantly bundled up in scarves and waterproof suits; many of the families carried bouquets of huge yellow maple leaves, which all Russians seem to gather at this time of year. (Leaf collecting amounts to a craze here. I recently came across the old woman attendant in the library cloakroom pressing leaves with an iron to decorate her windows. And in all my friends' apartments summer flowers have been replaced by vases of leaves.) As always, I passed great numbers of lovers strolling through the trees or embracing in clearings. Half of them seemed to be university students; the rest, well-dressed middle-aged men and women. Seeing them made me think of a conversation I'd had with my friend Zhenya. We were talking about sex, and I asked him if it was true that the lack of privacy in communal apartments made most Russian lovers delay sex until marriage.

"Not true," he said. "Nobody waits." Then he explained that lovers, young and old, found privacy in the woods. "The things that you can see in the woods on a summer afternoon!"

"What about the winter?" I asked.

Zhenya shook his head. "We have an expression," he said. " 'In the summer, the bear eats; in the winter, he sucks his paw and dreams of summer.' We say this about making love. In winter, there's no place to go. All you can do is wait and think about the woods."

In a few minutes I came out of the trees onto the Lenin Hills. This is one of the best views in Moscow. It looks northeast. Under the long crescent of wooded hills that rise so abruptly and strangely in this flat landscape, the Moskva makes a single immense curve. On the other side lies the main part of the city. As an entity, spread out in a view, Moscow is not a beautiful city. Its beauty lies mainly in old neighborhoods invisible at this remove—haphazard clusters of wooden or plaster houses that were preserved from the mass construction of the fifties and sixties. From a distance, Moscow gives most of all an impression of denseness—not height —and industrial vigor. Barges and riverboats move constantly up and down the broad, dull waters of the Moskva; watching them, I thought of the historical importance of this river, which from medieval times has linked Moscow to trade routes leading to Central Asia and the Baltic. Back then, the city must have been scarcely visible from these bluffs above the river. This was true even in 1914, when Baedeker described the same view:

> VIEW. In the foreground, surrounded by fields of vegetables, is the small white Tikhvinski Church; farther off is the Church of the Redeemer; in the background is the many-towered city of Moscow, with the Kremlin; to the left (N.) is the Novo-Dyevitchi Convent; to the right (E.), on the high, wooded bank of the Moskva, is the Merchants' Poor House.

Well, the vegetable fields, the churches, and the poorhouse have vanished, and many-towered Moscow has spread to the other side of the river. The Kremlin is hidden behind a new wall of apartment houses, but the bright bricks and bulbous gold domes of Novo-Devichy Convent still shine in the distance. Beside the convent is the round white Lenin Stadium, being renovated for the 1980 Olympics; in the background is the Ministry of Foreign Affairs, a Stalin Gothic tower that seems to be the twin of the university building. Otherwise level, Moscow is dotted with these horrific pointed towers, which give the city a sinister appearance on misty nights.

I stopped running and began jogging slowly when I reached the overlook, which, as usual, was crowded with tourists, mainly Soviet. They gave me some strange glances: a female runner is very unusual in Moscow. There was a group that looked as if it might be from Soviet Georgia; the men and women had dark Mediterranean good looks, and their clothing was stylish and expensive by Moscow standards. From the corner of my eye I saw two Russian students laughing at them, and I thought of the undisguised hostility with which Russians regard Georgians. (Zhenya describes them as "rich, dark, and dirty.") I remembered a popular expression I'd recently learned: "*Vy iz aúla!*"—meaning "You must be from the *aúl!*" An *aúl* is a mountain village in the Caucasus; Russians often use this remark to ridicule someone acting especially uncouth.

I left the overlook and ran along a tiny path that traces the crest of the Lenin Hills. Below me, a rich sweep of autumn foliage descended to the river. The path was bordered by rowan trees, with their rust-colored foliage and clusters of red berries. Sparrows and huge magpies flew wrangling around the fruit, and I remembered that the traditional name of this area was Sparrow Hills.

The Sparrow Hills used to be imperial forest. Ivan the Terrible is reputed to have had a summer palace here, though no one now can point out the site. But there are palaces still standing. Every day, when I cross the river on the metro, I see a cluster of domes in the unmistakable prerevolutionary yellow, high on a wooded slope. A cabdriver told me that this was formerly the home of a minor member of the royal family; it is now a physics institute, closed to the public. Today I circled this building, which is hidden by a high yellow wall, and followed a path into the woods behind it. In a few minutes I found what I was looking for: traces of a formal garden. Following a muddy path, which showed a bit of red brick, I entered a clearing waist-high in goldenrod and camomile. At one end stood a sad ring of disheveled lilacs. Among the trees at the other end I saw the remains of an old orchard, the shaggy fruit trees overshadowed by birches and maples. A group of little boys stood smoking cigarettes nearby. I caught my breath in the hot sunlight. For some reason, the ruins of gardens always move me much more than ruins of buildings. Perhaps it is simply that the neglected plants still live, and so preserve some of the life of their past; perhaps that in a wilderness of new growth, they stubbornly trace out the formal patterns of man. The clearing was a pleasant place, filled with the bright silence of midautumn, when the frosts have killed the summer insects. A brindled cat came by and looked up at me, and suddenly I realized my jacket was covered with burs. After I pulled them out, I set off for home.

It was almost five, and a rosy-brownish glow had begun to spread over Moscow and the river. A big gibbous moon had risen to my right, and far ahead of me I could see the gleaming yellow walls of Mosfilm, the Soviet Union's largest film studio. Near the overlook, I passed a bridal party that had come to be photographed in the Lenin Hills. The bride was red-cheeked and pretty, with a long braid, a clumsy white gown, and platform shoes; her husband was an earnest young man in a brown suit. They opened champagne, they kissed, and their relatives photographed them against the view. A Chaika waited nearby—one of the hideous chrome-encrusted limousines that Stalin introduced; rented for the day, it was decorated, as usual, with balloons and a bride-doll attached to the grille. To be photographed in the Lenin Hills immediately after the ceremony is a very popular custom in Moscow. Countless friends of ours have shown us what is essentially the same bridal picture: "That's me, Mama, Yurochka, Papa—and that's Moscow behind us!"

I was tired and eager to get home. The light was already gone from the woods, and the cold was surprising. It made my ears sting. I pulled my fingers inside my jacket sleeves and ran faster. There was a smell of burning leaves; through the trees I could see university grounds workers, big women in quilted coats raking and spreading embers. In one grassy clearing, under the lopsided moon, six young men were tumbling after a soccer ball. At last I came to the edge of the woods, where the preposterous bulk of the university tower loomed in front of me, and there I stopped to pick my own bouquet of maple leaves. The electric lights were just coming on as I walked up the steps.

Two Soviet Women

I. Elena

October 26

Elena is the kind of woman Millet would have painted picking apples if he had come to Russia. Physically, she is a classic Central Russian: a muscular body; short, powerful legs; and a flattish face with a touch of Mongol about the cheekbones. The modeling of this face is extraordinary. The strong, broad cheeks, clear-cut lips, and heavy eyelids give it both gravity and intensity; it is the face of a passionate dreamer. Lena lessens this impression, however, by dressing with the coy primness favored by female Komsomol members and by coiling her hip-length tawny hair into a tight bun.

Lena is an "official" Russian, a young woman for whom the system is working very nicely. She is an instructor at the university, teaching the Russian language to foreign students—a position

that, because of its constant exposure to corrupting capitalist influences, can be held only by someone of reliable orthodoxy. We
met in one of her classes and became friends, drawn by one of
those inexplicable attractions that two people sometimes have
for each other. Our friendship has been full of the suspensions
of logic, the tactful silences, and the frequent deceptions that char-
acterize friendships between Americans and loyal Russians. From
the first, we tacitly agreed not to discuss politics. This was less of
a problem than was the fact that I knew she was required to turn
in reports on me—something that, in her conscientious way, she
surely did. The constant wear of this falseness—my inability to tell
her where I've been or what I've done—has perceptibly thinned
the fabric of our friendship. Before it vanishes entirely, I would like
to set down a bit of what I have found in Lena.

She could be a model for the Party to hold up to Russian women
everywhere: attractive; ambitious; married to a stout young factory
worker; mother of an exceptionally plump child; owner of a hair
dryer, a television set, and an East German stereo; writing her
dissertation with the same energy with which she attacks house-
work. These are the sides of Lena that leave me cold. What I like
are the unorthodox things about her—traits that show through
when she is lazy, soundings from a deeper Lenochka, clues that fulfill the promise of that face.

These appear most frequently when she is at home. This fall
I've taken to visiting her one or twice a week in the afternoon. It's
the best time for us to talk freely, since her husband, Misha, is not
at home. Misha is a tall, immensely solid man with tremendous
red hands and a round, rather handsome face. He is the absolute
type of those massive figures who are always plunging forward or
straining to lift bulky objects in Soviet political posters; his
mind, unfortunately, is cast in the same conventional mode. He
has a heavy touchiness, an underdog complex about the Soviet
system, and suspiciously regards the most innocent question by a
foreigner as a possible gibe. When I asked, "What kinds of radios
does your factory make?" he pondered awhile and then growled
back, "I'm sure they're not as fine as all your fancy American

brands, but let me assure you, they're excellent sets." Misha disapproves of me, Lena has told me, because I seem frivolous, because I seem to be trying to impart a kind of Western frivolity to his wife. I dislike him because he brings out the worst in Lena. In the evening, when he is there, she sits up straight and titters.

No, the afternoon is by far the best time to visit. The streetcar lets me out at Vavilova Street, and I pass through a leaf-strewn apartment courtyard, filled with old women and tiny children, to climb four flights of damp concrete stairs. Lena and Misha have an excellent four-room apartment, which they share with only one other tenant; it is large, westward-facing, in good repair. The walls of the main living-dining room are covered with the same tan figured wallpaper that a thousand "good" apartments in Moscow display; there is the same uncomfortable straight-backed divan with a strip of Georgian carpeting thrown over it, the same laminated dining table protected by figured oilcloth, the same bare wooden floor, shiny from countless scrubbings. Lena greets me at the door, kissing my cheek, bringing me a pair of battered slippers. Almost immediately we sit down to lunch: clear soup with small bits of meat in it, a mound of boiled potatoes with fried carrots or pickled mushrooms, black bread. Lena eats greedily, bending over her plate, mumbling through food in her mouth. This greediness endears her to me: in it I see back to her ancestors, to the endless, unappeased hunger of the Russian peasant who has endured the privations of winter, war, and collectivization, and who thanks the stars and stuffs his mouth when he sits down to eat.

Once, Lena's father came by when we were eating. He is a short, gnarled *kolkhoz* (collective farm) worker, with the silent, deferential shyness of the real peasant. Looking at his black-jowled face (with the full lips and hazel eyes of his daughter) and his rubbed fur hat, quilted coat, mud-stained rubber boots, and heavy olive-green rucksack, I understood what Lena had meant when she told me she was born "outside Moscow." I could envision the town, with its single fruit-and-vegetable store full of half-frozen cabbages, the sagging wooden houses with carved windows and eaves, the rickety new apartment buildings, the bare concrete platform where the electric train stops, the lonely propaganda center with its bedraggled red flag.

Sometimes Lena's little son, Sasha, is there for an afternoon visit. (Most of the time he lives with his grandmother in order to free his parents for working.) Sasha is a small, perfectly round boy of two who seems destined to grow up into the same heroic mold as his father. He's a smart, healthy child, a shrieker. Lena dresses him in the universal Russian baby costume: woolen tights and a short tunic, which make him look medieval. Although Sashenka is being raised according to Dr. Spock—*Baby and Child Care* is the rage among advanced young Russian mothers—Lena does not feel that the good doctor stresses affection enough. She makes up for this by spoiling Sasha extravagantly in the traditional Russian style: stuffing him with candies, giving him endless mouth-to-mouth kisses, calling him her little bird, her little paw, and a hundred variations on the nickname Sasha. She sits proudly bouncing him on her knee in the sunlight as he recites his favorite nursery rhyme: "Kitty is crying in the hall . . ." It's a pretty sight. By this time of the afternoon the autumn sun warms the walls of the room and gives an even, amber tone to Lena's face and hair. When I see her this way, I think of a remark made by an American friend of mine, a young man hopelessly in love with a Russian girl. He said, "There is a kind of glow about Russian women which I have never seen before. It's simplicity, it's sentimentality, it's mystery. Damnit, they are just the most alluring women in the world!"

Sasha naps, and Lena and I sit and talk about music and literature, the vagaries of fashion, scandals among our friends, the habits of our husbands. Lena is twenty-seven, and seems at once older and younger than that. Her figure seems about to ripen into the dense solidity of those squat, ageless women who patrol the streets of Moscow with brooms. Two teeth are missing from that lovely jaw. The sunlight shows a net of wrinkles under her eyes; the hair over each temple has a faint spray of gray. I know that physically her life is far harder than mine: besides teaching and working on her dissertation, there is the eternal round of standing

.n line for bread and *kefir*, meat and vegetables; putting up pre-
serves; cooking; scubbing dishes in harsh washing soda; launder-
ing the family's clothes in the bathtub. When she talks of these
chores and I cannot respond in kind, there is one more barrier between us. Once, I complained that she treated me like a child.
She laughed, and said in a half-envious, half-chiding voice, "I can't
help it! All of you American women seem like little girls to me.
So slim and careless—even the grandmothers!"

At the same time, there is much of the *jeune fille* about Lena.
She can be naïve, with a barbaric simplicity that almost transcends
questions of age or sex; she is like her father at these moments,
the grizzled *kolkhoznik* wandering cautiously through the great
world. Once, when I gave her a moderate-sized bottle of Eau de
rochas, I came back the next day to find the bottle nearly empty.
"What happened?" I asked. "Did you spill it?"

She looked placidly back at me. "No, I used it," she said. "We
went to a party at my friend Tanya's, and I wanted to smell nice.
It takes a lot to cover all of you."

Another time she showed me a box of colored wax crayons and
asked whether this was what American women used to paint their
faces.

She is astonishingly prudish about sex, blushing and growing
silent whenever I mention the subject. Recently, when I told her an
anecdote about an American here whose name is constantly mis-
taken for a ribald Russian term, she laughed nervously, turned red,
and finally told me to hush. "I can't bear talk like that," she said.

Like many Russian women, Lena walks arm in arm with her
best friend, giggling and whispering like an American fifteen-year-
old. But there is an untouched, almost virginal quality about Lena
that runs deeper than these adolescent gestures. A dreaming, questioning, expectant look comes over her face at unguarded moments: it is the look of a very young girl who is forever interro-
gating the romantic future. When we listen to music, to the
Gypsy singers or the old Russian romances that are her favorites,
she slumps forward in her straight-backed chair, resting her breasts
on the scrubbed oilcloth with her face in her hands, her head,

with its magnificent coil of hair, bowed. She listens with the extravagant emotion of Russians, who seem to know no self-consciousness.

The expectant expression is often on her face. I have seen it when she sits with Misha in the evenings; it shines from her eyes in a fugitive flash during her language classes. It is a queer, out-of-season expression for a woman already middle-aged by Russian standards. The only thing that banishes it completely is the presence of her child. "I want many, many children," she told me once, almost fiercely. "I would like ten! That's impossible because of the housing shortage. We are waiting, however, for a larger apartment. If we get it, we will have at least three."

Last week Lena showed me her photograph album. It was fat and full: pictures of the infant Lena sleeping in the arms of her father; Lena with her mother, a worn beauty in an Orenburg shawl; Lena in a rabbit costume at a State nursery school; Lena in a starched school uniform with an immense bow perched like a moth at the exact center of her head; Lena at Pioneer camp; Lena at sixteen, startlingly, almost professionally beautiful in heavy makeup for a class play; Lena as a snow fairy in a Komsomol skit. Then there was page after page of wedding pictures: Lena and Misha at the Palace of Weddings—Lena a sphinx in a white gown, Misha wearing a huge, embarrassed grin.

"How did you meet Misha?" I asked.

Lena turned her clear hazel eyes on me and then looked out the window. "It was at school," she said. "He was in a class with my brother. I was very young and very *seriozna*, as we say. One day I came into my brother's classroom after school and began to lecture him on how to be a good student. I told him he must work harder and improve. Misha was standing beside my brother as I spoke. He says that I was wearing black-rimmed glasses and a long braid down my back, that I was very pretty and very strict." Lena giggled. "He was fifteen and I was thirteen. Misha fell in love."

"And did you?"

Lena continued to look out the window. "I was in love with

another boy at school," she said. "I loved him until I went to the university." She turned to the back of the album and pointed. "Here he is—Volodya." We stared in silence at a young man holding a guitar in a circle of friends. Some spark of animation in his face, his posture, seemed to draw the rest of the group around him.

"He's handsome," I said.

Elena slid her hands into a patch of sunlight on the table. "Yes, he was," she said. "The girls at school used to call him 'Graf'— 'Count.' It was a joke, you know."

"Was he in love with you, too?"

"He said he was, so I suppose it was true. But he went into the Army and he didn't write to me for a long time. And then I found he had written a letter to Olga Ivanovna, a girl at school. So I broke things off."

"And then you fell in love with Misha?"

Lena looked at me. "No," she said. "I did not fall in love with Misha. I married him because I thought that other men would be worse. I had heard stories." She paused, and poured out two more cups of tea. "Take some more of this jam. It's very good. And have a candy." She sipped her tea. "I didn't love him at first," she continued. "But then we had Sashenka, and Misha was good to me. I was very tired, and he helped me with the baby. Most men don't do that. So I began to love him. He's a good man."

"And you've never heard anything more about Volodya?"

Lena tossed her head. "I've heard a little about him, of course, from friends, neighbors. He's an engineer and has gone to work in Siberia." There was a cough and a murmur from the crib where Sasha lay napping, and Lena rose, pushing aside the red velveteen curtain that divides the family's tiny sleeping room from the rest of the apartment. I heard her soothing and kissing him. She returned and sat down, smoothing her hair. "I'm sure he's done well, though—Volodya," she said, with her grave half-smile. "There was something about him ... Do you know that sometimes when I teach my class for foreigners, there are young men who remind me of him. They're from England, France, America—they seem like princes from abroad. Sometimes I get crushes on them!" She turned red and laughed self-consciously.

I laughed, too. "What about Misha?"

She was grave again. "Misha is a hard worker. I don't think he will go very far, but he is a good husband. He picked those mushrooms you had today, and dried the apples you ate in the compote. He's better to me than any man I could imagine."

II. Vera
March 8—Leningrad

On the eve of International Women's Day, a bright windy Saturday with four inches of slush in the streets of Leningrad, I went out shopping with Vera for the ingredients for a festive dinner. All day, indeed all week, the radio had been blaring sentimental songs, generally sung in a fruity bass, in praise of women; along the breezy thoroughfares flapped colorful posters of women and flowers, and the trolleys were crowded with shoppers for this rather tame holiday, which is a bit like a large-scale socialist-style Mothers' Day. Vera and I, equipped with a string bag and a small plastic suitcase, were headed for Srednii Prospekt, where there is an excellent meat-and-poultry store. Vera has made friends with one of the counterwomen by bringing her packs of foreign cigarettes that she wheedles from hapless American acquaintances like me, and as a result can buy ducks, Polish chickens, and cuts of lamb that never make it into the hands of ordinary customers without bribes.

We hopped off the trolley and plowed through the muddy snow to the shop, where there was a line extending out the front door. Vera's eyes brightened. "What are they selling?" she asked. A woman clutching two tremendous bags of potatoes told her: beef liver, a delicacy so rare and popular that it is usually reserved for hotels serving foreigners, and the stores restricted to Party members. Vera debated for a minute, then shrugged. The line of slow-moving women was too long—there'd be at least a fifty-minute wait. We made our way over to the line for poultry, where after fifteen minutes, Vera's friend produced a duck she had saved for us under the counter. We got in the cashier line, paid for the duck, waited in line to pick up the duck, and walked back to the trolley stop. Vera was jubilant. "We're lucky!" she said. "Ducks are generally hard to come by."

If you stand in a hallway when classes change in any faculty of Leningrad State University, ten girls like Vera will pass by. She has the sturdy compact body, the pale, attractive, slightly hard face, the single aluminum tooth, the fringe of hennaed hair of thousands of young Russian women. She dresses in knit sweaters, strongly scented with cigarettes and sweat, a very tight rather grubby denim skirt, and a cherished pair of Italian ankle boots, obtained through intensive black-market maneuvering. Vera is a student in video-journalism, a garrulous young woman with a hearty, raucous voice that can shift, paradoxically and charmingly, into a tinkling flirtatious laugh; her skill at badinage and understanding of what a well-timed present can do has earned her friends in shops from Vasilevskii Island to Nevsky Prospekt. Outside of school, her passion is shopping—darting from store to store to lay hold of odd bits of quality merchandise with the swiftness of a sparrow pecking up crumbs, her round dark eyes scanning the streets for lines that mean some new delicacy or luxury (Hungarian peppers! canned arroz con pollo! those cute painted thermoses from Japan!) has found its idiosyncratic way in over the Soviet border. Like other perapatetic young Russian women who spend their free hours scouring the city in search of good food and stylish clothing, Vera has made a fine sport out of necessity.

The next stop on our Saturday expedition was a wine store, also on Srednii, where the proprietor, another friend of Vera's, had saved three bottles of sweet Georgian wine. ("Thank heavens," said

Vera. ("It's impossible to get anything in this town without friends!")
Next we stood in line for bread, which we tested for freshness by
pressing it with a little metal spatula, and after that we went to a
dairy store crammed with shoppers where we stood in line again
for sour cream and butter. Then we took a trolley ride to a small
peasant market in the northern section of Vasilevskii Island, where
Vera haggled with the vendors over the exorbitant price of winter
cucumbers (fourteen rubles a kilo) and exchanged quips with an
old man selling comb honey. By the time we left the market, the
plastic suitcase was heavy with big winter beets and cabbage; we
each clutched a strap as we fought to keep our balance on the
crowded trolley back to the dormitory where Vera lives. The whole
way back, Vera lectured me on how to bake in a typical Soviet oven
—one with cranky or nonexistent temperature controls. "A pan of
water under the baking shelf is the important thing," she said. By
then the streets outside were getting dark. The shopping trip—to
buy a duck and a few groceries—had taken five hours.

Much later, munching a drumstick in the neat brown dorm room
she shares with two other young women, Vera talked with Tom and
me about Soviet life. She is a second-year student in the Leningrad
faculty of journalism, a distant acquaintance, in fact, of our Moscow
friend Grigorii; like him, she is an active Komsomol member, but
she is a bit more relaxed, a bit freer in her opinions. Seated at dinner, she was extraordinarily forceful and articulate in her speech,
describing herself as a patriot, but critical of some aspects of her
country. She complained especially about the difficulties of every-
day existence. "You saw how it was buying food this afternoon,"
she said. "The time, the loads, the effort. And it all falls, all of it,
on the shoulders of us women—when we're not sweeping the streets."

Vera is a self-professed liberated woman who, when she is not
shopping or studying, can work herself into a fine rage about the
status of women in Russia. According to her, the relative equality
of men and women in the labor force has not changed traditional
attitudes. "Basically we women have two roles," Vera said, pulling

off a piece of duck meat and eating it with relish. "We work all day alongside men, and then the bell rings, the men go home and open a bottle of vodka. What do we do? We start our second lives: standing in lines, carrying bundles, cooking, knitting, sewing, scrubbing, serving the men at the table. They're smart. They give us International Women's Day—posters and flowers once a year—and never lift a finger the rest of the time."

Three years ago, Vera divorced her husband, an agricultural scientist from the steppes of Russia's Kuban region. "He was a Cossack," said Vera, who is half Cossack herself. "I married him at eighteen, and he thought, in the good old tradition, that I should wait on him and remain calm when he beat me." She looked at Tom and me matter-of-factly. "My girlfriend Tanya's husband beats her all the time. But she accepts it. Most women do."

Vera's present boyfriend, an amiable blond engineering student named Arkadii, grinned tolerantly as Vera spoke. He had helped her set the table and had contributed to the feast a huge cream-filled cake from a bakery. "I think that men should help their women," he said. "But I'm traditional. I think a man should always be head of the household. There are some tasks that women should do alone. My mother did them. Why can't modern women?"

Vera threw a piece of bread at him. "Hopeless!" she laughed. She began telling us about a short film about women's liberation she made with two or three other young women from the journalism faculty. I interrupted her to ask whether she knew anything about the women's movement in Western Europe or America. She said: "Very little, of course. I know that bourgeois capitalist women have it easier than we do, that often they don't have to work. Why then should they need liberation?" We discussed the subject for a while, and a little later Vera said: "It all seems a bit refined and romantic to me. Fighting for equal pay scales I can understand. But all this business about work for self-fulfillment seems like capitalist luxury. We Russian women have always worked hard—twice as hard as men. Liberation for us means freedom from being brutalized, from having to work so hard. The time has come when we would like to be a bit more feminine—not workhorses any more. You see the women on the construction sites. All of them wear lipstick now, all of them are dying to be a little more feminine—attractive, not beasts!" Vera was flushed; she banged her wine glass sharply on the table.

"My grandmother lived through the Revolution, the Civil War, and two world wars. She worked like a slave alongside men, yet she never sat down at the table with my grandfather. It's this type of attitude that has to change, if the Soviet Union is to become truly civilized. Russian men have to give Russian women a little more; we have to be comrades at home, not just on the job!"

Because Vera is paradoxical Vera, she ended this tirade with a giggle and a flirtatious glance at Arkady. Someone turned on the radio, and a shamelessly treacly baritone poured into the room, singing the kind of song one is flooded with on International Women's Day:

> You're our flower, our flame,
> our inspiration,
> Soviet Woman, this is for you!

The program changed, yielding to a series honoring Soviet female heroes. The third woman described was a factory worker from Simbirsk who was attacked by a wolf last winter as she walked home from a rural bus stop. The woman had been carrying bundles of food home; when the wolf attacked her, she dropped these, grabbed the wolf by the tongue, and dragged it two kilometers down the snowy road to her hut. There, she singlehandedly bludgeoned the wolf to death with an axe handle.

Vera listened to all of this in silence, switched off the radio, and poured us each another glass of Georgian wine. "I propose yet another toast to Soviet women!" she said, with a grin that showed her aluminum tooth. "We can do anything on our own!"

Mayakovsky Billboard

In Mayakovsky Square, not far from the Tchaikovsky Concert Hall, a big computerized electric sign sends various messages flashing out into the night. An outline of a taxi in green dots is accompanied by the words: "Take Taxis—All Streets Are Near." This is replaced by multicolored human figures and a sentence urging Soviet citizens to save in State banks. The bright patterns and messages come and go, making this one of the most sophisticated examples of advertising in Moscow. Even on chilly nights when I pass through the square, there is often a little group of Russians standing in front of the sign, watching in fascination for five and ten minutes as the colored dots go through their magical changes. The first few times I saw this, I chuckled and recalled an old joke about an American town so boring that people went out on weekends to watch the Esso sign. With each month I live here, however, I'm more and more tempted to join the spectators in Mayakovsky Square.

Tourists I've met here invariably refer to Moscow as a "gray" city: this impression, when I examine it, does not come entirely from the weather—I've lived through grayer Novembers in Paris—or from the color of the buildings, a surprising number of which are painted in charming pastels. It springs more from the unbeautiful aspect of the crowds (Russian bodies and faces are heavy; Russian clothes, when not actually hideous, are monotone and forgettable), and most of all, from the lack of Western-style advertising. Advertising, of course, is the glamorous offspring of capitalism and art: why advertise in a country where there is only one brand, the State brand, of anything, and often not enough even of that? There is nothing here comparable to the glittering overlay of commercialism that Americans, at least, take for granted as part of our cities; nothing like the myriad small seductions of the marketplace, which have led us to expect to be enticed. The Soviet political propaganda posters that fill up a small part of the Moscow landscape with their uniformly cold red color schemes and monumental robot-faced figures are so unappealing that they are dismissable. (It's interesting to try to figure out exactly whom these posters are aimed at. Every Russian I know, even the most conservative, finds them dreadful; perhaps they're intended for a future race of titans.)

I realize now, looking back, that for at least my first month in Moscow, I was filled with an unconscious and devastating disappointment. Hardly realizing it, as I walked around the city, I was looking for the constant sensory distractions I was accustomed to in America. Like many others my age, I grew up reading billboards and singing advertising jingles; my idea of beauty was shaped—perniciously, I think—by the models with painted eyes and pounds of shining hair whose beauty was accessible on every television set and street corner. In Moscow, I found none of this easy stimulation—only the rarer, more demanding pleasures of nature and architecture: rain on the gold domes inside the Kremlin walls; yellow leaves stuck to a wet pavement; a decayed stone grotesque on the peeling front of a mansion in the Arbat; a face in a subway crowd.

Living in these comparatively simple surroundings has made my inner life more intense. Tom and I have found that our dreams have gained color and our memories have become sharper; we are both more attentive to beauty. I finally understand in part the Russian phenomenon of staring: now, when I see a well-cut dress (terribly rare), a handsomely bound book (still rarer), or an attractive face, I stare with amazing persistence, until my ravenous eyes are satisfied. Tom and I have found that we can sit for an hour looking—just looking—with lingering pleasure at the most banal American magazine—*Good Housekeeping,* for example—stunned by the attractiveness of its layout and photographs. Last week I received a tiresome dunning letter from the alumni office of my university; I was about to throw it away when my Russian friend Olga snatched it, stared at the elaborate graphics of the letterhead, and said, "It's so beautiful . . . may I have it?" Later I found she'd pinned it up beside her bed.

Everywhere we go in Moscow, we find a frantic enthusiasm for any kind of natural or man-made beauty. At parties, pretty girls are feted with an innocent, extravagant adulation from men and women alike; ordinary people show a passion for art and literature which might be suspect as a pose in America. The deepest roots of this quality of Russian life are hard to discern, and I am setting aside the ugly fact of government censorship of the arts, which obviously plays its own perverse role in intensifying enthusiasm for beauty. I mean to observe here only that a more austere environment seems to favor sensitivity. This isn't a new idea at all, of course. People on islands, in prisons, in monasteries have all discovered the same thing. But it's a remarkable feeling to have my mind clearing up week by week, like a lens that was filmed and dim, until, just as the year goes dark with winter, I've started to see the subtle points of light in this gray city.

Hippies

Yesterday, around three o'clock in the afternoon, I was standing waiting for Misha in front of the Manege, near the Kremlin. It was a dark, wet afternoon with a fine sleet in the air; Russians of all ages crowded up the steps of the Manege, a huge yellow building that was formerly the imperial riding school and now holds exhibits of contemporary art. Misha and his friends were supposed to come by and take me to a café, the Aramat, near Gorky Street, and they were late. I scanned the crowds and thought once again how much nicer Russians looked dressed for cold weather: they are ungainly and ill-at-ease in their badly cut summer clothes, but winter in Moscow means fur, rich fur, everywhere, spangled with melting flakes of snow. Suddenly a slight start went through the crowd. People paused to look, an old woman nearby said, "*Gospodi!*" (My Lord!), and a policeman standing in front of me turned his head thoughtfully. It's them, I thought, and sure enough, I saw Misha waving his big hand as he made his way nonchalantly toward me. Behind him came a little troop of six men and women dressed as he was, their long hair blowing in the sleety wind, their bells and beads tinkling and rattling.

"Hi!" Misha said in English, cheerfully taking my arm.

"Hi!" I said. "You forgot the *shuba* today, huh?"

This is a joke we have. A *shuba* is a heavy fur coat. Whenever I see Misha, I reprimand him for his light clothing, and he promises he will dress in furs for the next meeting. Today he wore his usual outfit: a thin purple jacket embroidered with the English words "Love" and "Rock Explosion" and a pair of tattered orange pants.

The others had gathered in a circle around us, and Misha began to make introductions. "I would like to present you," he said, quite formally, "to some more of our people, *nashi hippi.*" As always, it seemed strange to hear the English word "hippie" used in a Russian sentence. Misha and his friends, however, are adamant about their identity. They are *hippi* (for them, the word is a collective plural and is pronounced "heepee"), and their adoption of the word suggests their fascination with Western culture. Misha took me around the circle: "This is Petya, Kolya, Vitya, Natasha . . ." Looking at the austere young faces, the beads, the long, tangled hair, and the bright clothes gave me a sharp thrill of nostalgia; I thought of the streets of Philadelphia, Rittenhouse Square in 1968, when I, too young to join in seriously, had watched the hippies drifting by—knights and their spacy ladies bound on some quest I burned to understand. But this was Russia, ten years later, and the dated look of the whole assemblage was almost ludicrous. I felt like a traveler who has chanced upon an outpost in India where Victorian England still survives.

We set off down Gorky Street, leaving a wake of stares, turning heads, and muttered comments in the afternoon crowd. The public reaction was rarely hostile; it was more one of unabashed curiosity, which Misha and his friends blandly ignored. "Russians never get used to anything," Misha had told me earlier. "There have been *hippi* for years now. But still they stare like peasants, and still *babushki* stop me on the street to scold me about my hair." I was walking with Misha and his girl friend, a Lithuanian named Aldona, who had a cherubic face and a mass of frizzy brown curls, with a narrow black velvet band tied around her forehead. Misha was telling me about traveling; he talked very loud and fast, and made the rest of us scuttle to keep up with his rapid, bouncy walk. Misha is from Orenburg, a city in the Urals. He is nineteen, tall and thin, with long, stringy black hair, a pimpled face, and an expression of genial astonishment at the rest of the world. He left Orenburg a year ago, because it was boring and because his parents did not understand his desire to be a hippie. Since then, he's been hitchhiking around the Soviet Union, moving from Central Asia to the Baltic with his little migratory flock of friends. He spent the summer in a tent near the Black Sea, then came to Moscow, where he's been staying with friend after friend. "But it's getting too cold here," he said, tugging down his sleeves. Soon it will be time to move on to Kiev, and from there to Samarkand, with its sun and melons and that famous Central Asian hash.

I asked Aldona how she became a hippie. In a small, shy voice, she told a nearly classic story. She is seventeen and has been away from home for four months. A little while ago she was living with her family in Vilnius, attending an institute for advanced study of English. She was bored and unhappy; her father had recently remarried, and his new wife hated Aldona. "I couldn't stand it," she said. "I heard about the life of *hippi*, and I decided to leave home." Like Misha and the rest of her friends, she has a strong, if vague, reverence for Tolstoy—whom she has never read. She and a friend left Lithuania and hitchhiked to Yasnaya Polyana, Tolstoy's estate, near Tula; she had heard rumors that a great hippie gathering would take place there to celebrate the hundred and fiftieth birthday of the author. The gathering took place, but because of their hair and clothing, the two hundred hippies who showed up were denied entrance to the estate. They paid homage to their idol by setting up camp for two days in the woods outside the gate. Here Aldona met Misha and his friends. "It was a paradise," she said. "Such gentle people, so loving and kind. I left my friend, and when the *hippi* came to Moscow, I came, too." Now Aldona wears a bell around her neck and a pair of Soviet jeans with English words embroidered on the knee. "It says 'This Little Light of Mine,'" she told me. "A spiritual. Mahalia Jackson. Ah, so beautiful." In Russian and in English, "beautiful" is one of Aldona's favorite words.

"And what will you do in the next few years?" I asked.

Aldona gazed at me uncomprehendingly, and I was struck by the beauty of her wide brown eyes and childish mouth. She pulled her short velvet jacket tighter around her. "Well, I guess I'll be a hippie for the rest of my life," she said. "And do you know what my father says? He says that I am right—that if he were younger, he'd be a hippie, too!"

By now we were rounding the corner onto Tverskoy Boulevard, which, with its central strip of iron-railed park, has the look of Paris. The brown leaves left on the maple trees were rattling with sleet, and a keen wind had started to blow. Taxis swooped by, splashing through puddles. The Café Aramat is near the square where Herzen Street intersects the boulevard; there are two churches there, and the magnificent Art Nouveau house where Gorky once lived. The café itself is a hole in the wall which you go down two steps to get into. Inside are five or six round tables and a counter where a surly old woman sells tea and buns. As the eight of us piled inside, blowing on our cold fingers and stamping our feet, she called over to us, "So you're going to buy something today, are you?"

Misha said, "Yes, Grandmother, we'll drink tea all afternoon." To me he whispered, "They hate for us to come here. Often, in the evenings, they get the police to throw us out."

I had heard bad things about the Café Aramat. Friends had told me it was a place that foreigners should stay away from, because of police surveillance and frequent raids. Misha and his friends are very fond of the Aramat. Their name for it is *Vavilon* (Babylon), because they claim that like the ancient city, it is a meeting place of all nations. "Here you can find hippies from all over the Soviet Union," Misha once bragged to me. "Sometimes from all over the world!"

The place looked innocent enough, with its pink walls, half-empty tables, and students and middle-aged people reading newspapers or chatting. We sat down, and Misha started lecturing me in a whisper about the police. Russian hippies have the same obsession with the police which American hippies once displayed; *hippi* and *militsiya* have a dependent, almost symbiotic relationship of mutual irritation. Misha's friends speak of their police skirmishes with the expert fabling of soldiers who have seen action. One of the first questions Misha ever asked me about the United States was how the police are there. He laughs with delight whenever I tell him rude words for "cop": "pig," "flic."

By this time we were clutching hot cups of tea. Misha and his friends all added many lumps of sugar and drank greedily, sharing a few small buns. I reached for my bag and offered a carton of milk I'd just bought. At first everyone declined scornfully, but then Aldona reached out shyly for the carton. In a few minutes they were all gulping down the milk; I guessed that for most of them it was the first meal of the day. I studied the faces around me and saw that every one of them—except Aldona's, with its radiant young complexion—was blemished and haggard from lack of sleep. I thought of Misha's queer elusiveness when he is asked where he lives in Moscow—"With friends, with friends," he always says—and tried to imagine the life of transients here: panhandling; sleeping on splintery floors, on sagging chairs, in the bleak, high-ceilinged vestibules of Soviet apartment houses. An interesting thought is that in the Soviet Union such a life style isn't as much a rebellious departure from a social norm as it was for hippies in the United States. Even middle-class Russians are always putting friends up for the night, always borrowing or lending money for living expenses. The communal life forced on most Russians by the housing crisis makes the hippies' close-knit groups seem like a continuation of, rather than a break with, tradition. Besides, the Protestant ethic has never quite caught hold here. The Russian nature seems to hold fewer reserves of guilt about not working or about living off someone else; characteristic generosity and interdependence have placed such situations almost in the common run of things. I know a number of older Russians whose lives are as precarious as the hippies'.

Inevitably, we started to talk about America. Misha and his friends have the typical Soviet fascination with things Western—especially the counterculture of the sixties. The talk quickly became an interrogation. Allen Ginsberg—what's he doing now? What about Jerry Rubin? Jane Fonda? Eldridge Cleaver? What are American hippies doing now? Do young people still live in communes? Hitchhike? The faces of the group bent in toward me, their eyes searching mine ravenously. I felt a curious embarrassment as I tried to describe to them the changed temper of the seventies. It was a near-sad feeling, as if I were the bearer of tidings to an isolated group of believers that their leaders had lost the faith. They laughed at me in open disbelief when I said that Rubin had married a rich woman and was living with her in a luxurious apartment in New York. "What about the revolution?" asked Petya, a young man wearing a hood.

"Most American radicals from the sixties have decided to work for a change within the system," I answered glibly.

There was a pause. Misha pushed back his hair and lit a cigarette. (On his wrist I could see one of those woven-yarn charms that I myself used to wear nine or ten years ago—good karma). "I understand that most of those people are old now," he said. "Almost our parents' age. But what about the *hippi?*"

"There are not very many hippies any more. There are people who have decided to live in a different way. But they are not hippies."

"But what is the youth doing?" he asked.

"It's dancing in discotheques and hoping to get into law school," I said.

The dark afternoon had got darker, and the fluorescent lights in the café came on. The *babushka* had several times waddled over to us to say threateningly that if we weren't going to order more tea, we'd better go. The group at our table was a fluid one, with people constantly arriving and leaving, new arrivals bearing little gusts of cold air on their coats. One of these new arrivals, a beautiful girl with a cascade of hair under a drooping felt hat, whispered to Misha that we could go to the apartment of a friend of hers. The place was just off Gorky Street; we jogged the short distance, hurrying to get out of the sleet. I found that this is the way that Misha spends most of his days in Moscow: migrating between the Aramat and various apartments.

The place belonged to a young artist named Slava. He was a slight young man with a beard and a mild, sarcastic smile. We all sat down around a table in a small room with peeling walls and a bed heaped with clothes in one corner. By a window were some examples of Slava's work, which was very bad: psychedelic pastel drawings alternated with murky religious scenes, apparently painted with a stick. We drank more tea, and Misha, Petya, and Aldona started teaching me how to panhandle. "Hey, man, can you give me ten kopecks?" The group doubled up with laughter at my repetition.

Slava put a Jefferson Airplane tape on a very fancy West German machine. He had a huge collection of tapes, mostly American jazz or sixties rock. He grinned when he saw that I was impressed. He borrowed Western records whenever he could, he said, and a friend at a music store taped them. We were all talking about the problems of the *hippi* with the *urla*, their name for working-class toughs. These men, short-haired young factory or construction workers, like Western hard rock but hate hippies and Hare Krishnas. (Yes, there are Hare Krishnas in Moscow.) Everybody seemed to know somebody else who had just been beaten up by the *urla*. I was interested in the stories about the *urla*, and still more interested in what Misha had to say about drugs. It seems that Soviet hippie culture places a lot less emphasis on drugs than the American hippies of the late sixties and early seventies did. It's obvious why: scarcity and strong government suppression have left most Russians unexposed to drugs. (Just recently a student friend asked me whether I'd ever "shot up" marijuana and whether I was all right after the experience.) Misha and his friends have smoked marijuana—which they call *trava* (grass)—and hashish a fair number of times; they say it's not hard to get hold of either in Central Asia. Harder drugs—cocaine, heroin, LSD—they had not tried. The group laughed knowingly about different names for marijuana, but it was clear that getting stoned means very little in their lives. It was strange for me to see and hear all around me vestiges of the American drug culture of a decade ago—the psychedelic drawings, the fantastic clothes, Grace Slick wailing on the tape player—and to know that the core of the experience was missing. This seemed like one of the latest examples of Russia's borrowing form but not content from the West.

Misha and his friends like being crazy more than being stoned. Their vision of the ideal state of things is the universal hippie dream of a kind of gentle anarchy, where every mortal does his own divinely inspired thing in an atmosphere of peace and brotherhood. Because present normality accepts violence and repression, it follows that the insane must be on the right track. In the course of the afternoon, Aldona said to me, "I want to be crazy. I hope I am." A pretty typical desire, I thought, remembering our own adolescent crowning of insanity in the sixties. But it became a sad joke when I found out that Misha and two of his friends had spent time in insane asylums—a popular Soviet method for controlling intractable young people as well as older dissidents. Being locked up was a convenient—perhaps a deliberately courted—fate for these young men, since it helped them avoid the mandatory military service at age eighteen. But aside from a few jokes about haircuts and lack of knives, they wouldn't talk about the experience.

"Was it bad?" I asked Misha.

For a minute his face lost its expression of vague good will. "Yes, very," he said.

Aldona stared at him with wide eyes.

As it got later, we started to talk about dissent. Misha and his friends discuss political protest against the Soviet government with the same vague, eager enthusiasm with which they talk of any rejection of convention. In the same way, they—and most of my other young friends—are religious. They wear crucifixes and go to church regularly, partly because the Russian Orthodox Church provides the kind of pageantry that hippies are drawn to, and partly because church attendance is an act of nonconformity. Even church lingo has become an in thing. Misha mockingly crosses himself when something surprises him, and some of his friends say goodbye by raising a hand and intoning, "God be with you, children." The double attraction of pageantry and rebelliousness also draws the *hippi* to the culture of the prerevolutionary past. They adore anything old: peasant huts, the crumbling mansions near Arbat Street, icons, jewelry.

In politics, things are simple. There are the good guys—the young, the crazy, the gentle fans of Western music and culture. And there are the bad guys—the KGB, the Komsomol, parents, policemen. Misha and his friends are fuzzy on the Jewish question, and disapprove of violence, but they applaud any kind of dissident behavior as moving toward the new Eden they envision. "Overthrowing the Party would mean happiness here," Misha told me, leaning across the table with a beatific smile. "Everyone could do what he wanted."

Certain incidents have become symbols or touchstones for them the way Kent State or the Chicago riots did for American youth. One of these is the folk-rock-concert demonstration that took place last summer in Leningrad's Palace Square. Petya had been there, and he described how Voice of America and the Leningrad newspapers had announced that Santana, Joan Baez, and the Beach Boys were coming to Leningrad on July 4, how hundreds of kids—workers, students, hippies—had made their way to the city from all over the Soviet Union; how when the concert, without explanation, failed to occur, the angry and disappointed crowd began chanting and refused to disperse. (I found out later from American friends that the concert had been aborted early in the planning stages by Soviet officials, who quite naturally disapproved of anything having to do with Western music, youth, and the American Independence Day. The announcement in the Leningrad press was a profound error, which must have cost some journalist his job.) "We were right under the windows of the Winter Palace," said Petya, running his fingers through his hair. "It was a real nation of youth. And do you know what happened? We were all angry and determined to stay. I was there with my good friend. We had been chanting 'Santana! Santana!' Then, farther up in the crowd, they started chanting 'Down with the Party!' After that, we all started to yell it, and then the *militsiya* came with fire hoses."

"Did you get beaten up?" I asked. I had heard five or six versions of this story, with and without chanting and fire hoses.

"Of course," Petya said modestly.

Next, the group took turns telling me about Kaunas, Lithuania. This is a city that has gone down in dissident lore as the scene of two days of rioting in May of 1972, after the funeral of Romas Kalanta, a Lithuanian Roman Catholic who had set fire to himself to protest Soviet rule, especially the suppression of Catholicism. "Thousands of young people marched through the streets," Aldona told me. "The police beat them up, and arrested hundreds. The Russians sent in parachute troops and KGB units."

"And what do you think about that?" I asked, remembering that most Lithuanians I know are fiery patriots.

Aldona gave me her lovely, naïve smile. "I think freedom is a beautiful thing," she said.

I had to go and said so, but Misha pressed me to stay for a minute. "We have something to show you," he said. He reached into his shoulder bag and produced a large school notebook. He opened it and said, "This is our book." It was a neatly kept scrapbook of the American youth movement in the late nineteen-sixties. There were pictures of Rubin, of Leary, of Peter Fonda, squinting over motorcycle handlebars, of Joplin, of Hendrix, of the archetypal hippie girl with beads and cascading blond hair. The neatly clipped pictures were grainy and distorted—culled, I was sure, from the most improbable sources. The Cyrillic lettering under each picture was large and childish. Looking at this curious monument to the sixties, I felt amused and a little melancholy.

Misha and his friends walked back to the Arbatskaya metro station with me. The sleet of the afternoon had turned into a stinging hail; the lights of the cars coming up Arbat Street showed up the pellets whirling through the dark. "My God!" said Misha, trying to pull his collar up around his ears. "What a wind!"

"It'll soon be time to move on to Central Asia, right?" I said.

"You're right. There's still sun there. And melons."

Beside us, Aldona scurried along silently, her red cheeks buried in her fur collar, her hair streaming out under her headband.

Petya was taking long strides ahead of us, clutching his ragged hood and talking about Bulgakov to a girl named Tanya. In front of the metro (the brick-colored entrance near the Praga Restaurant), we stopped and said goodbye. Rush-hour crowds came shouldering by us, pausing to stare at the *hippi* with their fanciful clothes and bedraggled hair.

"How do you like our café and our people?" asked Misha.

"I like both very much," I said.

Aldona gave me a kiss, and a blond boy with a steel tooth said, in English, "I dig it the most!"

Then all the members of the group, much to my dismay, and much to the intense curiosity of the subway crowd, raised their hands and gave me a peace sign. I watched them, and wondered how this graft of the American past on the Russian present would survive. I wondered, too, about their future under the system— these children whose clothes and behavior can win them a stint in a mental hospital. But I couldn't just stand there, so I raised my hand and returned the sign, wondering what, exactly, I meant by it.

Gori
(Soviet Georgia)

Stalin's birthplace, the town of Gori, is a dusty, haunted village forty miles northwest of Tbilisi. The sunny town square holds what is surely the only life-size statue of Stalin remaining in the Soviet Union. The figure strides energetically forward, the thick mustaches and slightly receding chin pointed confidently at the mountains, but the only people who see it are the women in black scarves crossing the square to a little fruit store at one end and the occasional small groups of tourists who visit the town. Gori is the site of the Soviet Union's single remaining Stalin museum, which is now a monument less to the dead leader than to the Soviet power of forgetting what it is inconvenient to remember.

The museum at Gori is a beautiful Renaissance-style building of tawny Georgian sandstone, constructed in 1957, four years after Stalin's death. It stands in a formal landscaped garden, and to one side, under an elaborate marble pavilion, is the two-room plaster hut where Stalin was born. Farther away is a large hotel, now closed. The whole display has a muted air—none of the banners, flags, or elaborate souvenir stalls of the countless Lenin museums scattered across the Soviet Union. The buildings lie peacefully in the mountain sun, and a sullen-eyed guide takes visitors on a brief tour. She is an attractive young woman, with the plump, compact body and Mediterranean features of Georgian mountain people; her tone as she talks is quietly defiant, as if daring visitors to mock her subject. Like her, many Georgians retain a fierce loyalty to Stalin, and that is one reason for the existence of a barely concealed hostility between Georgians and Russians. Kiosks in Tbilisi openly sell illicit Stalin memorabilia: plastic-covered postcard portraits; prints of Stalin and his mother. A Georgian friend told me, "There's a reason the museum at Gori exists. The Russians know there would be a riot if they tried to close it down."

Inside, the museum is unexceptional. There are endless photographs of the young Soso Dzhugashvili, who could be any of the urchins playing in the streets of Gori today. There are his old exercise books. There are manuscripts of poems he wrote while he was a student at the Tbilisi theological seminary. There is the first article signed with the pseudonym "Stalin." There are notes from Lenin. Above it all hangs a series of bland commemorative paintings that chart the emergence of a formidable will. Adjoining the main room of the museum is a display of craftsmen's tributes to Stalin during his lifetime. There are lamps, rugs, tapestries, carvings—many bearing portraits, and all in astounding bad taste. The worst of these is a radio that was presented to Stalin in 1938 by the workers of an industrial town: it is set into a gilded foot-high representation of a mountain topped by a small steel replica of a tank, and the whole thing is crowned by a large lamp with a fringed shade. Looking at this monstrosity, which was supposedly a favorite of the former leader, one inevitably thinks of the outrageous ugliness of the "Gothic" buildings that Stalin caused to be erected throughout Moscow. A Russian friend has given me a word to describe this barbaric bad taste—*meshchansky*, which can mean both "philistine" and "of, or belonging to, the petty bourgeoisie." Both senses apply, of course. Seeing the two whitewashed rooms where the Dzhugashvili family lived, and strolling through the humble streets of Gori, one can easily envision an ambitious boy gradually evolving a vast, vulgar dream of opulence and power.

The exhibit makes a number of smooth Soviet transitions that ignore the fact of the purges. Questioned about them, the guide fixes you with a level look and replies in a chiding voice, "I'm sorry. We don't discuss such questions."

What is most striking, certainly, is not the museum exhibits but Gori itself, sleeping with its secret in the dusty sunlight like a lost kingdom—unremembered, almost unvisited, a part of Russian history deliberately set aside. Although families live here, in a few high rises and crumbling two-story plaster houses, the air has a lifeless feeling: it reminds me of those unlucky sunny spots in America where old people cluster to die. And, in fact, it is an Elba, a San Clemente for a dead man; it feels unhealthy.

Valerii

For those of us exchange students who from time to time crave an infusion of American culture, there's the Friday night Marine Bar at the U.S. Embassy: American drinks and dance music served up to the youth of Moscow's foreign community by a dour crew of Marines, all this in a setting that combines the atmosphere of a PX and a disco in, say, Sioux Falls. Each time Tom and I go, we have a magnificent time gorging on canned corn chips, drinking screwdrivers made with frozen Florida orange juice, and dancing among our short-haired young hosts. Back in the States, Marines seemed as foreign to me as Russians did, but now I have a queer, glad feeling of recognition when I see their unfailingly healthy faces and hear their polite Southern and Midwestern accents. Like the rest of the ingrown embassy world, where few staff members speak even passable Russian, the Marines bear no relation to the realities of life in the Soviet Union. They go about their duties in wintry Moscow, strangely enough, wearing jungle camouflage uniforms. When I dance with the Marines, or stand in the embassy commissary, with its rows of peanut butter jars and boxes of sugared cereal, or walk among the big shiny Detroit cars in the embassy driveway, or talk to the earnest, affable bureaucrats who work in the offices, I feel as if I'm seeing part of a dream America: the dear, blind, brash, innocent America of television shows and commercials—the kind of vision that we simple souls in exile would naturally long for, and unfailingly re-create.

Last Friday night there were four of us crowded around a table in the Marine Bar: Tom and I; another American student; and our Russian friend Valerii, passing as an American. Twenty minutes before, we had walked him into the embassy, past the Soviet guards who are there to keep unauthorized Russians from entering the big mustard-colored stronghold of American power. There have been many cases of Russians seeking sanctuary in the embassy—the most sensational episode of late being that of the family of Baptists who escaped into the embassy and actually lived there for several weeks—and so the guards are attentive and tough. There was little need to worry, however, that Valerii would be recognized as Russian. His short light-brown hair and regular, boyish features give him the air of an American textbook illustration of the 1950s, and with his plaid jacket, his Levis, and his painstakingly polished slang, he seemed almost more authentic than the rest of us.

Valerii is in fact a young man with two lives, a Moscow State student whose situation is an example of the sometimes-fatal love affair many young Russians have with the West. He is a student of philology at the university, in the inevitable position of studying the English language. The English division of the Philology Faculty is one of the most difficult to get into, partly because of the huge popularity of the English language, and partly because groups of students are sometimes allowed to travel in England. "You travel in a group filled with spies, and you are given so little money that you can see nothing of the country on your own," Valerii once told us. "But still I dream of going. It would be worth anything to be in the West."

His parents, a pair of low-ranking technical engineers, have none of the special privileges of the Soviet elite; Valerii got into the English program because he is an extraordinarily gifted and conscientious student, and an equally conscientious Komsomol member, so well thought of that he is permitted to lead groups of foreign students on tours. He is also an extraordinary hypocrite, someone who, to me, incarnates the very idea of lip service. Tom, who is rereading 1984, found an apt description of Valerii in Winston Smith's reflections on his lover Julia:

> She hated the Party, and said so in the crudest words, but she made no general criticism of it. Except where it touched upon her own life she had no interest in Party doctrine. . . . Any kind of organized

revolt against the Party, which was bound to be a failure, struck her as stupid. The clever thing was to break the rules and stay alive all the same.

Valerii's evasion of the Party, like Julia's, is not overt; rather, he has used the official *apparat* to gain himself the best possible life. Unlike the ambitious Grigorii and our other Komsomol friends, who flirt with an interest in the West but are deeply conservative inside, Valerii mocks the system of which he is already such an efficient functioning part, and holds the West in his imagination as a shining door of escape. His vision of America and Western Europe is almost pitifully defined by material things: his collection of denim and corduroy jeans (corduroy, incidentally, is the newest fad among a very few spoiled young Russians who have actually become satiated with black-market blue jeans); his British umbrella; his Western records; his Frisbee. In his stylish clothes, he is often approached by Soviet black marketeers who think he's a foreigner. This "passing," as he calls it, is one of his greatest pleasures; when he describes it, his eyes flash with an almost hysterical brilliance.

Valerii shares in the very fashionable contempt that I have seen several young Russians display toward anything native to their country. "It's the best kind of dance band," I heard him say once. "They don't play a note of Russian music." Attitudes like this prevail in his fast circle of friends, most of whom, like himself, are young native Muscovites of a "middle-class" background. Growing up in the capital, they have been exposed to a great many foreign influences. "I've always been curious about the West," Valerii told us as we chatted on a stroll one recent afternoon. "When I was little, I used to catch sight of the diplomats in their big cars and beautiful clothes and wonder where all that came from."

Girls find Valerii very attractive, with his American clothes, his word-perfect imitations of "The Voice" (Voice of America), and his dangerously thin hypocrisy about the Komsomol. Double lives are very chic in his circle. But the worship of things Western takes its toll. Two years ago Valerii's girl friend abandoned him to marry a Soviet Jew who promised to emigrate to New York and take her with him.

As he entered the Marine Bar the other night, Valerii paused for an instant in the doorway, in the face of the colored lights and disco music and the laughing, dancing, drinking, casually dressed crowd of foreigners inside. He had been cool and relaxed as we walked him through the guards, but now a spasm of emotion crossed his face. I couldn't tell whether it was nervousness, fear, or the indefinable, troubling sensation one experiences when one is suddenly confronted with something one has dreamed of and wondered about for a long time. He clutched Tom's arm for a minute. Soon we were sitting around a table near the dance floor, drinking gin-and-tonics, and watching British, Swedish, and American nannies and secretaries cavorting with Marines to "Le Freak," the song of the evening. One of the dancing Marines, a tall blond with a rawboned Appalachian face, gave a rebel yell every time the chorus came on: "Yee—haw! Freak out!" Near us, a balding embassy staffer in double-knit pants was trying to strike up a conversation over the music with a strapping British girl; she kept tossing her head with the dangerous coquetry of women who live in foreign outposts where they have been given exaggerated notions of their own charms. A half-opened window behind them let a channel of cold air into the hot crowded room, and through it I could see the lights of the snowy Sadovoye Kol'tso, where a few trolleys were passing. The Soviet guards at the front of the embassy must have been able to hear the laughter and music, and I wondered what they were thinking, standing down there in their gray woolen coats in the snow.

Valerii drank a few gin-and-tonics (curiously examining the plastic mixers) and stared at the dancers. After we'd all danced and had kidded around awhile, he drew the three of us close around him and began to talk to us in a flood of words which grew progressively more bitter in tone. Like many of our Russian friends, he plunged directly into a discussion of turbulent emotions without the least preliminary. "I don't know if you can understand it," he said. "I don't know if you can possibly understand what it's like for me to be here. For you this is something pleasant, something usual, and it's a joke, kind of a lark to bring me along. But for me, it's as if I'd entered a dream world—you know, it's like in *The Master and Margarita*, when Margarita steps into what seems like an ordinary apartment, and it's infinite inside, it's hell. Only this is heaven—not exactly, but something I've shaped in my thoughts and carried around with me for a long time. And now, to be here and only halfway belong . . ." He took a sip of his drink, glanced around at us, and gave a tight smile that contorted his young face unpleasantly. "Don't worry," he said. "The Embassy bugs can't hear us through the music. I'm an expert about eavesdropping. I have to hand in my little reports on the tour groups I lead. It's as painful for me to mix with the foreigners on those tour groups as it is for me to be here with you tonight. All these Scandinavians, English, and Americans—they're all so rich and free and casual about life. I know that they can do whatever comes into their heads, and it makes me angry, it really does.

"You see," he continued after a slight pause, "to succeed in the Soviet Union, I'd have to be settling down by now. Doing more Komsomol chores, volunteering, fawning. And then I'd marry a suitable girl, move in with her parents, produce a child for the State. And when I was fifty I might have a post at an *institut*, with a three-room apartment and a few trips abroad. That isn't enough for me. I'm getting more and more turned off to life here. Even Russian girls don't interest me any more. I've had affairs with two foreign girls, and they were different—so lively and exciting . . ."

It was strange to hear this anguished, entirely Russian confession in English, from the lips of a fresh-faced young man who could have posed for a Pepsi-Cola commercial; stranger still to hear it against a background of disco music and flirtatious chatter as the Marines behind the bar laid out rounds of drinks and the pretty girls on the dance floor bobbed in time to the beat. I thought of Valerii's frequent talk about emigration: he told me once that he will probably try to arrange a marriage of convenience to a foreigner, or—like his former girl friend—to a Russian Jew who is planning to apply for an exit visa. In a low voice I asked him about this, and he gazed off over the heads of the dancers. "What holds me back is my parents," he said finally. "I'm not sure I could stand never seeing them again. We've discussed it and they say they're prepared for anything I decide. But the authorities might make them suffer in some way if I emigrated. So I really don't know what to do. Sometimes I think I'm a little crazy."

Later that night, as the big sound system thumped out the soundtrack of *Saturday Night Fever*, we tried to explain the plot of the film to Valerii. "A young working-class American—you know, a worker—who feels that he's caught in a dead end . . . a pointless, unprogressive . . . life," I said, stumbling over my words in embarrassment as I suddenly saw the parallel to Valerii's own situation. But Valerii didn't notice; he was too busy watching the dancers.

"What amazes me about Westerners, especially you Americans, is the freedom with which you move," he said. "You're not worried about what anybody might say. Russians couldn't move like that." He frowned suddenly, ran his fingers through his hair, and said, "Why am I always speaking such dirt about Russians? Now you see what happens to us Soviet kids. We turn on to Western stuff and start to hate ourselves."

Still later, the Marines stopped the music and shut down the colored lights. As we went down the stairs and walked through the embassy courtyard, it flashed across my imagination for one instant that Valerii might break for it and run, might try to seek asylum like those hapless Baptists. But he passed calmly through the exit, as if nothing had been said inside, as if it all, indeed, had been a lark. It was after one in the morning, and a light powdery snow was falling. "Goodbye, America!" said Valerii flippantly, tossing a cheeky grin back at the Soviet guards who stood motionless against the tall yellowish building. "Back to the fortress!" We caught a taxi back to Moscow State.

The Movie

We went to the movies today with Volodya and his wife, Anna. The four of us shoved our way to the front of a tremendous crowd to buy tickets, and then bought ice cream to take into the theatre. Volodya told us that this *kinotheatre* was one of the best in Moscow; it was a large pink room with plaster friezes of athletes, filled with rows of hard wooden seats. The film was French, an absurdly didactic reworking of the poor-little-rich-child theme. A confused, wispy-haired newspaperman is "bought" as a toy by the spoiled eight-year-old son of a newspaper magnate; after a series of high jinks in a garishly overfurnished château, the story leads us gently to the conclusion that the little boy is, in fact, *not happy* with his icy bejeweled mother and his potentate father—he loves the journalist best! It is easy to see why this film is being shown at a large downtown theatre: it is a socialist bedtime story, with rooms of huddled office workers thrown into contrast with the vast cars and gilt curlicues of the big boss. The audience giggled appreciatively each time the boss slapped at a secretary or capriciously fired a worker, there were satisfied murmurs at the end, when the little boy left his father's big Mercedes to cling to the humbly dressed newspaperman. But this was a French film, and there were suggestions of bedroom farce that, for the Soviet audience, were never fulfilled. The journalist would encounter the boss's beautiful wife in one of the long velvet corridors of the château, exchange a few flirtatious words, and—poof! jump!—we found our hero in another scene entirely. There was a strange stuttering feeling to the action which could not, I felt, be wholly because the sound was dubbed in Russian.

Walking back to the metro, I asked Volodya if he thought the film had been cut. He gave me a peculiar look and said that it was hard to tell, that he thought it was an excellent film, and that, as always, there was no sex. Tom and I mentioned a French spy comedy, *The Tall Blond Man with One Black Shoe*. Anna said yes, yes, she knew it, one of the funniest things she'd ever seen. Well, what about the sex in that, we said, that hilarious scene where he's fooling around with his friend's wife? No, that scene had not been in the version they saw. I thought of the odd mental talents a diet of such films must develop: an ability for elision, for constant suspension of logic. Only a people ravenous for foreign entertainment could accept a French farce with the romantic scenes deleted. Volodya started to laugh in amazement as we described the cut scenes in the spy movie. "We Russians aren't old enough for that yet!" he said. "We are children!"

Victor Louis

Two sappy songs keep running through my head: one about Ded Moroz, the Russian Santa; the other about a little Yule tree. Both are played on Radio Moscow constantly these days, sung in the high, squeaky children's voices that sentimental Russians love. It's the holiday season here now with a vengeance, as everyone gets ready for New Year's, the great Soviet winter celebration. The stores are packed with customers, special booths in metro stations sell New Year's cards with pictures of Ded Moroz, and "bazaars" have been set up around the city to sell scraggly Yule trees. A friend of ours bought a set of small metal tree ornaments; they included a silver soccer ball and a tiny gilt cosmonaut.

While all the New Year's preparation goes on around us, some of us Westerners have been quietly celebrating Christmas—a holiday that for Tom and me ended up being a strange one indeed. Christmas Eve we spent initiating Russian friends into the mysteries of eggnog. (They had all heard of it, and thought of it as an arcane drink made from an immensely complicated recipe.) On Christmas morning we ate an American breakfast at the Intourist Hotel while two Swedish drunks sang "White Christmas." Then we took a train out to Peredelkino, twelve miles southwest of Moscow. We were carrying our skis the whole morning; we had been invited to spend Christmas Day in the country with Victor and Jennifer Louis.

Long before coming to the Soviet Union, I'd heard of Victor Louis—mysterious journalist, Soviet millionaire, so-called mouthpiece of the Kremlin, man of so many roles and faces that it was difficult to keep track of them all. It was in the early sixties that Louis first caught the attention of Western journalists, who were fascinated by his peculiar position as a Soviet citizen who was the Moscow correspondent for the London *Evening News* and whose byline occasionally appeared in foreign periodicals like *France-Soir* and the *Washington Post*. Since then, he has become known as the official conduit by which maneuverings inside the Kremlin are "confidentially" leaked to the West; for example, in 1964 it was Louis who revealed to foreign newsmen the fall of Nikita Khrushchev. Louis is much more than an unofficial Party spokesman, however. In *Ten Years After Ivan Denisovich*, Zhores A. Medvedev asserts that Louis was a central figure in the persecution of Aleksandr Solzhenitsyn. Medvedev also states that it was Louis who, presumably acting on KGB orders, dampened the sensation of Svetlana Stalin's 1967 memoir, *Twenty Letters to a Friend*, by arranging the Western appearance of a pirated edition months before the official publication date.

Louis is known as much for his lavish personal life as he is for his political activities; a 1971 *Newsweek* article describes him gloating almost obsessively over his luxurious country household, his expensive foreign gadgets, his travel privileges. Thousands of tourists know him from still another side—as the co-author (with his wife, Jennifer) of *The Complete Guide to the Soviet Union*.

Though Louis and his wife move mostly in journalistic and diplomatic circles, they occasionally entertain a few of the exchange students from Moscow State at their house on holidays; this was how Tom and I came to be visiting them.

When we told Russian friends about our Christmas invitation to Peredelkino, the response was usually a laugh and a shrug. "Everyone knows what *he* is," people would say. "It's not even worth a joke."

My friend Olga gave more of a warning. "If you go there, you'll be walking right into the mouth of the KGB," she said. "They'll talk very freely, almost like *dissidenty*. But they'll be listening to *you* the whole time. Don't talk about what you're doing, whom you know. Yes, of course Victor Louis is KGB. How else could a

Soviet journalist write for Western papers? And how else could a Soviet family live like landed gentry?"

Jennifer Louis picked us up at the station. She is an English-woman who came here as a governess with a British diplomat's family in the mid-fifties and married Louis—in spite of his name, he is Russian—a few years later. Being picked up at the station by Jennifer Louis was somewhat like being picked up at the station of an English place like Tunbridge Wells when you're coming out for a weekend of riding, walking, or sitting near the fireplace in a very large house. The icy platform, though, was crowded with Russians in felt boots and worn winter coats, who turned to stare at her as she herded us into the car. She is a small, robust woman of forty-six, with a narrow, ruddy face that reminds one, pleasantly, of a fox or a ferret. Her eyes are very bright, and her voice and her movements are brisk, with a kind of impatience to them, as if she were constantly waiting for the rest of the world to catch up. She wears Scottish sweaters and tweed skirts, and in a crowd of English or American women with well-bred accents she would be indistinguishable, but in the Soviet Union she is unique.

She drove us to her house, past the writers' colony at Peredel-kino, past the cemetery where Pasternak is buried, up and down the lovely frozen hills. On the way, we chatted about her three sons. The eldest, Nikolai, is a history student at Moscow State University.

"What period is his specialty?" Tom asked.

Jennifer paused to shift gears. "Contemporary. I thin.'. that's nice, don't you? The contemporary period's much the best to study —because dear old Uncle Lenin wasn't around to comment on it! The students have more freedom." She gave us a pleasant smile. En garde, I thought, remembering Olga.

We turned onto a short snowy road lined with tall pine trees and high green gates. The tops of big houses showed over the fences, and there was that feeling of concentrated privacy one finds in the neighborhoods of the very rich. Jennifer glanced at us. "These houses were built for victorious generals of the Second World War," she said. "As you can see, they're enormous and frightfully old-fashioned, even for Russia. The generals died off in the fifties and sixties, and there's nothing left of the military now. Editors of *Pravda* live here . . . and here. And we live here!"

We pulled into a large circular driveway, the car wheels crunching on the snow. A dog barked a greeting, and before I looked at anything else, my attention was caught by a gigantic, beautifully carved wooden doghouse, with the closely joined logs and lacy carving of an antique Russian hut. "Isn't it beautiful?" said Jennifer, following my glance. "We have a man who does the most exquisite woodworking. You'll see more inside."

The main house was enormous and sprawling, and was painted a bright turquoise. Across from it stood a garage, also painted and carved in the traditional Russian *izba* style; we learned later that it contained living quarters for several servants, and held the five family cars, which included a Mercedes and a nineteen-twenties touring car. In a few minutes we found ourselves seated inside with cups of tea in our hands, staring at a twelve-foot Christmas tree. Jennifer Louis had stayed outside to direct a Bulgarian maid in the cutting of more Christmas greens. Soon she came in and offered us a plate of gingerbread cookies. "We have the cleverest cook who makes these things," she said, crunching on a cookie and looking at us with an alert tilt of the head. I thought I caught a glint of humor in her eyes, and I wondered if it amused her to watch the struggles of first-time guests to control their amazement at her home.

The room in which we were sitting was long and high-ceilinged and light, with a good view of the woods of Peredelkino in the distance. Closer to the house we could see a tennis court turned into a skating rink for the winter. The room was furnished with a mixture of traditional English and antique Russian furniture; there were big vases of fresh flowers on the tables and Oriental rugs on the floor. In a corner stood a grand piano, and on a wall nearby hung a magnificent collection of early icons. On another wall, dominating the room, hung a large rug with the seal of Imperial Russia—a double-headed Romanov eagle bigger than Jennifer Louis.

Victor and Jennifer Louis are collectors, and are among the canniest in the Soviet Union. The assemblages of old Russian wood carving in State museums seem sparse next to their private collection, which is intimidatingly vast: room after room full of dark wood bristling with faces, breasts, leaves, beards, wings. Jennifer took us on a brief tour, talking lightly about her holdings—not about dates of masters but about means of possession. They'd found this table out near Suzdal; for that desk they'd had a fight with another collector, a friend from *Pravda*. In between explanations, Jennifer chatted about the doings of the international women's group that she had helped to found—a social and charitable organization for wives in the foreign community. As I listened, I forgot for a giddy moment where I was. It seemed impossible that two hours earlier we'd been pushing through a crowd of workers on the metro in a city—a country—where these concerns, this house, this way of life were not supposed to exist. Now we were talking with the mistress of a country estate, and the Workers' Paradise had vanished. I looked hard at Jennifer to see if there was anything in her face that showed an awareness of the discrepancy between her way of life and the State ideal. No, there was nothing. She continued to chat imperturbably, the hint of amusement I had glimpsed earlier either having vanished or having been only a product of my imagination. Such obliviousness, I thought, must come either from extreme stupidity or from a self-control tougher than anything I could summon up. Jennifer Louis did not seem stupid.

Later, we skied through the pinewoods and rolling meadows around the house, Jennifer far ahead of us, a small, birdlike figure in a red parka, shouting "Come on!" She skied well, with the sturdy, fearless strides of a young boy. Other guests had joined us: a Danish journalist and his beautiful pregnant wife; an Indian diplomat; an American correspondent. The sun set behind a snowy ridge, and we all trudged back to meet our host for Christmas dinner. Tom and I changed our clothes in our hostess' bedroom, a pink-and-ivory place whose night tables, true to the perverse form of this household, held several "forbidden" books put out by émigré presses in the United States and France.

When we went down, Louis was waiting for us in the study, beside a silver tray of caviar. Victor Louis is a man of fifty, stocky, of medium height, with a pleasant-featured square face and narrow eyes. Except for the eyes, the face is unremarkable, almost indescribable, as some Russian faces are—faces that have absolute symmetry without beauty, without some twist or exaggeration of feature to add humanity. But Victor Louis' eyes are unusual, giving him a faintly Oriental look that adds to an impression one receives of intense reserve, of behavior compelled coldly by a disciplined will.

We sat down to dinner, and Louis entertained us with anecdotes about his travels in Europe and America. He seemed bored and indulgent with those of us at his end of the table; he got up occasionally to talk rapidly into a telephone in a mahogany box behind him. On the phone he spoke Russian, but English was the language of the dinner and the day. The table glittered, and there was every conceivable fork.

While two Russian maids served a Dickensian Christmas dinner, I talked to Nikolai, who is eighteen and a graduate of an English public school. He and his brothers are all slim and fresh-complexioned, with a modest, chirping British accent and graceful manners. He wore a Levis jacket, freshly pressed, and sat up very straight in his chair. We talked about skiing in Switzerland, which he had done on a family trip last winter. He said he preferred Swiss resorts to those in Soviet Georgia, because in Georgia the lifts were so primitive. As we talked, the servants kept returning to his side, offering him the choicest portions of the dishes; they spoke to him only in Russian, and used affectionate diminutives. Nikolai smiled and said, "They take good care of me."

I asked him about his studies at the university, and he said that he liked history and would almost surely work toward a higher degree after he graduated. This made me think of something I'd heard from Russian friends—that one way the Soviet elite assures high status for its offspring in this society in which wealth and honors can't officially be inherited is to make sure that they get a higher university degree. With that degree, Nikolai, the young master of this fief, could be assured of advancing into a privileged position in the Party *apparat*.

We talked more about school. "I drive in every morning from Peredelkino," he said. "Or sometimes I spend the night in Moscow. We have an apartment there."

"What do you do on weekends?"

He flushed and looked down. "Oh, I mostly just hang out here."

Nikolai seemed to me to have a lonely life. I found it hard to imagine him shoving his way through the drably dressed crowds of students at Moscow State, having driven in from the country in his own car—an inconceivable possession for a young Russian. He belonged to a different category from the so-called Golden Youth of the university, the spoiled students who hang out at the Sinyaya Ptitsa, flaunting their Western jeans and their foreign cigarettes. There are only a few at the university like him: shy rich kids with understated clothes and exquisite English, whose manners show a peculiar mixture of unshakable poise and fundamental reserve. I wondered how the Louis children had been affected by their odd life: the unlimited privileges in a country of repression; the father whose activities they can never fully know; the half-public existence in a household flooded with foreign visitors. Earlier that afternoon I had been skiing beside the youngest son, a boy of nine or ten. I fell, and as I got to my feet he asked suddenly, "Who do you belong to?"

I said, "I belong to that man in the green hat behind us, and he belongs to me. Why did you ask that?"

He kicked some snow off the sled he was dragging, and stared at me with a small, serious, red-cheeked face. "It's just good to know," he said finally, in his polite British voice. "There are so many new people here all the time that one never knows who belongs to anyone."

The superb dinner ended with plum pudding, tiny mince pies, and Central Asian melon. We all went off to a corner of the living room to drink coffee and cognac. We had been listening earlier that afternoon to the children's Elton John records blasting from a fancy German stereo; now we watched a tape of a British television program. Sitting in front of *The Two Ronnies*, with a savor of hard sauce still in my mouth, I found it difficult to believe that we were not recovering from Christmas dinner in Hampstead or some other chic London suburb. Victor Louis came out from telephoning in his study and sat down in an armchair. Through the doorway of his study I could see a tremendous carved desk; there were, I knew from my tour, other offices, with similar desks, in the basement. These rooms are lined with shelves of books in English, including a collection of American and European scholarly works on Soviet politics and society worthy of a professor of Soviet history. A rapid-fingered Bulgarian typist sits at one of the basement desks daily, updating Victor and Jennifer Louis' famous travel guide to the Soviet Union. The typist also turns out final drafts of Victor Louis' articles for Western periodicals. Touring the rooms, I had wondered whether Louis' 1969 article denouncing Solzhenitsyn was composed here.

Now Louis was in a sociable mood. He watched *The Two Ronnies* with us and talked about his problems with taped programs. Only after a long search, he said, had he found a Japanese machine that played both American and British video cassettes. There was a note of pride in his voice which had been absent from his wife's when she commented on their possessions. I recalled his bragging and posturing in the *Newsweek* interview, and thought: At last we've caught you out in something natural, something *nouveau*. But looking at his unchanging eyes, I found it hard to decide whether this all-too-Russian lapse into boastfulness was not itself a pose.

The program ended, and Louis kept talking. He had apparently decided to open up to us, and though there was little warmth in his manner, there was a certain heavy joviality. He laughed a lot, and played very deliberately with his coffee spoon. We asked him how he had got started in journalism, and he answered at length, in an expansive, confiding manner.

"Well," he said, "first I was schooled in law, and then I attended an institute to get training in English. As I started to read Western newspaper reports on the Soviet Union, I felt that I could write about my country better than they could. I know the language, I know the people, I'm familiar with all the channels of information, and I know the ropes for getting around here. This was in the mid-fifties, when the government was still not used to the idea of letting Russians work as foreign correspondents. But I convinced them that it was better to let a Russian write about this country than to leave the job to a foreigner. And now the government is very happy with my work. And I can offer the foreign papers several advantages over the foreign correspondents here. When news is made, I find out about it faster than the others, and I just send the stories off by telex to London or Paris."

The odd thing about this conversation was that Louis talked about himself as if he were an ordinary journalist, when all of us knew that in fact he was far more than that. He referred often to the American correspondents Robert Kaiser, Hedrick Smith, and David Shipler as his "colleagues," and his comments on the Soviet government seemed designed to present the image of a freethinking Soviet reporter. When we mentioned Saratov, a "closed" Volga town, which we, as foreigners, couldn't visit, he laughed and said that the entire closed-region system was something of a farce, since all spies knew about secret military installations from satellites anyhow. "Saratov is a lovely town," he said. "It's a shame you won't be able to visit it. It's a wonderful example of the old noble provincial town, quite different from the awful new towns built after the Revolution and the war. What do the new towns have to offer? Only another bust of Lenin and a tomb of the unknown soldier. Jennifer and I only visit the old towns."

He poured himself more cognac, and in a few minutes he was telling us that he didn't understand why a masterpiece like *Doctor Zhivago* couldn't be printed in the Soviet Union. He said this with a smile and a tone of voice which suggested that the Soviet government was amusingly stuffy in its views. A bit later, in speaking of dissidents, he used the same suave tone. Many demonstrations against the government—so-called "spontaneous" demonstrations—were in fact carefully planned and orchestrated by dissidents in conjunction with foreign journalists, he said. "Of course that's so. The whole thing takes place in five minutes. They unroll their banners at the assigned spot, shout a few slogans, provoke the police—who are dull-witted, like police everywhere— and everyone goes home in time for dinner. Including the journalists, who have known about it for weeks in advance." He took a sip of coffee. "Mind you, I'm not condemning dissidents. I have a large number of friends in the dissident community. Last year, following a demonstration, I went to the Mexican Embassy and found S. [a dissident painter] there. S. and I are good friends. In fact, that is one of his paintings over there on the wall—it's from the 1974 exhibition that was bulldozed. Well, the two of us had a couple of cocktails, and I started to tease S. 'My friend,' I said, 'how can you call that a spontaneous demonstration? Why do you even bother to unroll your banners, since the newsmen already know what they say?' " He laughed heartily and sipped his cognac.

It occurred to me that we were finally getting to see how he operated—as a fine-mesh disseminator of received opinion to those who might be put off by a hard Party line. Almost no one would have been deceived by his weightless criticism of the regime, but his remark about the dissidents was more subtle: while preserving his own image as an independent observer, it made protest against the government seem ridiculous and, above all, insignificant.

I looked across the room at Jennifer Louis, who was tending a silver kettle over a spirit lamp and chatting with some of the wives. She gave me a single penetrating glance in return, and I reflected that the chilling thing about this establishment was the sense of absolute orthodoxy which came poking its way through the mask of luxury and freedom of thought. Exactly what, I wondered for the twentieth time that day, was the official position of this place? That it was an official position was clear in the very flamboyance of the lives of the Louis family, in this country where privilege is hidden like a disease. Part of the answer might be that the Louis household is an island of European-style comfort and freedom which gives foreigners the momentary illusion of having left the Soviet Union, of being among their own kind, and, as such, is the perfect center for the measured diffusion of attitudes and information, and for the gathering of information as well. In this respect, Jennifer Louis, an Englishwoman with deep roots in the foreign enclave here (she is a pillar of the Protestant community of Moscow), seems just as useful as her husband. When I inadvertently mentioned a Russian friend earlier in the day, she stiffened and began to question me closely about his name, his address . . .

When it was time to leave, we asked Victor Louis what time the Moscow train left from Peredelkino. "I don't know," he said. "I've never taken the train." Another guest offered us a ride, and we shook hands with our hosts. "Merry Christmas!" said Victor and Jennifer Louis, in English and then in Russian. They stood on the threshold for a few minutes before the big door closed, and I carried that image away with me: the fiercely energetic, watchful wife and the husband with his bland cold smile, framed together in the doorway. Above them, the windows of the big house gleamed with light.

It felt good to drive away though the snowy woods and fields of Peredelkino. The clear, starry sky shone above the empty road, and I was glad to be leaving the Louis house behind. Once more we passed near Pasternak's grave, and I thought of how Victor Louis had used *Doctor Zhivago* to help establish his own liberalism.

Back in Moscow, Tom and I caught the metro in Mayakovsky Square. A tremendous crowd had just emerged from the Tchaikovsky Concert Hall, creating inch-deep puddles of mud and slush by the metro entrance. Sweating miserably in our heavy coats, we packed ourselves into a subway car. Around us were the worn faces I saw every day in the city; no one knew or cared that it was Christmas night in the Western world. I fought to keep my skis upright, and stared at my fellow-passengers as if I had just arrived in the Soviet Union. On all sides, old women, students, families, lovers, drunks were thrust together in an almost visible atmosphere of garlic, cheap tobacco, damp fabric, and ancient sweat. All of us rocked back and forth in the dimly lit car, pinned against our neighbors.

"Here we are," whispered Tom. "Welcome back to the Soviet Union." It did seem as if we'd been away in some other country. The house at Peredelkino, with its space, its creature comforts, its English speech and celebration, had enfolded us for a day like some warm, bright capitalist dream, and now here we were. But later I felt differently. We may have left Russia, I thought, but we certainly moved a lot closer to the heart of the Kremlin.

Seryozha (II)

Today we saw our friend Seryozha again, three months after he was denounced by his wife's family. As he had promised, he sent us an unsigned letter giving us a time, and we met him by a certain pillar in a metro stop near Arbat Street. This afternoon it was a sunny, windless thirty-five-below-zero Fahrenheit; our cheeks were cold as we kissed each other, and on the street we had to run to keep our fingers and toes from freezing. Seryozha didn't dare take us home. Instead we went to drink tea in a friend's apartment on stylish Kutuzovsky Prospekt. The apartment belonged to Andrei, a plump, well-to-do philosopher, who was in the country that day. It was big and bright, with the beige walls and glass-fronted bookshelves of the best Moscow apartments, but it was very cold—heating systems were breaking down all over the city. The three of us wore hats and gloves, and huddled around a gas stove with lit burners.

Seryozha looked bad. He is thinner, and his delicate face is pimply and drawn. Although he usually dresses so nattily, today he met us in a cracked black leather coat with a couple of sweaters underneath. Over tea, he told us the long, complicated story of his divorce and of how his wife's parents had denounced him to the KGB. He sketched diagrams to illustrate which family members took which sides. We couldn't follow it. He said that no one could. The upshot of it, though, is that he is indeed losing his apartment. (It is typically Soviet that it is much more of a tragedy to lose your apartment than your job.) He has lost something else as well: the sort of vitality that he had before. Seryozha is far from being shattered, but it really seems that the strand of energy in him that used to vibrate in such a sprightly way has been broken. Bending to warm his fingers over the blue gas flame, he looked aged and peevish. Much of his talk was querulous: he complained of a stomach disorder he had developed from tension. Several times, as we sat in the cold, sunny kitchen, he had to get up and run to the toilet.

We asked about Seryozha's father, and found that neither the father's job privileges nor his elevated Party position had suffered as a result of the son's disgrace. He had, however, almost entirely rejected Seryozha. "Both of my parents try hard to make me feel guilty," Seryozha said. "There is a lot of bitterness between us." He also said that he had now definitely decided to try to emigrate. "I used to resist the idea, but I feel certain now that if I stay, I'll end up in prison." How to emigrate was a problem—perhaps by marriage to a foreigner or a Jew. We discussed this for a while, drinking our sixth cup of tea and listening to Mick Jagger on the stereo for old times' sake. It was strange to think of Seryozha as he had been—mischievous, snobbish, mercurial, prancing to the same music—back in September. I looked at his haggard aristocratic face and recalled what a friend once said about him. "It's cruel for him to be tortured this way," the friend had said. "Doesn't anyone realize he isn't even of this era? If only he could have been born a hundred and fifty years ago. Then he could have died properly, in a duel."

It got late, and we had to go. We asked Seryozha when we could see him again. Would it still be dangerous? "No," he said. "I'm only careful out of habit. Right now I could do anything I liked, and it would all be the same. My life as a respectable citizen has ended." He sat silent and began to gnaw his fingernails—another unfortunate new trait. Outside the window, in the freezing sunset, we could see hundreds of plumes of rosy steam hovering almost motionless over the apartments along Kutuzovsky. I recalled a rumor I'd heard that Brezhnev lived out this way. Seryozha, with a laugh, said it was true. We put on our coats and went down in the elevator. It was deadly cold in the street, and as we walked we had an argument with Seryozha about his seeing a doctor for his stomach.

Teaching

Note: The following section is the record of a month I spent conducting a clandestine English class for Soviet Jews about to emigrate. As luck would have it, this was the month that Tom and I spent house-sitting in an apartment in one of the diplomatic enclaves, a setting that allowed me to be much more easily observed by the authorities. Things happened so quickly during this period that I kept a journal record of almost every day; the entries from January 4 to February 8 in fact make up a small, self-contained narrative.

January 4

Yesterday Rima came to me with a new idea. "Some friends" of hers are leaving the country and are willing to pay many rubles apiece for a month of lessons in American English. What if she and I were to teach them together? After this suggestion, Rima looked at me with her usual air of being poised to retract everything she has just said. I started to laugh, and said, "Who are these friends? Aren't they Jewish if they're leaving for America? And if so, won't it be dangerous for us to teach them?"

Rima took my hand and began to talk persuasively. She is a somber-eyed part Georgian poet who for five months has been one of my best friends, and though I laugh at her, I trust her absolutely.

"Yes, they are . . . mostly . . . emigrating Jews," she said at length. "But that's not a problem for you. If there is any danger, it will be for them and for me, not for you. For that much money, I'm willing to chance it." Her eyes lit up at the thought of so much money, at the meat and peace of mind it would buy. She looked intensely at me, and I looked away. Already I could feel myself drawn into the vortex of one of her schemes.

"I'll consider it," I said.

January 5

I mentioned my teaching plans to my friend Valerii, who said that I was crazy to be thinking of it. "It's suicidal for a foreigner to get involved with emigrating Jews in the Soviet Union," he said. "Few people are more certain to be watched and harassed. And a *group* —you could be charged with political conspiracy and thrown out of the country. Your students could be denied their exit visa." He scratched his head. "I don't understand you," he said. "There are so many illegal things Americans can get away with in this country. Sell your jeans. Smuggle icons. Sell dollars. Just leave the Jews alone."

January 7

First meeting of the class today, in an apartment belonging to Yura, a well-to-do chemist. The place is located in the ritzy Moscow neighborhood off Kutuzovsky Prospekt; by Soviet standards it's luxurious, with clean tan walls, a shiny kitchen, and two living-sleeping rooms filled with books. There were seven students, Rima, and me. I asked the students to introduce themselves, and immediately lost their names in a blur of nervousness. What I made out was that they were mostly male, mostly from Odessa, and mostly scientists and engineers who seemed to specialize in bizarre areas like Concrete Control. An exception is Iulia, an eleven-year-old girl whose mother, a dissident art collector, is planning to leave the country in a month.

The students were shy and rather respectful. Miracle of miracles, they actually sat and repeated the dialogue I had written (we have no textbooks). With the insecurity of a beginning teacher, I had thought that they would burst out laughing and refuse. Rima and I signaled happily with our eyes. In the discussion period, we talked about American literature. "Which modern writers do you like?" I asked. The answer was Arthur Hailey and J. D. Salinger, two writers whose work seems to penetrate Soviet censorship with some regularity. One student, however, asked me my opinion of Heller's *Something Happened*. His name is Zhenya; he is a plump young man of about twenty-five, with a heavy, rather handsome face. All of his remarks are sarcastic. At the end of the lesson, he demolished my polite pretext that this is a normal class for people with a normal position in Soviet society. Glancing through *The French Impressionists*, a picture book I'd been using for teaching, he put out his hand and covered up the first part of the word *Impressionists*. "This is what *we're* interested in," he said, and showed me. The word read: "sionists." He glanced at me mischievously and ironically.

January 10

My evolving method of teaching: a new dialogue every day, dealing with some aspect of life—romance, job hunting, attending a snobbish party, marketing. Then composition, and finally a debate or discussion. Their English vocabularies are growing; more than that, they seem delighted with the class, with the fact that we laugh a great deal. Rima tells me that this doesn't happen in Soviet classrooms. Most language classes, in elementary schools or in the special institutes, depend on rote drilling of incredibly boring texts. Soviet educational techniques seem based on rigid discipline, on the humiliation of slow students and praise of the obedient. My students, all (except for Iulia) adults in respectable positions, act embarrassed and humbly apologetic whenever they make a mistake. Now they've started laughing at their own more humorous errors, but with a daring sound in their laughter and a covert, wondering glance at me, as if I were suddenly going to chastise them.

January 11

A queer thing happened in class today. A young man showed up whom no one quite knew, an indecisive-looking character with a beard and wispy shoulder-length hair. His English was good, and he was interested in joining the class. He told us that he was a rock musician employed in a dance band at a restaurant off Leninsky Prospekt. He was enthusiastic in class and afterward walked back to the metro with me. For a few minutes he talked about his band, which he said I must come and hear. Suddenly he broke off, turned to me, and said in unaccented English, "Have you ever taken any illegal drugs?" The minute he said this, his face flushed and he looked terribly embarrassed. I laughed off the question by saying that we Americans, of course, were all heroin addicts. This afternoon I described him to Rima's boyfriend, Vasia, who made a disgusted noise. "That guy! I know him. He's a *stukach*—a stoolie—and a *provocateur*. Everybody says he works straight out of Lubyanka.* I met him three years ago under highly unpleasant circumstances. He denounced a friend of mine."

I felt alarmed. "What will I do? What if he reports us?"

Vasia, like many of my young Soviet friends, was casual about surveillance. "Don't worry about it," he said. "If he comes back, get somebody to kick his ass out of there."

---

*The prison is also the KGB headquarters in Moscow.

January 13

As it happens, our rock musician friend hasn't shown up again. Other unnerving things have happened, however, making me sorry Rima persuaded me into this venture. Today I came to class about twenty minutes late, having run through the snow all the way from the Kievsky metro stop. I stopped to catch my breath at the top of the stairs, and saw a strange man leaning against the wall outside Yura's apartment. He was well dressed, neither tall nor short, with the terrifying lack of distinctiveness in appearance that only an agent can have. He was smoking a cigarette, and continued to smoke as he looked me straight in the eye. I remember distinctly that he did not smile, but that his face gave the impression of a smile—and not a pleasant one. It was a frightening moment. When Yura answered the door he looked scared. Yura is a very short dark-haired man, with a shy, neat way of moving, and the gentlest of dispositions. He led me into the kitchen for a minute, and told me that it was impossible for him to continue with the class. He loved it and was learning from it, he said, but it was interfering with his work. I looked at him, and he looked unhappily back at me. "It's been a little hazardous for you, Yura," I told him. "Oh no, oh no—oh, not at all," he said sadly.

While the class was writing an essay entitled "My Weekend," Rima grabbed my arm. I told her about the man in the hall. "KGB," she said. "It's certain. There was also a woman who came by before you arrived. She knocked and came in and said she had the wrong apartment. Yura and I knew what she was, however." I looked at Rima and she looked back at me. Her face was pale and her eyes had dark rings around them. But she didn't seem particularly scared. "It's such a nuisance," she said. "These stupid agents. They just want to shake us up a bit. But now we have to find a different apartment for the class." Just then the phone started to ring, and Yura and the others looked up from their writing. "Better not answer it," said Rima.

January 15

Our new location is far away in the suburbs of Moscow, a half-hour bus ride from the metro station near Izmailovo Park. The apartment, in one of the indistinguishable white high rises that stretch endlessly outside of Moscow, belongs to Vilen, a professor of biology. It consists of three largish rooms, a kitchen and a bathroom. Four people live here: Vilen, his wife, his daughter, and his son-in-law. The airy, well-lit rooms have the standardized tan wallpaper typical of most luxurious Moscow apartments; they serve varied functions which seem queer to American eyes. One room combines a serious study area—complete with typewriters in several languages—with a large, flirtatiously carved double bed. The room we work in is the living-dining room, which contains a laminated wooden table, an uncomfortable red divan, and an enormous modern buffet—one of those monstrous all-purpose pieces that Russians love, with shelves for books, knickknacks, and flowery china. Many of the books are foreign art books which I've seen selling for two hundred rubles apiece; Vilen is obviously quite wealthy.

The final membership of the class is six. They are all Jews who have applied to emigrate, and who are in the final stages of waiting for a visa—a process which takes up to two years. They are:

Vilen

Our host: a tall man of fifty, with shrewd eyes behind thick glasses and wild hair that stands up in wiry spikes. His smile is sweet and boyish; there is a large gap in his front teeth in which he often absent-mindedly rattles his pencil point. Vilen's family for generations back were Odessa intellectuals with a radical bent; in fact, Trotsky, during his student years in Odessa, was once engaged to Vilen's grandmother. (The match was broken off by the young woman's disapproving father.) Vilen's own father, a staunch Bolshevik, is responsible for his peculiar name. "It stands for V. I. Lenin," he told me with a grin. Rima whispered to me, "Such a name! And now he's leaving the country!"

Andrei

Vilen's son-in-law, who shares his apartment. Andrei, a very good-looking plumpish young man, has a beard and long hair and a large wardrobe of expensive American jeans. He is said to be a gifted chemistry student, though how he progresses I don't know, since he is amazingly somnolent, drowsing through class in various dull states from which he occasionally awakens to give answers with a foggy grin. Vilen treats him with the exaggerated patience of a father-in-law saddled with a doubtful case.

Raiza

A friend of Vilen's family. Raiza, a woman in her forties, is a mathematician at some small *institut*. She learned English by memorizing flash cards on the metro each day for ten years. Raiza has a faded, gypsyish beauty, a dark-browed, straight-planed face that must have been devastating when she was younger. Even now she is striking, in spite of steel teeth and the uncontrollably weary eyes of all middle-aged Soviet women. She has a half-coquettish shyness which makes her blush and refuse to speak when she fears she will make a mistake. But when she does speak, it is with passion and intensity. She knows an amazing amount about Western literature, and has questioned me about Iris Murdoch. Raiza is originally from a small White Russian town destroyed by Germans during the war. She married a Muscovite and had two sons, whom she worships. She says, "I am first and foremost a mother." Her voice trembles with feeling when she says the word "children."

Zhenya the First

I've already described him, with his heavy face, his fat body, his wit. Rima and I like him very much. There is a funny kind of self-parody in his speech and behavior—sometimes he carries his big belly with a lumbering stately air like a bear or a church dignitary. More than any of the others, he complains about Soviet life, usually to me as we take the bus together. His complaints get monotonous, but he has a point. As an experienced young engineer, he's making one hundred rubles a month—just above minimum wage. Zhenya has a wife and a baby daughter; on their combined salaries he and his wife can barely support their tiny family. "We young engineers have a name for ourselves," he says. "Because we know how blacks are treated in America, we call ourselves 'enginiggers.'"

Zhenya the Second

Zhenya the Second is much older than Zhenya the First. He was born in 1932, in Odessa. He is a professor of chemistry, and a lifelong friend of Vilen. Like Vilen, he is prosperous, with a high position on the faculty at Moscow State University. Zhenya is a slight, dark-complexioned man, with hazel eyes in a handsome, eager face. He is perhaps the most delightful of the students to teach, because everything that is said to him makes an immediate, almost miraculous impression. Zhenya's mother died during the war, and because his father was at the front, he spent a number of years in an orphanage in Central Asia. Perhaps that is why, in spite of his dapper clothes, he always has a slightly disheveled waif-like appearance.

Iulia

Our sole, beautiful child. Iulia is eleven, with the blond hair and slanted green eyes of a Finnish angel. All the adults want to control her, in the domineering way of Soviet adults, but she doesn't allow it. Iulia is a true waif, with grubby clothes and lank, unwashed hair. She has an urchin's tough cockiness, too. Her mother, the divorced wife of a high-ranking Party member, is an art dealer "on the left" who doesn't have much time for a child. Their apartment is a bohemian chaos, full of poets, painters, musicians, foreign diplomats, and the odd hangers-on of the world of unorthodox Soviet art. Peculiar, and peculiarly rich world for a child. Iulia (who has left school during the waiting period for the visa) can swear like a truckdriver and discuss Bulgakov's *Master and Margarita* with equal ease. Ironically, she was also a Pioneer troop leader last year.

January 17

Today I assigned a written explanation of a picture which shows a young man standing empty-handed in a shop full of brightly colored folded material on shelves. Zhenya the First wrote: "We see here a young man who has just arrived in Vienna. He is a native of an Eastern European country. But he has left his home. He is standing in a shop which sells flags of all nations, trying to choose his new home. The colors are all beautiful, and he is confused. Which will he choose?"

January 18

We've settled into a sort of routine over the past few days. Every morning I take the metro to Izmailovo Park, where, with Rima, Iulia, and Zhenya the First, I take a bus to the Moscow suburbs. Izmailovo Park is very beautiful on these clear January mornings, with the sun shining through the snowy birches and little troops of schoolchildren passing on skis. Zhenya, Iulia, Rima, and I chatter away freely in Russian and English, ignoring the KGB agent who is usually hovering somewhere behind us. The agent, a different hard-faced man or woman every day, is near us on all of our trips to and from Vilen's apartment; I have no idea what he or she does during the three hours of class.

I have become almost as fatalistic as my Soviet friends about being spied on. It's going to happen if I continue to do what I'm doing, and I have no intention of stopping the class. The one precaution I have taken, to avoid conspiracy charges, is to forbid any mention of politics.

Zhenya and Rima make jokes about KGB tactics. "Nothing subtle about *them*," said Zhenya yesterday, indicating our "escort," who was leaning nonchalantly against the bus shelter a few feet away. "That guy is typical. They just want us to know that *they* know what we're doing."

"Can it be," Rima asked me mockingly, "that buses in America are not the same valuable sources of information that they are in the Soviet Union?"

I can't respond to all this with jokes and the bitter laughter of acceptance. I am too new to the phenomenon of being watched and followed. Instead I am becoming aware of an intense anger forming like a stone in my guts. This isn't my normal rational indignation over the brutalities of the Soviet system; it is a personal anger based on fear. I often catch myself in fantasies of hitting, kicking, or shooting a KGB man these days. And I've become alarmingly paranoid, turning ferociously on the peasant women on the metro who sit inspecting my clothes with innocent curiosity.

January 19

A dialogue on the bus. I am standing with Zhenya and Rima, watching little Iulia, who sits reading a few seats ahead of us. In her fluffy white hood she looks innocent and much younger than her eleven years.

Zhenya to Rima: "At what age did you first realize that you had to keep your mouth shut—on the bus, on the street, at school? I remember it very clearly. My parents warned me not to talk to the teacher about some books we had at home."

Rima: "What a good memory you have, Zhenya! There was no such date for me. I think I was born knowing that."

January 20

With the goons and all the scary business in the street, I'm starting to turn to the class itself for comfort. Vilen's little apartment smells pleasantly of sunflower-seed oil; when I take off my thick coat and snowy boots in the front hall, and put on the slippers his wife, Galya, provides for us, I am conscious of a passionate relief at being inside, warm, among friends. I now fully understand the distinction Russians make between the intimate world of home—where they are princely hosts and loyal friends—and the impersonal hostility of the outside world. The street is so very cold that, as in a wartime romance, we cling to each other behind doors.

Teaching, I am faced with the temptation of the novice instructor whose method is a success. My pedagogical triumphs give me a buoyancy that, I'm afraid, turns into cocksureness at certain points. Things are complicated by my position as an American among Soviets, a position with which many Americans in the Paris of the twenties could empathize. "Let's face it," said an American friend of mine a few nights ago. "In this country we're gods." Unfortunately, this is true. I don't believe that the American diplomats and correspondents feel it as exchange students do, simply because they lead lives insulated from any real contact with Soviet society. But we who live—and in my case, work—among Russians find at every step the universal, awestruck belief in the barbarous wealth of Americans.

After formal class, we have a discussion session that quickly turns into a question-and-answer period about the United States. Galya, a slender, fresh-faced woman, serves us black coffee and tiny cabbage pancakes while the group bombards me with questions. How much does an art book cost in America? What kinds of clothes do people wear? Is it true that many people own houses? What salary would an engineer make? What happens when one gets sick? What exactly is a credit card? A check?

These questions are understandable from people denied any knowledge at all, who are about to start off life in a new country. What unnerves me is the eager assumption in their voices and eyes that they are leaving not simply for a freer country, but for the blessed land of silver streets, God's kingdom on earth. I try, cautiously, to present some of the negative as well as the positive sides of American life, but they will have none of it. What they really want, I find, is more of the materialistic bragging found in the literature put out by the American Embassy here.

"Don't tell us about the problems," Vilen said today, gulping down his coffee. "We know all about your racism and unemployment from *Pravda*. Tell us again about that bookstore in your city —the one that has books in all languages. And what about more names of cars; we know Cadillac, Chevy, Mustang, Rolls-Royce . . ."

These sessions leave me exhausted. When I complained recently to Rima about their insatiable questioning, she patted my arm sympathetically. "Poor thing!" she said. "It's bad for you, but you have to understand that they're leaving everything, *every*thing that they know, behind them. Right now they have to believe in America as a paradise, don't you see? They have to make up a dream to travel to. Otherwise they'd lose their nerve."

Nevertheless, there are times when their dreams can't stretch enough to accommodate American reality. This happened yesterday, when Andrei asked me to describe where I lived as a child. I said, "When I was little I lived in a house with my family."

"A house, not a flat!" said Zhenya the Second. "How many square meters of space were there?"

"I don't know. There were five of us, and there were eight rooms."

There was an audible intake of breath. Even Rima, with all of her

Western connections, looked a little awed. I felt extremely embarrassed.

"But surely the state owned the house," Raiza said, very softly.

"No, my family owned it," I said.

There was a moment of silence, while everybody stared at me. I could tell they didn't believe me.

January 24

The students get more and more comfortable with one another; we're becoming quite a family. Vilen and Zhenya the Second, the old school friends, bully and tease each other, at the end of a debate occasionally embracing in the passionate way of Russian male friends. The group makes fun of Raiza's coquettish refusals to speak when she feels shy, and of Zhenya the First's constant cynicism. Toward Iulia, much to her annoyance, everyone behaves like a parent.

A conversation:

Raiza (*reading*): "'My little horse must think it kveer/To stop without a farmhouse near—'"

Vilen: "Queer, Raya, *que*er. What an accent you have, my dear. Worse than Odessa!"

Raiza (*in Russian, shaking her hair around her face*): "No. I won't read, I can't. Don't make me do any more!"

Me (*composedly*): "Raya, you were reading very well. Please don't stop. Say 'queer.'"

Raiza: "Kveer." (*In Russian*): "There, see: I can't. They'll never understand me in America. I'll let my son talk . . ."

Zhenya I: "In America they understand all things. Especially in Texas."

Me (*startled*): "What does *that* mean?"

Zhenya I: "I dream about Texas. I want to settle there and be— what do you call it?—a Ranger."

Zhenya II: "Zhenya is a dreamer and Raiza is a coquette."

Vilen: "And you are my friend the *hooligan*."

Me: "Let's go on, please. You read, Andrei."

Andrei: " 'To stop without a farmhouse near—' "

Iulia (*pushing her untidy blond hair out of her eyes*): "What's a farmhouse?"

Andrei (*in Russian*): "A peasant hut."

Me: "Speak English, please. Not exactly. There are no peasants in America. And a farmhouse can be a big house with many rooms."

Zhenya I: "Even the peasants are rich in America."

Zhenya II: "Don't be silly, Zhenya." (*To me, seriously*): "It seems to be that this Robert Frost has written a very Russian poem. Peasants, the forest, a sleigh—"

Iulia (*breaking in*): "I'm going to be rich!"

Everyone (*in English and Russian, variously*): "Iuluchka, don't interrupt!"

January 26

Yesterday was frightening. The scare-tactic business has reached a peak, and I am beginning to think that I may have to quit the class. Rima and Iulia and I were followed home very obviously today by a big guy in a Soviet fake-denim jacket. His face—what a face! Utterly unremarkable except for the rigidity of the features—the actual skin seemed stiff, as if something had been injected underneath it. When I got back to the apartment, the phone began to ring. I picked it up, and there was breathing and then a click. Disconnected. This happened six times over the course of an hour. The seventh time, I picked up the receiver and said clearly and slowly into it the worst Russian obscenity I could think of. Then I replaced the receiver. A minute later the phone rang again, and a woman's voice repeated the obscenity to me in English, in a vicious, heavily accented voice. I held the receiver silently. In a minute the woman asked in Russian, "Who are you? What are you doing?" I said, "You should know." The phone went dead.

After that I took the receiver off the hook, drew all the curtains, made myself a cup of tea, and sat. Tom came home about an hour later, and I began to tremble as I told him. He told me to cut off the class. I said no, that I was already too attached to my students. "In that case," he said, "you'd better start thinking about a book: *Conversations with the KGB*. Or maybe you should start studying American culture—because we're going to get kicked out of the Soviet Union."

It was hard for me to sleep last night. I felt that the darkness was full of eyes and voices. Twice I saw flashes as if cameras were in the room. But it was only my nervous eyelids jerking as I dozed off.

I told Rima and Zhenya the First about the telephone incident. They weren't as alarmed as I was. "They are just thugs," said Rima, looking at me with her straight Georgian gaze. "They just want you to know that they see what you are doing. They won't dare to do anything else."

Zhenya grinned and patted me on the shoulder. "What you said was good," he said. "You showed your claws—just a little bit. Now they'll think twice."

January 28

Phone calls continuing—some of them ludicrous. Yesterday evening I picked up the receiver and the familiar feminine voice said, in English with insulting emphasis, "You are a *very old rascal!*" I laughed. I suppose I am becoming hardened.

January 29

On the bus today little Iulia told me a story about vampires. She has developed a crush on me, and loves to corner me with fantastic stories. This one told of bloodsuckers terrorizing a town in Central Asia, the exotic territory which for Russian children is full of mystery and adventure. When the tale, which was in English, had reached its gory conclusion, I asked Iulia why she never talked like that in class. Iulia shrugged. "Class is boring," she said. "Besides, I already know enough English."

"When are you leaving?" I asked.

"Soon. We have the visa. Mama still has to pay for the pictures."

Iulia's mother is trying to take nearly a hundred paintings with her as capital to start her new life; for these, she has to pay about eight thousand rubles in duties. The money is coming in slowly, mainly in contributions from friends.

"And will you live in New York?"

"No, North Dakota at first. We have friends there."

Iulia's slanted green eyes shone with excitement as she said "North Dakota," and she pronounced it with a roll of the tongue, reveling in its strange sound as Zhenya the First revels in the sound of "Texas." It is hard to imagine this urban child in North Dakota.

"Are you scared to go?"

"No." Iulia tossed her head and then came over and squeezed my arm. "I'm not afraid of anything."

I thought of what I knew of Iulia's life: her estranged father, high up in the Party; her brilliant, garrulous mother, chain-smoking and always just completing a deal on icons or paintings; the times when I'd seen Iulia napping on couches in rooms filled with Moscow's avant-garde poets and painters, or moving self-assuredly through groups of foreigners at parties. I think she can take care of herself anywhere, though she's surely going to miss salon society.

"Why should I be afraid?" demanded Iulia, hugging me and staring up into my face. "Are there vampires in North Dakota?"

January 31

The telephone harassment ended a few days ago, on a genuine note of farce. I had invited Rima home with me; she is one of the few Russian friends who dare visit me at the apartment, which we all know is bugged. We were eating lunch when the phone calls began again. After the third call I was thinking of taking the phone off the hook, when Rima said, "Let me try something." When the phone rang again, she picked up the receiver and said in a loud, authoritative voice, "I am an active Komsomol member and I'm going to file a complaint!" She put down the receiver and smiled at me. "That ought to put the fear of God in them," she said.

"Fear of Lenin," I said.

It was like magic. The telephone was silent for the rest of the afternoon. When I told my friend Valerii what Rima had said, he said, "The KGB wouldn't be stupid enough to believe that!" Stupid or not, invoking the Komsomol worked wonders, as it does anywhere else in this rank-conscious society. The phone calls have stopped, and even the tailing is much less obvious.

February 1

With surveillance and harassment lessened, we are all happier. The final week of class is approaching, and without quite knowing how it happened, we find ourselves bound together by a strong affection. Iulia has become the pet of the entire class; when we take breaks, she entertains us with songs from school. Her favorite song begins: "In the blue sky/There is a golden city . . ." The tune is haunting, and Iulia's voice is strong and true. The members of the class look at her tenderly as she sings. I think we are all starting to realize that the time we have together is short, and that these moments are sweet.

February 2

Since we are still afraid of a conspiracy charge, we continue to stay away from politics in our discussions. Often we discuss what Zhenya the First calls "the only interesting topic": family life, the relations of men, women, and children. I unwittingly uncovered a hornet's nest today, when I mentioned something a Russian journalist friend had told me: that a women's liberation movement exists in the Soviet Union. Rima, up till now sphinxlike, speaking in class only to give grammatical drills, burst into a cascade of remonstrances against men, and against the life of women in general. Raiza, and even little Iulia, joined her, while the men looked astonished. Rima said, "Yes, there is such a movement in this country, though mainly in our minds. We younger women are getting fed up! What kind of life is it to work all day alongside our men, and then to come home to cook, clean, and care for children while they don't even lift a finger?"

"You forgot to mention shopping," said Raiza. "We leave work and then stand in line for two hours every day. I *hate* to stand in line!"

A heated argument began. The men in the class got over their amazement and began to defend themselves. Vilen said that housekeeping had been women's work from time immemorial, and that there was no reason why it should stop under socialism. "That's a crazy attitude," said Zhenya the Second to his old friend. "Naturally, if a woman works, it must be a man's duty to make things easier for her at home. Yet I still believe that a man must be master of his household. That must be clear in the family. The husband must be older than the wife so that he can instruct her in the proper way to behave."

Andrei recalled the advice his grandmother once gave him: to marry an illiterate girl who would always know her place.

The argument went on and on. "What do American women want?" the class asked me. I mentioned several things; one of them was equal opportunity in the job market. Raiza said, "I hear that many American women don't have to work. What a luxury! Why on earth do they want jobs?"

Rima turned to Zhenya the First, who had been silent throughout this argument, his face bland and inscrutable. "What do you think, Zhenochka?" she asked. "You have a little daughter. How are you going to raise her?"

Zhenya said, "My daughter is tiny. In a few months she's going to be leaving this country. She won't remember anything of the Soviet Union, and I'm happy for that. I don't want her to have to endure what her mother and her aunts did. Whatever life is for American women, I want it to be her life. I want her to be an American girl."

February 3

As the class draws to an end, the subject of Jews and Jewishness comes more frequently into our conversation. At first, by a tacit agreement among all of us, there was silence on the subject. Now that we have only a few days left, we talk more freely. Raiza asked me about Jewish writers in America, and I mentioned Roth and Malamud, among others. The class had never heard of Roth, but were thrilled and enthusiastic when I described the plots of some of his novels. They were amazed to find that Singer had won the Nobel Prize. "A writer in *Yiddish?*" said Vilen. Throughout this conversation, the class members glanced anxiously to see whether or not I looked hostile. When I did not, the good humor of the company gradually expanded. Listening, I was struck once more by something I had recognized earlier: how little the group seemed to know or care about Jewish religion and culture. For them, as for many Soviet Jews, Jewishness has been reduced to a matter of blood alone, a reason for persecution, or a means of emigrating to a better life outside the Soviet Union. Except for Raiza, the class members are atheists who consider the Torah an artifact of a historical period long past. Even Raiza has little knowledge of Judaism. When I left yesterday, she was trying laughingly with Vilen's wife to list the Jewish holidays. "I can't do it, I can't remember," she was saying, counting on her fingers. "No, this makes me very angry. What is the holiday that comes before Yom Kippur?"

February 5

Today, during one of the breaks from our endless drills, Raiza and I started to chat. "What is the name of your town in Byelorussia?" I asked.

Raiza looked at me earnestly. "It doesn't exist any more, so the name doesn't matter," she said.

"That's a terrible thing," I said. "How did you escape?"

"I was very small then. I had three younger brothers and sisters. My mother took all of us and traveled to Central Asia."

"So many refugees went to Central Asia!" I said.

"Yes. There was food there, and it was warm."

"How did you travel?"

Raiza pushed her dark hair back with both hands, as she always does when she starts to get excited. "We traveled by truck, by wagon, by train, but mainly on foot," she said. "On foot, if you can imagine it, with four children under the age of five. And that's not the worst way we traveled. We escaped from our village in a cart full of dead soldiers."

I looked at her silently. She looked back at me, a short, plump middle-aged woman with her beautiful faded gypsyish face, and steel teeth framed in bright lipstick. There was a peculiar expression in her eyes, an anxious eagerness, a desire to tell, as well as apprehension that I would be bored. She said, "I don't want to bore you with these stories. My children tell me that they are tired of them. But if I could only tell you how terrible it was!"

"I don't mind," I said. "I want to hear."

"For a month we had no food. Nothing. And my mother was insane, delirious with hunger, and crazy at seeing her children starve. And then the news came that the Nazis had captured our village. What did they do to the old people, our friends and relatives? They shut them up together in a small house and set it on fire."

We all listened to Raiza. After a while Zhenya the Second broke in with the story of how his mother had been killed in an air raid in Odessa. Vilen told us about his uncle, captured by the Nazis, who escaped and returned to Moscow, only to find that he was regarded as a spy. He was sent to a Siberian labor camp, where he stayed for twenty-three years. "He was a brilliant man, a chemist," said Vilen. "But they changed him into a lumberjack. Now he lives in Moscow again—an old, rough-mannered man. His health is destroyed, his wife married another man, and his children are strangers to him. And this is his grand reward for fighting for Stalin!"

The name made us all pause. We looked at each other a little guiltily, remembering our vow to avoid any controversial topic. "Well, well," said Raiza, sighing a little. "It's boring for a young person. But this is the baggage we're taking with us to your country, this kind of memory. We have all suffered, and we are the lucky ones."

February 6

Question for discussion: Are you a patriot?

Zhenya the First replies: "There is one man in me that loves this country strongly, very strongly. I am, after all, a Russian. But there is another part of me that wants to live and cannot do so here. Life is too hard. I can't go on being divided like this."

February 7

Our last discussion. I said, "There is a subject that I'd like to propose. It is: How do you expect America to be? You have asked me so many questions. Now I am curious about *your* impressions."

Raiza: "We think about it as little as we can. It is a frightening thought. We have to close our eyes and jump."

Vilen: "I think of America mostly as a place in which to do my work. In the Soviet Union it is difficult for anyone who does good work and has any respect for himself. I am not talking about anything dissident or illegal. Just good work. There are too few rewards for working well. I know four or five colleagues at the university who do no work at all, and receive exactly the same pay and benefits as I do. They can't be dismissed, and it makes the rest of us—who do work—feel degraded. I'm a little afraid of the caprices of American bosses, who, I hear, can fire anyone any time they like. But I want to be rewarded for doing a good job."

Zhenya II: "What you should understand by now is that a man's chances for success in this country are limited almost entirely by who he is, whom he knows. You have to be a Party member to get anywhere. We have in the Soviet Union a group we call a *klan*. It means the rulers and their relatives, and their children who will inherit the power. My nephew wanted to be a journalist. He couldn't get into the school of journalism at Moscow State University—the places there are always filled by children of our ruling class. So he studied at an institute for English language, and now he's a translator. He's a good writer, so he's been writing articles and reviews for *Literaturnaia Gazeta*.* He gives them to a friend of his who works for the paper, and they are always published— under the other writer's name. That's all he can do. He'll never be a journalist on his own, not if he publishes a thousand articles. That's why I look forward to life in America, because in my country there are few chances for a talented man on his own."

"You keep saying 'my country,' " I said.

"It is my country," said Zhenya the Second. "Still."

Zhenya I: "Where I plan to live in the United States it is hot and sunny—like Central Asia. I imagine it full of dust storms and big cars. My friend who lives there wrote me that the people there are ignorant, that they never read, only watch television."

"Where are you going to live?" I asked.

"Texas," he said. "There are jobs for engineers there."

Andrei: "I hear that Americans are very unfriendly and anti-social. Every night each family shuts itself up alone, and there is very little visiting between friends. This frightens me a little. Is it true?"

"I think that friends stay for a shorter time when they visit," I said. "That's all. There are not as many parties of ten or twelve

*A leading weekly newspaper published by the Union of Writers.

hours, with people sleeping on the couch. Here, friends live with each other. In America, they visit each other."

"Americans don't have deep, warm friendships like ours," said Vilen in an authoritative tone.

"That is because they are more materialistic," said Raiza. "They value money above all." She glanced at me in embarrassment. "Excuse me, I didn't mean you, of course. But I know your countrymen are like that."

"I don't think that's true," I said. "I've been forced to talk about money far more in these past few months in Russia than I ever have before. I have my clothes and possessions appraised constantly. My Russian friends spend much of their time discussing salaries and prices, and I find it a little tiresome. You do it yourselves."

"Oh no," said Vilen. "In a capitalist society, you can't help but think about money—to the detriment of friendship. We Russians are poorer. Our lives are Spartan, and because of that, we have more time to consider things of the heart."

Everyone nodded approvingly. I muttered, "Oh, you're all steeped in *Pravda!*" The discussion made me a little mad, and I told myself that the class had gone on quite long enough.

Thinking back to my irritation this morning, I suppose that I was especially annoyed at finding in these future émigrés the same attitudes I find in my conservative Soviet friends. A typical Russian attitude toward the United States is that Americans may have modern kitchens and toilets, but we don't have the heart, the soul that Russians have. In other words, we sit isolated at our shiny plastic tables counting credit cards, instead of joining in one of those boozy, bear-hugging Slavic fellowships over a bottle of vodka and some salted fish. It's a good defense for a country with a chronic inferiority complex, where everyone who can is busy thinking up excuses to leave. This sounds bitter . . . but it hurts to be called materialistic, when over these months in Russia, I've been exposed to the rankest form of materialism: the curiosity and desire of the have-nots.

Class, I love you dearly, and hope for your health and wealth.

I am eager to see what befalls you in your terrifying first steps into the fleshpots. I can't imagine what seeing New York would be like, with one's total experience of flashing signs limited to Moscow's sole electric billboard in Mayakovsky Square. For such a step, you need good armor, of course, and perhaps this is the best: feeling oneself the bearer of "heart" into the meretricious land of capitalism. Anyway, I hope that Russian heart and your own healthy ambitions never have to collide.

February 8

Our last day. After a final dialogue and pronunciation drill, we had a party. I was touched to see that everyone had dressed up, the men wearing suits and Raiza wearing a new dress and her best amber brooch. Even little Iulia wore a clean set of stylish blue-jean overalls. We put a white cloth on the table and ate mutton and pickled mushrooms. Zhenya the Second had picked the mushrooms and pickled them himself. Raiza had bought the mutton. "How did you find such excellent meat?" someone asked. "I bought it over a month's time," answered Raiza proudly. She had visited a meat store every night for three weeks and bought a tiny piece of mutton—all that was available. She had kept it all frozen by hanging it in a bag outside her window.

We drank a bottle of French cognac that I had brought, and we all felt happy. Galya had baked a cake filled with cream, and she pressed huge slices on me. We proposed toasts. I toasted their English, which was very good, and their new life. Everyone looked back at me with shining eyes, and then Vilen, whose wiry gray hair stood more and more erect on his head as he drank cognac, proposed a toast to Rima and me. Then they brought out a present. It was a traditional Russian harvest doll woven of yellow straw, as such dolls have been for generations on end; she had a long braid down her back and carried a wheat straw like a teacher's rod. I looked at it and thought what a very Russian present they had chosen for me—they, the avowed non-Russians who were leaving this country behind.

We drank a little more and felt happier and sadder. Iulia sat on my lap, swinging her long legs and taking sips from my glass of cognac. "It's bad for the child," said Raiza, but Zhenya the Second said, "Let her taste!" We told jokes. Zhenya the First and Vilen told Radio Armenia jokes, Radio Armenia being a mythical broadcast that gives politically pertinent answers to dumb questions. Example: Radio Armenia defines a musical trio as a "quartet which has just returned from a tour in the West."

I told two Polish jokes, and slightly offended Zhenya the First, whose mother is Polish. But he said never mind, because it turns out that many American Polish jokes are told in the Soviet Union as "police jokes." So Iulia told us how many policeman it takes to screw in a lightbulb, and Andrei showed us how a policeman ties his shoe.

Raiza started giggling, and said she wanted to sing. Raiza's face was flushed and merry, and her lipstick was very red, and with her amber and her tousled dark hair, she looked more like a Gypsy than ever. Everyone begged to sing "Jingle Bells," which I had taught them long ago, and which they loved. So we sang, a bit slowly but with perfect pronunciation. Zhenya the First loves the phrase "bells-on-Bobtail-ring," which he chants loudly, his sarcastic eyes gleaming with pleasure. Then Galya and Vilen sang part of a duet from a Russian comic operetta. Then I sang "On Top of Old Smokey," and Rima intoned part of a Georgian folk song through her nose, but got embarrassed and forgot the last part. Finally Raiza, carried away by the exciting noise of the music and the clapping, began to sing "Hava Nagila." "Come on, everyone!" she cried. The others stared at her for a second. No one else knew the words.

"You go ahead, Raiza," said Vilen. "You're the only authentic Jew among us!" In a minute we all started clapping and humming "Hava Nagila" as Raiza sang, looking at one another happily and rather defiantly. After that I persuaded Iulia to sing her special song. " 'In the blue sky/There is a golden city . . .' " she sang, and after that we all hugged her tearfully, smoothing back her matted blond hair and gazing into her green eyes. Then it was time to go. We put on our coats, embraced, all of us, and promised to see each other in America. When the door shut finally on Vilen's apartment, I felt that an important part of my life had ended.

On the way to the bus stop, I was silent. It was a beautiful sunny afternoon, with a new fall of snow glittering between the bleak apartment buildings. I was thinking about the class members, wondering about their preparations for departure, their misgivings, their farewells. I pictured them arriving in Vienna, staring at the streets that would seem so bright after Moscow; making their way in America on the strength of those crazy dialogues. Thinking of that, I wanted to laugh and cry at the same time.

"What are they all going to do?" I asked Rima, who was walking beside me.

"Who?"

"The class, of course."

Rima pulled her flowered scarf more tightly around her face. "They'll make their way very well," she said. "And so will I, if the time ever comes."

"Would you seriously try to emigrate?"

"Perhaps," she said thoughtfully. "But it would take so much effort. And the strange thing is that I love this awful country. If I left, I would always be torn, as they all will be—wait and see."

Up ahead of us, little Iulia was running in the snow, skidding and waving her scarf. "Come on!" she shouted. "The bus is coming!"

We got on the bus and rode to the metro.

Ibrahim

A midwinter thaw in the last week has broken the January cold spell and brought us three glorious days of warmth. Although I know that months more of winter will follow this break, I can't help feeling a ravishing, unquenchable happiness that seems to spring from my bones. It's partly the light that does it—the fact that the sun now appears over the buildings before ten o'clock and vanishes later in the afternoon. All over the city, roof-corners drip incessantly with snow-water, and the huge red-faced women who struggled to keep the sidewalks clear all through the deadly frost now easily chop their mattocks and shovels through the rotten ice. At the *rynok* yesterday a few Georgian women were selling new lettuce. We are halfway through our stay in Russia now.

It was warm enough for me to leave off my snow boots last night, when we went off to visit Rima and her boyfriend Vasia. Tom and I even went without hats, ignoring the disapproving stares of every Russian we met. (Russians seem to think that going hatless before April and after October is inviting certain death.) Feeling light without our normal winter weight, we hopped and skipped giddily through the darkness on our way from the metro. Vasia lives on the very edge of town in a run-down neighborhood that is a mixture of shoddy high rises from the early sixties and old wooden peasant houses; there are groves of huge pine trees that suggest the lushness of the forest there in the past. When we got to the apartment, everyone was sitting in the kitchen: Vasia,

Rima, Rima's friend the beautiful Nadia, and an Ethiopian student who introduced himself as Ibrahim. It was the first time I'd seen Rima since the end of our English class, and she quickly pulled me aside to whisper some gossip about the class members. For some reason, lights were turned off in the apartment, and only a few candles illuminated the tiny kitchen. "We've been playing the saucer game," Rima told me excitedly. "Vasia had a conversation with Mandelstam in which the poet told him, 'Continue'— that must mean with his poems. And now everybody wants to talk to Akhmatova."

The saucer game is the equivalent of playing with a Ouija board: the fingertips of the company touch a kitchen saucer that glides over a lettered wheel sketched on paper and spells out messages.

Tom and I had brought a bottle of Smirnoff from the diplomatic store and everybody was eager to try it. (Strangely enough, the American-produced Smirnoff vodka is rumored, here in the land of vodka, to be the best in the world; Russians tell us this is because the Smirnoffs were once official vodka makers to the royal family.) Vasia had a bottle of *samagon* (home brew) which was said to be 150-proof. So we sat in the candlelight around the rickety table and drank, and ate up a bowl of murderous-looking but very tasty pickled mushrooms and a pan of unsalted cornbread that Rima had made from a Georgian recipe. Against the wall slept Vasia's dog Hemingway (pronounced *Gemingway*), big and furry and yellowish white as a polar bear; he occasionally opened his eyes and blinked his stiff white lashes.

The kitchen window was still sealed with cotton and brown paper against winter winds, but through the air vent came an almost springlike smell of mud and damp concrete that made us all feel lively. The beautiful Nadia, especially, was smiling radiantly. She is a girl of eighteen or nineteen, with blond hair and full, very red lips that give a surprising richness to her face. She works in a minor sales job and is said to be cynical and promiscuous, but last night there was in her expression so much freshness, so much evidence of beauty's simple delight in its own existence, that seeing her was like drawing in a lungful of the damp thawed air. The saucer and lettered wheel lay on the table, but we were all busy talking to Ibrahim. He was a very tall, thin young man in his late twenties, with a huge mass of frizzy hair, brown cheeks decorated with several precisely set black moles, and the beautiful linear features of the saints in ancient Ethiopian church frescoes. Toward me he showed the absolute lack of interest with which many Africans greet American blacks. Ibrahim is a student at Patrice Lumumba University, the school set up in southwest Moscow to educate Third World students in advanced technology and Communist ideology. He has been in Moscow for five years, and his Russian—spoken very swiftly in a soft voice—is excellent. When we asked him how he liked the Soviet Union, he gave a short laugh and thoughtfully ate the last piece of cornbread. Licking his fingers, he said, "It would take me a long time really to answer that question. Most of my African classmates hate it here because of the climate, because we live here under miserable conditions, and because the·Russian *narod*, the masses, call us black devils and spit at us in the street. One African hated it here so much that he went home and wrote a book called *Seven Years in Prison*. I've suffered here, but that doesn't concern me now. What I'm most full of worry and bitterness about is my own political situation."

Ibrahim's political situation, it turns out, is that he is not really Ethiopian, but Eritrean—part of the rebel state now battling to secede from Ethiopia. Ibrahim arrived in Moscow when the Soviet Union was backing Eritrea, but a few years ago, when the USSR switched allegiances in favor of Ethiopia, Ibrahim became *persona non grata* in Moscow. By moving out of his dormitory and administering a few bribes, he has managed to stay on to complete his education (he receives his degree in June) but his situation remains precarious and dangerous.

"What will you do when you get home?" asked Tom.

"Fight," said Ibrahim, joining his long, dry-skinned brown fingers together on the tabletop. "My brother was already killed; now I have to serve. I'm very afraid for my country. Our secession was based on regional differences, but the conflict now is between the Soviet-backed government in Addis Ababa, and our non-Soviet secessionist troops. In my five years in Russia, I've come to hate everything about the Soviet system. Life here is a misery of repression—you yourselves know it. And so I'll be fighting from my Moscow experience as well as from my love for Eritrea. The Soviet Union has educated me, though not in a way it intended."

"Aren't you afraid to fight?" asked Nadia, after a pause.

"My own life isn't so very important. I wouldn't mind losing it, although I'd feel bad for my mother and father. As I said, my brother was already killed."

His matter-of-fact tone chilled me. In the candlelight, his unmistakably Ethiopian face, with its thin nose and black-rimmed eyes, had the almost uncanny austerity of a man who is ruled by a single idea. He really wasn't afraid, I thought, because it had never occurred to him to be. The big dog Hemingway rolled over with a groan, showing us his yellowish belly in the corner beside the stove. The rest of us were quiet; our giddy mood had evaporated. Ibrahim went on talking, outlining for us government factions and military movements, of which he somehow managed to keep abreast during his secretive life in Moscow. I couldn't follow him; all I could envision was a dry landscape, stark as an abstraction, in which troops of soldiers with faces like Ibrahim's marched and countermarched, and bodies lay mummified in the sun. It occurred to me, as it has occurred to me countless times this year, that in Russia, matters of life, death, and freedom always come pushing their way, like uninvited guests, into the most frivolous gathering. I remembered something Rima once said to me: "No conversation here is light for very long." The constant encounters Tom and I have had with people who are willing to risk their lives for something—whether they are dissidents, or loyal Soviet citizens prepared to fight for the motherland, or flotsam and jetsam like Ibrahim, washed up in Moscow from obscure warring

Third World states—are what have given touches of a particular solemn darkness to the last six months.

We finished the bottle of Smirnoff and brightened up a bit. Tom and Vasia went into the front room to listen to Pink Floyd, and Nadia, Rima, and I persuaded Ibrahim to play the saucer game with us. Ibrahim (who had lost some of his awesome seriousness) balked, saying it was stupid to invoke dead poets who gave advice in gibberish. "Well then, we'll talk to a spirit from your country, Ibrahim," said Rima in her most tactful tone. "You call the spirit and ask the question in your own language, and the rest of us will just use our powers of concentration to receive the message in Russian. Go on, go to the door and say the name three times." Rima was flushed, her odd face very solemn in the candlelight; she loves spells and conjuring of all kinds. Ibrahim reluctantly went to the kitchen doorway and said something three times softly in a language we couldn't understand. He came back to the table, and we all rested our fingertips on the saucer and waited. "Who did you ask for, Ibrahim?" whispered Nadia, smiling at him meltingly.

"I've called my brother," said Ibrahim.

All of us were stunned.

"Why, that's bad luck," said Rima. "It should have been a famous person, someone you didn't know . . . But never mind."

Under our fingertips, the saucer suddenly took off in the startling way of possessed things, and skeptic that I am, I found myself wondering whether it was Rima or Nadia who was pushing it around. Although certainly the kitchen with its peeling walls and big black stove was somber enough to attract any spirit. Ibrahim said something under his breath in the same strange language, and the saucer slid from one letter to another on the wheel of the Russian alphabet. I was gripped by sudden excitement.

"Oh, it's gibberish!" exclaimed Ibrahim. "Just gibberish."

"Wait," said Rima. "It's still moving." The saucer slid from side to side, and at the fifth letter, Nadia gave a shriek and snatched her hand away. The saucer had spelled out *smert—*

"death." Rima also took her hand away, jumped up, went over, and switched on the electric light. "This is a stupid game," she said. "I don't want to play any more."

All of us blinked in the bright light. "What question did you ask?" said Nadia timidly to Ibrahim. He ran his hand through his bushy hair and grinned. "I asked my brother what I could expect when I went home."

Tom and Vasia opened the door of the bedroom and came out to see what was going on. None of us explained. As soon as I could, I took Rima down to the end of the hallway. "That was a bad joke," I said. "Did you do that?"

"No, I didn't do it," she said, twisting her fingers in her long braid. She was almost in tears.

Later that night Tom and I walked with Ibrahim back to the metro. It was real thaw weather: damp, with a huge buffeting wind that ranked and regrouped the clouds and carried that same fresh hopeful scent of mud and wet pavement. Ibrahim wore a thin parka and an odd-looking striped hat that seemed to be made out of cat fur. He jumped over puddles with us, but his face in the streetlights was as abstracted as ever, and he was talking again about his country. "I have to get there," he told us. "It doesn't matter what happens. Just to fight, to know that I have done something, is all that is important to me."

When we said goodbye to him at the Gorky Park metro station, he strode off quickly down the corridor, his cranelike figure already bearing, I noticed, a military set to the shoulders. Two *babushki*, who were manipulating an enormous electric sweeper, paused in their work to study him with a hostile stare, but he passed without appearing to see them, as if he were entirely alone.

Leningrad

When we got to Leningrad, two weeks ago, the branches of the trees around the Winter Palace were still white with the famous hoarfrost of this damp region; above the frozen Neva, in the stunningly clear light of a minus-thirty-degree morning, the blue-green palace looked like the final step in a theorem proving that cold weather would be the eternal state of the world. As our taxi crossed the bridge to Vasilevsky Island, I saw people strolling on the ice of the river, all of them as bundled up as I was in fur coats and hats and tightly wrapped scarves. (I've found that by far the best way to deal with temperatures below twenty degrees Fahrenheit is to wrap my face like a mummy until only my eyes show, and then to breathe the warmed air coming in through the cloth.) Far behind them, the gold spires of the Peter and Paul Fortress shone under the blinding sky like a signal to even colder countries, farther north.

Even then, the length of the days betrayed the approach of spring. Every day the twilight comes a bit later and hangs longer over the city, and in the afternoons, everyone, starved for light through the darkness of December and January, is out strolling along the streets and canals. After our arrival the weather swiftly grew warmer, the temperatures rising daily, until now the snow has turned to puddles of slush and it is possible to go outside in what Russians call a *"demi-saison"* (many of their fashion terms are French), a wool coat, instead of a fur or sheepskin. I paid careful attention to the Neva, so as not to miss the breakup of the ice. I imagined that I would be awakened one dawn by the fabled cracking sounds like gunfire that would mean that the river had wrestled itself free from winter. Instead, as I paused one sunny afternoon on the Dvortsovyi Bridge, I heard a light tinkling, like crystals in a chandelier, and looked down to see an open channel about two feet wide in the thick gray ice; inside was a swift eddy of brownish water where dozens of tiny pieces of ice were caught and ringing against one another. This delicate chiming seemed to be an apt voice for this ravishing artificial city of pastels, balanced on its marshes at the top of the world. The combination of Mediterranean colors and architectural shapes with the high white skies of the North gives Leningrad, to me, the disturbing glamour one finds in exotic hybrid fruits and flowers—wherever the hand of man has tampered outrageously with nature.

There is the Leningrad of Rastrelli and the Bronze Horseman, of Nevsky Prospekt and the Winter Palace, and then there is our corner of the city: a working-class neighborhood on Vasilevsky Island, which was filled with barricades during the revolutions of 1905 and 1917. We are staying in a small dormitory for Russian and foreign students that is set inconspicuously among brick apartment buildings and snowy open spaces that are becoming seas of mud as the snow melts. Our window looks out on what seems to be a boys' *gymnasium*: we often see the boys outside in their school uniforms, goose-stepping through some quasi-military drill. They also like to gather upstairs in the lavatory to laugh and smoke cigarettes and try to push one another out of the windows. Once there was a *skandal* when some of the pupils threw snowballs at one of the school cleaning women: she charged into the yard, her white kerchief flapping, yelling and flailing at them with a mop.

Shopping in the stores in this neighborhood makes it clear that we're no longer in a relatively privileged community, as we were in Moscow. There are fewer leather boots and blue jeans on the clientele, and more *valenki* (felt boots) and black quilted workmen's jackets. The stores are filled with crowds, strong smells, and puddles of soupy mud near the doors. Entering the *gastronom* on Malyi Prospekt, where I shop almost daily, one is assailed with the stink of stale meat and turning milk, of crowds who eat too much sausage and wash infrequently. Behind the counters, big slatternly women—who usually have crudely bleached hair above exhausted faces shining with grease and perspiration, faces whose fine-textured skin is a startling reminder that these women are quite young, perhaps thirty or thirty-five—slice kilos of cheese, weigh butter, and bring out the greenish bottles of *kefir* and acidophilus milk. The people in the endless jostling lines are constantly shouting orders and thrusting out their cashier slips, but these women in their bedraggled white coats do everything with an insolent slowness. Foul-tempered beyond any American's nightmare of a rude employee, they pounce, with shouts of abuse, on any customer whose demeanor offends them. In the line itself, there is always some nimble old woman who tries, without any subtlety, to dart to the front; a proper reaction might be to say *"Grazhdanka, vui byez orchered!"*—Citizeness, you're out of place in line!—or one can simply shove. (I prefer the latter response.) In the middle of the crowd, mothers in lacy knitted headshawls try to keep tabs on toddlers bundled in immense wooly coats, with scarves tied around their middles. Workmen with black-jowled faces and missing teeth line up for salted fish. Behind the welter of bodies, glass sale cases display huge yellowish pigs' heads.

In this uncertain transitional weather between winter and spring, this end of Vasilevsky Island, with its streets full of dirty snow and its dingy apartment buildings streaked with moisture, can seem intensely depressing, a bit like an American slum, though one devoid of any flamboyant signs of vice or suffering. Here, there is just a sense of incessant struggle, of the constant burden of a harsh life that squashes men into mean shapes. Yet something of the magic of Leningrad penetrates even to this lowly corner. The early evenings can be lovely. I get off the metro in the middle of a crowd and push my way outside through the masses of damp wool coats at the station door. At this hour dozens of people are waiting for the trolley on Sredny Prospekt. Some of the girls and young women have their heads uncovered for the first time since October, and their necks and faces look vulnerable and delicately colored after a winter of protection. The sky over Sredny is blue-white with a roseate tinge to it; the air is moist and cold, scented with whiffs of cabbage-flavored steam from a nearby cafeteria. By the bus stop stands a small open-air flower market, run mostly by Moldavian women; they sell hyacinths and red tulips, which the crowds carry away like torches. Across the street, there is often a line waiting to get into a candy store that has a mild blue neon sign depicting a squirrel. There are few cars in Leningrad, compared to Moscow, and so one can look far up the street, where slushy puddles gleam in the sunset, and watch the trolleys as they rattle from block to block, striking showers of sparks between the dark buildings.

Tolya

Yesterday I went out for a jaunt with my best friend in Leningrad. His name is Tolya, and he is a Komsomol member so highly respected that he heads his own study group. Like many young Russians, he is also, in his off hours, an aficionado of things American. His collection of American jeans—fifteen pairs, with every lace, strap, buckle, stud, appliqué imaginable—far surpasses my own, as does his stack of rock records. In his tiny apartment, off Sredny Prospekt, bottles of American after-shave and mouthwash and cans of American air freshener are artistically set out, like so many bibelots. Tolya, who is twenty, has told me that he checks his calendar every morning. If there is no Komsomol meeting that day, he can dispense with his Russian suit and "dress American"—that is, in denim everything. Yesterday he was resplendent in black-market plumage: an American Air Force parka, the inevitable jeans, a denim vest, desert boots, aviator glasses, and a jaunty denim hat. He carried his lunch in a plastic bag with WRANGLER emblazoned on it in huge letters.

Tolya and I took the train out of the city to Pushkin, formerly Tsarskoye Selo (the "Tsar's Village"), and strolled through the muddy fields and woods around the palaces there. Several weeks of thaw have melted much of the snow in the countryside; now the woods are full of dripping vapors, and the ground sucks at your feet. The Catherine Palace was under reconstruction, closed to visitors, but we squeezed through a wooden barricade and walked around staring at the rows of big blank windows and their blackened gilt decorations. A battered carriage stood propped up in one corner of the courtyard. We went over to inspect it. Outside, it was splintery and peeling, but on one door were still visible an ornate gilt A and the numeral II. "Aleksandr the Second!" said Tolya. The interior of the carriage was dry and still upholstered with a springy cloth. We climbed inside and began to eat bread and sausage, giggling, and terrified that we'd break an axle. Tolya began to bounce up and down. "Hey, I dig this!" he said in English. "Who do you suppose rode in this?"

"I'd say a very minor courtier," I said.

We joked and ate. There was a cold drizzle falling outside, and we felt happy and warm inside the carriage, with the wet blue plaster palace outside the window and piles of dirty snow and lumber nearby. Tolya told a story about some old carriages he had seen in a Leningrad square, where a film crew was shooting one of Tolstoy's short novels. "There were some old women nearby, and they started to cry when they saw the tsar's carriage with its gold crowns. One *babushka* muttered, 'Oh, those dear old days!' "

I knew that Tolya himself thought of them as "dear old days." He is fascinated by the photographs and relics of tsarist times, and often speaks of his drop of noble blood, from one of his great-grandfathers. In the carriage, he stroked the door handle dreamily and gazed out at the palace.

He changed, we both changed, when we began the political dialogue about China and Russia and the United States which I've had with so many of my Russian friends.

"What do you think?" I asked.

Tolya said, "What I think is what I teach in my study group."

"What is that?"

"That there will be war. Inevitably. In the next decade." Tolya took off his glasses and looked at me shyly but intensely. "We young Russians live with that assumption now. We have to attack China before China develops too much nuclear strength. That will mean war with America. But we believe we can win."

We were both silent for a minute. "Do you really believe that?" I asked.

Tolya began to talk faster. There was something rattling and rhetorical in the terms that he used, but his tone was sincere. "What you Americans don't realize is that we'll win because we're not afraid to sacrifice everything for winning. We lost twenty million people in the Second World War, but we beat the Germans. And that spirit of sacrifice still exists—the government has made sure to keep it alive in all of us. Mention the war, and people still weep and shake their fists. They grieve, but they're ready to do it again. We are ready, too, in our economic life. Everything—everything goes into the military. That's why life is so bad here."

"And so you will win."

"Yes, we will win, because, if you don't mind my saying so, America is decadent. I'm not saying this because I've been taught to; I'm speaking from my own perceptions. Your dollar is low, your reputation is low, you don't seem to believe in anything any more. You're soft. And so we'll win, and I think it's very sad, because you have such a wonderful culture." He looked at me owlishly, out of breath.

There was silence, and then it was too absurd, and we both started to laugh. "Who will sell jeans to Russian black marketeers after America falls?" I asked.

We climbed out of the carriage and walked into the muddy park.

A bit later, in a costume museum in the park, we strolled through room after room of clothing from households of the tsar and the nobility. There were hussars' uniforms; coronation robes; Chinese silk dressing gowns; morning, afternoon, and evening dresses in styles ranging from crinoline to the lily-shaped Poiret *moderne*; immense cavalry helmets bearing double-headed eagles. The museum is remarkable for an especially poignant atmosphere, which springs, I suspect, from a lack of funds. The clothes are not shiny and perfectly restored, but have a faintly rumpled appearance, as if their owners had just stepped out of them and were standing by, invisible. For atmosphere, some inspired curator has added a short, scratchy tape of heartbreaking waltz music that plays over and over again.

The dreamy look returned to Tolya's eyes as we wandered through the exhibits. He was especially taken by an ivory embroidery box with enameled spools and thimbles. I came up behind him as he stood staring at it, and whispered, "So, do you think there will be American museums like this after the great victory?"

He turned and looked at me. "I'm so sorry," he said earnestly. "I didn't mean to offend you. But I do believe that what I say is true. For me, Americans are like these people." He gestured at the exhibit. "They cast a spell—oh, a wonderful spell—and they must inevitably die out."

The Beriozka

The diplomatic food store on Vasilevsky Island is located on an exceedingly drab industrial street where there are several factories, and a steady stream of poorly dressed men and women going by with huge bundles of food and necessities in bulging plastic suitcases or net bags. Many of these people slow down to stare as they pass the diplomatic store, which has the veiled, suggestive appearance of all Soviet *beriozki*. On this muddy street, filled with pits and rubble and lined with shabby buildings, the unmarked store window, with its snowy pleated draperies over a tasteful arrangement of pebbles that looks almost Japanese, is a mysterious and angelic presence, a visitation of luxury to a world that lives without it. Outside the store are often parked a few shiny foreign automobiles with diplomatic or business-community license plates—or equally shiny Soviet cars, usually the discreet black Volga. These are minutely examined by the heavily laden passers-by. Occasionally a workman with a gnarled frostbitten face will eye the cars and spit scornfully, muttering, "Foreigners!"

Inside, the shop consists of two rooms, and to enter them from the street is like passing into another dimension; the carefully decorated interior, in fact, has a suggestion of the feeling of intimacy and luxury found in an expensive Western boutique. The larger room holds every expensive brand of European and American beer, wine, liquor, cigarette, and candy, all artistically set out on mirrored shelves that reflect the soft lighting and the red carpet on the floor. There is a section devoted to Soviet beverages—Armenian and Georgian wines and brandies, flavored vodkas, the rare "balsam" liqueur from the Baltic region—many of which are unobtainable on the open market. In front of the shelves are a couple of comfortable armchairs, and near these is an attractive laminated wooden desk where normally sit two pretty English-speaking Soviet girls in stylish Western outfits. These girls greet customers, sizing them up with the expertise of snobbish salespeople around the world; sometimes, depending on the apparent rank of the customer, they actually fill and push the little shopping carts. (We students are definitely not important enough to have our carts pushed. Living among Russians and arriving on foot as we do, we form the lowest of the castes allowed in the store, slightly below, say, the African diplomats, who receive only the most perfunctory smiles from the young women.)

The second, smaller room is filled with canned goods—usually German, Russian, or Bulgarian—and an array of marvelous fresh meats, dairy products, and produce, all of which are Russian, and most of which are superior to anything one can buy on the open market or at the *rynok*. The beef is all prime, the hamburger particularly, so lean that fat must be added to it. There is liver, which Russians love, and which is almost impossible to buy for rubles, since it is reserved for restaurants serving foreigners and stores like this one. In the produce section are big bags of hot-house cucumbers and tomatoes, the same vegetables that have been selling for ten to fifteen rubles a kilo in the peasant markets this winter. In general, the prices at the diplomatic store are very low. The payment procedure is this: the foreigner pays his own currency for a booklet of ruble coupons redeemable for goods only in these special stores. Right now, a diplomatic ruble costs about a dollar forty. Even with the disadvantageous exchange rate, the store is full of bargains: a bottle of Cointreau costs about three rubles; a sack of precious tomatoes, about two rubles; a bottle of Starorusskaya (considered one of the best Russian vodkas), a ruble fifty.

Last week when I was at the store, a middle-aged foreign woman from the Brahmin caste that receives obsequious service from the salesgirls was doing some shopping. She had a finely made-up, rather imperious face, and was swathed in handsome sheared beaver, the kind of coat Russians rarely see, because the best Russian furs are exported. One of the salesgirls, a curly-headed blonde in a denim jumper, was pushing her cart and urging her to buy some lettuce. "It's just in today, madame," she said in her birdlike English. "Greenhouse lettuce! Our first this winter!"

"I don't know," said the woman, also in English but with an ambiguous European accent. "So far I've not been very impressed with your Soviet vegetables. But send some to me tomorrow." She raised a thin hand to her lips, and I saw her fingers glittering with diamonds. At the desk, the other salesgirl, a redhead, gently packed the woman's few purchases into a plastic bag, totted up the bill in graceful flourishes on a piece of paper, and reverently received the coupons. As the woman went out, the blond salesgirl sighed, and then said to her companion in rapid Russian, "That coat—oh, my goodness! And the boots, did you see the boots? All the women are wearing that style now. What a life!"

I had been pushing my own cart around. When I came up to the desk, they treated me with absent-minded civility, and I felt very annoyed. I was annoyed partly because I, too, longed for a fur coat and diamonds, but mostly because I knew that these young women shared with me a knowledge of the contrast between the two worlds of the Soviet Union: the hidden world where luxury and snobbery reign for privileged Russians—and especially for foreigners—and the harsh life of the working class on the outside, where even the plastic shopping bags from the *beriozki* are coveted luxuries. The workers on the street can't see inside the diplomatic store, and the foreigners, climbing into their cars and driving back to their segregated luxury apartments, can't possibly know what life is like for the average Russian. But I, trudging through the streets, speaking Russian and visiting Russian friends, know what both sides are like, and so do these young women, far better than I. So how, I wondered, could they sit there, so prettily painted and manicured, ready to shepherd rich women around this mirrored, carpeted room, without any trace of ugly cynicism crossing their faces? I told myself it was the universal Soviet pragmatism I've seen so clearly in Valerii and my other friends: the philosophy is to find your niche, make your adjustments, and then live without considering it. Like Intourist guides, and other Russians whose jobs involve close contact with foreigners, the salesgirls probably have KGB affiliations and probably, also, the privilege of shopping in the special "closed" stores for upper-level Russians. They are young, pretty girls, and the diplomatic-store job is clearly quite a pleasant one.

Just as I was leaving the store last week, something happened that occasionally occurs in these special stores. Normally, the doorman, a short, fat man with bulging eyes and a grotesquely upturned nose, is on guard to keep ordinary Russians from entering, but at that moment he was pausing to smoke a foreign cigarette and to lean over the desk to say something confidential to the two girls; the door, moreover, was open to allow some of the fresh balmy afternoon into the store. An old woman dressed in a worn black wool coat, a gray wool scarf, and a pair of rubber-shod *valenki*—unmistakably a woman from that stream of populace passing in the grimy street outside—appeared suddenly in the doorway. "*Ostorozhno!* [Watch out!]" hissed one of the salesgirls, and the guard leaped over to the door and began to back the old woman out, speaking in a firm, officious voice as if to a child. "Now, grandmother, this isn't for you. This is a special store, for foreigners . . ." The *babushka* pretended to be deaf and slow-witted, but it was clear that she knew what she was doing, and had been drawn there out of curiosity. As the guard backed her out, her head swiveled around and she took in the whole glittering two rooms. It was amazing to watch her wrinkled red face, on which there struggled a remarkable mixture of astonishment and avidity, as if she'd just discovered, and longed to plunder, an entirely new world.

The Blues Abroad

A few weeks ago we were lucky enough to attend a B. B. King concert in the Gorky Palace of Culture in Leningrad. B. B. King, correctly described by his publicity as the best-known blues musician in the world, had been touring the Soviet Union for three weeks, generating waves of enthusiasm among its citizens—who know jazz well but have little exposure to the blues. The tour began with a concert in the capital of Azerbaijan; it moved on to Yerevan and then to Tbilisi, where, according to a State Department aide, the impulsive Georgians nearly started a riot, shoving into the theatre until two people sat in every seat. In Leningrad, the excitement had been building up long before we reached the Culture Palace. There has been absolutely no advance publicity in the city, but all our Russian friends knew about the concert from Voice of America (another, not always facetious, nickname for this broadcast is "Voice of the Enemy"). The afternoon of the concert, a subtle excitement diffused itself through the crowds on Nevsky Prospekt. On the metro, groups of well-dressed people were eying one another and anxiously demanding the time. The horde of ticket scalpers encountered on the way to any Soviet performance extended this time all the way down into the subway. "Do you have extra tickets?" people were shouting on all sides. Our friend Tolya, who was with us, said that the street tickets were going for between fifty and a hundred rubles apiece.

Inside the performance hall, we found an ample display of Soviet fashion. There were endless pairs of American jeans, which women wore with the skinny-heeled Italian ankle boots that are the *dernier cri* of Russian style. The curious thing about the crowd was that it consisted not mainly of young people, as one might expect, but of people of all ages. There were many middle-aged men and women, dressed in their best baggy suits and polyester dresses. There were small children, and there were some of the oldest *babushki* I had ever seen, walking slowly, with pleased grins, their heads wrapped in shawls.

A slick-haired Soviet M.C. announced B. B. King ("A great *Negritanski* musician"), and then King was onstage with his well-known guitar—Lucille—and a ten-man ensemble. As King and the ensemble swung into "Why I Sing the Blues," one could sense the puzzlement of the Soviet audience. "Negro" music to them meant jazz or spirituals, but this was something else. Also, there was the question of response. B. B. King is a great, warm presence when he performs, and he asks his audiences to pour themselves out to him in return. King teases his audiences, urging them to clap along, to whistle, to hoot their appreciation, like the congregations in the Southern churches in which he grew up. But to Russians, such behavior suggests a lack of culture and an almost frightening disorder. Though obviously impressed, the audiences at first kept a respectful silence during the numbers, as it might at the symphony. (Only the foreigners shouted and stomped out the beat; we found the Russians around us staring at us open-mouthed.) Then King played an irresistible riff, stopped and leaned toward the audience with his hand cupped to his ear. The audience caught on and began to clap. King changed the beat, and waited for the audience to catch up. Then he changed it again. Soon the whole place was clapping along to "Get off My Back, Woman," and there were even a few timid shouts and whistles. King, who has carried the blues to Europe, Africa, and the Far East, had broken the ice one more time.

At intermission we were fortunate enough to talk to B. B. King. He rose when we came into his dressing room, a large dark-skinned man with sweat glistening on his forehead. King is one of the few performers whom it is not a revelation to see close up; he presents himself onstage exactly as he is, and his conversation has the same warmth and intermittent playfulness as his music. We asked him about his experiences in the Soviet Union, and he answered carefully, glancing occasionally at his manager, Sid Seidenberg, who stood by the door, and at an Intourist guide sitting nearby. (The backstage area was bristling with security people and Intourist personnel; Tolya said, "This place is full of KGB.") King said that although he preferred capitalism, he respected the Soviet system, and that he had been impressed by the cordial hospitality of the Soviet people. Audiences all over the Soviet Union, he said, had received his music enthusiastically. "The blues is likely something they've never heard before," he said. "I like to help them understand." He told us a bit about touring Georgia and Armenia—his favorite parts of the Soviet Union. His best memory, he said, was driving up to a mountain lake in Armenia, eating a fish dinner, and meeting the local farm people. "I grew up working on farms," he added.

We asked him what he felt he'd learned from touring the Soviet Union, and he seemed to give the question serious thought.

"I've learned two things," he said finally, leaning toward us. "The first is patience. The Soviet people are very patient. When things don't happen on time—if a plane doesn't take off for three hours, if a meal doesn't come—they wait. I've learned how to wait. The second thing I've learned here is that you can be a great musician and an amateur. I didn't think that was possible before I came to the Soviet Union. But we have listened to—and in one case actually jammed with—some very fine jazz musicians in Baku and Tbilisi. None of them were professionals."

When we asked him what he thought of Soviet jazz in general, he said he was impressed by what he heard.

"They were good technically—sure, that you'd expect," he said. "But these fellows felt the music, and that's what impressed me. I don't know where they got the feeling, but they felt it."

We said goodbye to B. B. King and left the dressing room to

talk with some of his back-up musicians. These musicians were less guarded in their comments. Like King, they were happy about the audience response, and they praised the jazz musicians of Baku and Tbilisi. But they generally agreed that for a touring musician, the Soviet Union is a boring place.

"There's nothing to do here," said one. "At home we'd finish up the show and go to some little after-hours joint and listen to some *music* or something. But there's nothing like that here. Everything closes down. It's hard to meet women. It's hard to meet *any*body."

Another player complained, "It's like a damn prison here. We go down to dinner in a big group, we go up to our rooms in a group, and there's two, three Russians watching us all the time. Are we followed? Hell, yes. I live in New York. I know the fuzz when I see it. Guides, they call them. They don't like us to do one thing on our own. I like the people, man. The people—especially those Georgians—are something else, if you can just get away from the guides."

By the second half of the performance, the audience was looser than any other Soviet audience I'd ever seen. People whistled, they hooted with delight, they clapped along, answering King's playful coaxing on the guitar. The guards standing against the auditorium walls looked uneasy. "This is exactly what they don't like," whispered Tolya. "This rowdiness. They're terrified of a riot." The music, already superb, got better and better. By the time King swung into his final song—the show-stopper—"The Thrill Is Gone," the audience was in love. Following the number, there was tumultuous applause, flowers were flung on the stage, and three Soviet hippies forced their way up onto the stage to kiss King's hands and to get his autograph. They were quickly wrestled away by a combination of American and Soviet security forces. King bent to shake hands from the stage, and the guards frowned some more as the crowd broke out into a roaring chant of "B. B. King! B. B. King!"

Quickly the guards fanned out through the audience, pushing people toward the cloakrooms and ending the wild applause before it really got going. At one point, during a lull, Tom and I had a chance to talk to our neighbor, a woman who had initially stared at our clapping. She was a well-dressed middle-aged woman who hadn't taken part in any of the "rowdy" behavior. Nevertheless, she had seemed deeply moved by the performance, and when we asked her how she had enjoyed it, we saw that she had tears in her eyes. "I have been studying American Negro music for years," she said. "I have listened to hundreds of records. It has been a kind of dream of mine to attend a live performance. Now—all that I can say is that I understand the music. One performance is worth a thousand records."

In the cloakroom line, we talked to other local people. The reactions were all enthusiastic and emotional. One girl said, "This is one of the greatest things that ever happened to me in my life! A friend gave me the tickets; I never expected to go. It's almost impossible for an ordinary person like me to see something like this. You have to be special—to have a lot of money or some Party connections—to get to a performance like this."

An older man in a baggy suit looked thoughtful as we talked to him. "B. B. King," he said, pronouncing the syllables distinctly. "B. B. King astounded me. This blues music—it's not like jazz. He poured his whole heart and soul out there on the stage. Such feeling is very Russian—we believe in emotion, in the soul. I never thought that an American could feel that way."

Yura

When I see Yura, I am reminded of a field of corn I once saw that had been exposed to radiation as part of an experiment. Like many of those cornstalks, he is tall, spindly, and twisted, with a spectral pallor. His figure is hunchbacked and pigeon-breasted, as if the hand that modeled him had suddenly grown impatient and crumpled its work. Beneath a bristly mouse-colored tuft of hair, his face is long, narrow, toothless, and innocent: at forty, he has a simpler nature than most people.

Yura works as an assistant in the tiny library of the Free Economic Society, a venerable tsarist Russian liberal institution whose archives have been preserved by the Soviet government. The library is an incredibly small, musty place with room for only two or three scholars at a time (right now, Tom is one of them). One gets there by taking Nevsky Prospekt over the Liteiny Bridge, with its glorious bronze horses, and walking alongside the Fontanka Canal until, entering a *dvor* (courtyard) through a typical eighteenth-century archway, one comes upon one of those hidden worlds of activity so common in Moscow and Leningrad—in this case, a children's clinic, with many grandmothers and toddlers waiting outside. To the left of the courtyard is another doorway, unmarked, dilapidated—in fact, a brownish vine has worked its way through the door hinges, and clutches the wall of the stairwell inside. Up the stairs is a second door, padded against winter drafts, and beside this is a tiny sign identifying the library. One rings a bell, and after a long wait, Yura opens the door. The first glimpse of his twisted body in the doorway is quite startling.

Yura was born into a peasant family in a forest village of Kalinin Province in the middle thirties. It is possible that his skeletal deformities are the result of deprivations caused first by collectivization, and then by the war as he was growing up. I have seen a number of such pinched and crumpled bodies moving through the streets, all of them about the same age—children of the years of starvation. He says he remembers little of the war, except that his father was killed. Right after the war he came with his mother to Leningrad, and was assigned to this library. Here he has been ever since. His job is to get books for the few scholars who use the archive, and to deal with a complicated shelving system, something he does with a great deal of pride. Most of his tranquil days are spent puttering at tasks of his own devising; he grumbles loudly if an overzealous scholar requests too many books.

When I first met Yura, we talked about the movies. Cinema is the main diversion of his odd life, and he has seen several American films, including *Cleopatra* and *Funny Girl*. "My favorite American actors are Henry Fonda and his daughter Janey," he told Tom and me. "Janey Fonda is a very, very pretty girl, and politically very good."

Tom said that that was so, and that, in fact, in America, we just said "Jane" Fonda.

"Well, what about her friends?" said Yura. "Surely they must call her 'Janey'!"

He asked us if we'd like to go to the movies with him sometime, since his mother didn't approve of his going on his own. There was a wonderful American movie playing—*The Great Fatherland* (*Velikaia Otechestvennaia . . .*); it was about the heroic role of the Soviet Union in World War II, and it was narrated by Burt Lancaster. Yura said that he was pleased with the fact that Burt Lancaster and other Americans understood how great his country was, then and now. "Life is good here," he said, and there was no false ring of propaganda in his voice. How, in fact, could someone like Yura not say what he really felt?

Later that afternoon, when I left the little library to run some errands, I realized suddenly how many people like Yura I encounter on my daily round of life in the city. There is the hunchbacked proprietor of the public scales in a Nevsky underpass; the shrunken, vague-eyed woman who is one of the *garderobchitsi* (cloakroom attendants) at the library; the dwarfish man whose occupation seems to be an undefined keeping of order at one of the metro stops. I can think of at least ten more Russians like these, who in America would probably be in institutions, but who are here included in the flow of daily life. I have no idea what the official Soviet policy is toward physically and mentally defective citizens, but I have been impressed for a long time by their acceptance here —as well as the acceptance of the aged—within the normal scheme of things. In America, it seems to me, we have a bit of the squeamishness of the inhabitants of Huxley's *Brave New World* about the old and the abnormal: we tend to care for them by relegating them to some clear point outside our own lives. In the Russia I've seen, there seem to be thousands of small niches for the Yuras and the *babushki* of society: simple, possibly unnecessary positions where they cling like barnacles in the crevices of a rock—out of the main surge of activity, but still alive, visible, useful, and commanding a certain respect. Deformed by nature or age, they are very often the strictest guardians of social form, many of them, like Yura, deeply patriotic. For him, life does seem good, perhaps the best it could be in any country. Ironically, it is other Russians, whose bodies are straight but whose beliefs have taken unorthodox twists, who have to suffer isolation from society and enclosure in asylums.

Tikhon Khrennikov

Late last Tuesday afternoon I was sitting in the upstairs buffet of the Hotel Evropeiskaya eating some of the lovely plump sardines they serve there, when Natalia Kirillovna, the old woman in charge, came over to me, told me rather roughly to move my chair aside, and seated three people at my table. I was surprised, not at the intrusion—since in Russian restaurants one is often doubled up with other parties, each group politely pretending that the other doesn't exist—but at the nervous agitation that flushed the old woman's cheeks and coarsened her voice. She was almost bowing as she seated these people, and she seemed to have forgotten that she knew me. Normally, Natalia Kirillovna, with her long, handsome old face, her straight backbone, her haughty blue eyes, and her skin as clean and fine-grained as freshly ironed linen, presides over the buffet like a queen accepting tribute. She is a fan of the arts, and took a flattering interest in me when I began eating lunch there because she had somehow gotten the idea that I was a member of a foreign dance troupe staying at the hotel. The troupe has long ago left the Soviet Union, but she continues to ask me where the rest of the corps is. I find it pleasant to be a dancer in someone's eyes, so I always answer, quite truthfully, "The others? Oh—they're off dancing."

The Evropeiskaya is an old-fashioned grand establishment that, like the Astoria, or Moscow's Metropole, has retained much of its prerevolutionary luxury: handsome paneling, frosted glass, brass fixtures. It is located right off Nevsky Prospekt, where the crowds flow up and down on these sunny late-winter afternoons, treading through pools of slush near the massive yellow walls of Gostiny Dvor, the shopping arcade built by Catherine the Great. In this area hover many black marketeers, skinny youths in flapped fur hats and dirty blue jeans who buttonhole foreigners in bad English about buying icons and selling records and Western clothing. I run this gauntlet to eat lunch at the Evropeiskaya late every afternoon, because it serves a truly formidable array of *zakuski*: cheese, sausage, chopped liver, herring, sprats, the sardines I mentioned earlier—things almost impossible to get on the open market. For this reason the buffet serves only foreigners and Soviet big shots: ordinary Russians who even try to enter the hotel are usually turned away by a doorman whose business is to limit access to the hotel restaurants, and to keep black marketeers away from the foreign guests.

I've seen many Leningrad celebrities devouring liver and fish in the buffet (which accepts rubles); one of them is the M.C. from the B. B. King concert. But the people who sat down at my table on Tuesday were clearly more important than these. All three were Russians: there was a stout man in his fifties wearing a magnificently cut gray suit; a woman of the same age, quietly and elegantly dressed; and a little boy of about eight or nine, with an alert, precociously intelligent face above a French-style velour sweatshirt. Contrary to the custom at these shared tables, they began to talk to me, or at least the woman and the little boy began to talk. The man sat spooning up soup with a mysterious abstraction on his broad face, which had cheekbones, as Turgenev once observed about another countryman, of positively antediluvian dimensions. He was balding, and covered with the kind of sleek plumpness that indicates much slow, deliberate feeding on rich foods.

"You are an American?" the little boy, speaking Russian, asked me in a sweet treble. "Oh, good. That makes twelve Americans I've met. My uncle and auntie here have been to America several times. My uncle is a very famous composer, you know." He was very appealing, with his large dark eyes and wise, rather peaked little face, and his poise of a child who had been too much with adults. I have not found Russians to have the same cult of naturalness in child behavior that we do; they don't seem frightened by precocious self-possession, but actually appear to encourage it.

"Stop chattering, darling, and eat your soup," said his aunt in French. Then, to me, still in French: "Are you a music lover? Oh, how pleasant. You may have heard of my husband, then. He is Tikhon Khrennikov."

"Very pleasant to meet you," said the man, nodding his broad head ponderously toward me. The name told me nothing, but I suddenly realized that every Russian in the small dining room had his eye on this table, and that the arrogant waiter, Sergei, from whom it is normally impossible to coax any service at all, had brought ice and Pepsi (one of the luxuries of this dining room) to all of us with an ingratiating smile. Khrennikov once more bent over his soup, leaving his wife to talk about him with the emphatic understatement one uses to identify a famous man to a poor ignoramus. "Tikhon—it is a very old Russian name—knows many of your American composers and conductors: Seiji Ozawa, Samuel Barber," she said, with a mildly chiding expression on her face, which was one of the lovely, faded images of refinement that one finds, in America, behind Junior League thrift-shop counters.

"Yes, and Auntie writes for *Literaturnaia Gazeta*—that's a terribly important paper!" said the little boy. "And my papa has just finished a book on American films. We're an artistic family."

They lived in Moscow, but were in Leningrad for the opening of a new ballet, *Gussarskaya Balada* (Ballad of a Hussar), which was to be performed by the Kirov company, and for which Khrennikov had composed the music. By the time the composer had raised his plump hand for the last slow journey from the soup bowl to his mouth (a process closely watched by Natalia Kirillovna and the rest of the staff), his wife, perhaps piqued by my ignorance, had invited me to a special pre-opening performance of the ballet on Saturday morning.

"Tikhon Khrennikov! At the Evropeiskaya! Ha, ha, that's a good one! She meets Khrennikov at the Evropeiskaya and gets invited to a closed performance at the Kirov with all the big shots!"

Alla Nikolaevna, mother of my friend Tolya, was frying some of her famous *sirniki* for Tom and me and Tolya when I announced the news. She is a muscular woman with high color in her cheeks, and a big, ringing laugh, and she immediately whooped when she heard it. "If that isn't just like you Americans! You are—if you'll pardon me—almost nobodies over in your own country: just two young students. And over here, just because you're foreigners, you get to eat in special restaurants and go to special performances with celebrities!"

"Well, who is Tikhon Khrennikov?" I asked. "I still haven't figured that out."

"My dear, he is the head of the Union of Composers and the official musical genius of the Party . . . And it shows," she went on in a lower tone, "in his work. A serious case of mediocrity. Here's an example." She began lightly to wave her spatula and sing "Lenin . . . will always live!" and Tolya, loyal *Komsomolets* though he is, laid his hand on his heart and sang mockingly along with her. "Oh, he's very, very important—a Hero of Socialist Labor. You've heard of Shostakovich, of course. Well, Khrennikov was one of the wolf pack who ruined Shostakovich. And now Khrennikov's on top. It shows how far a so-called artist can get on loyalty alone. But you'll see for yourself."

In the next few days we heard more about Tikhon Khrennikov from other friends. He has been head of the Union of Composers since he was appointed to the post by Stalin in 1948. Under Stalin, Khrennikov led the forces of repression in music in a campaign against Shostakovich, Prokofief, and dozens of other composers, attacking the free-ranging expression of originality and genius with a vindictive energy possible only to one who felt some lack in himself. Toward Stalin, Khrennikov seems to have behaved as a singularly obsequious vassal; there's a horrid scatological anecdote in circulation that describes just how far this devotion was carried. In the manner of born survivors, Khrennikov charted a smooth course through the upsets of the period following Stalin's death, retaining his own position and his undisputed power. At sixty-seven he has received all the highest prizes and orders of the

Soviet Union, and moves through Soviet society evoking some of the past brutal period of Stalin's heyday, like some Ice Age creature that has hung on into the present. "He carries with him the smell of the purges," said one friend.

The special closed performance of *Gussarskaya Balada* was held at nine o'clock Saturday morning. Tom and I got to the Kirov early, when the theatre was still closed, and took a stroll through the streets and up the Moika Canal nearby. It was one of those days that seem outside the range of seasons, the kind of weather in which winter is secretly preparing itself for the transition into spring—a grayish, mildish day with a penetrating chill lingering around the edges, and a faint odor of the sea. The deserted streets were bare of snow, and the melting ice in the canal was a filthy blackened gray, wrinkled and ungainly, like a snakeskin about to be shed. We stood near a wrought-iron bridge under a willow tree, and I noticed that the long naked branches were yellow and thick with buds. Tom was telling me about the midsummer night five years ago, when he roamed these pastel streets with dozens of Russian students on their annual holiday, all of them joyous, drunken, singing, playing guitars.

When we got back to the Kirov, a well-dressed crowd was going into the main entrance, watched curiously by a few passers-by. Tickets were waiting for us at the director's entrance, a small door to the side. When we entered, we found ourselves in a sea of fur coats, most of them far more elegant than anything we'd seen all year. Men and women, all of them obviously Russian, were waving to each other, lighting foreign cigarettes, embracing friends, and taking off their coats to reveal not denim, but expensive Western clothes. Tom and I, who have become used to feeling rather sumptuously dressed in our blue jeans and sheepskin jackets (since both are such luxury items here, people normally wear them to concerts and the ballet), immediately felt embarrassingly shabby, like a couple of urchins who had stumbled into a ballroom. Heads turned as we entered, and a red-haired woman smoking a cigarette in a long holder looked me up and down with an amused smile. In a corner, I caught sight of Khrennikov, looking more imposingly square and massive than before, half hidden behind a veritable ambuscade of men, who were all smoking furiously and talking to him at high speed. He stood out clearly from these lesser lights: there was a primitive vigor in his wide face and squat, powerful body, and a look of incarnated importance about him that made me reflect that in the Soviet Union, as in Africa and the South Seas, men of substance seem almost required to be truly substantial in flesh. I made my way over to him and introduced Tom, and he shook our hands with great gravity and meticulousness, with the air of conveying a distinction in the mere touch of his hand. I noticed that his flesh felt unduly heavy, as if he were already on his way to becoming a statue set in a public square. When we left him to enter the theatre, we heard one of his companions ask about us: "Who are they?" Khrennikov's reply was "Oh, just some kids."

The Kirov Theatre seems to have retained most of the gilt, the carving, the serene beauty of handsome proportions that it had before the Revolution. The stage curtain, a swag of blue velvet covered with an extravagant embroidered pattern in dense gold thread, particularly seems to sum up the sumptuous excesses of Imperial Russia. Now, however, there are gilded insignias of a hammer and sickle set over the stage and over the former imperial box, which is reserved for the most important Soviet dignitaries. The box was empty that morning, but the people around were clearly members of the official artistic elite. From a distance we saw Khrennikov's wife, surrounded, as he was, by a throng of friends and well-wishers. Then the lights dimmed and the ballet began.

Gussarskaya Balada was a very expensively designed ballet that used all the considerable resources of Soviet stage and costume design, and all of the exceptional talents of the fabled Kirov company, to tell a romantic and patriotic story about a Russian girl of the nobility who disguises herself as a hussar and rides off to fight during Napoleon's invasion of Russia. She finally captures Napoleon himself, as well as the heart of a young fellow hussar.

The story, based on a memoir of the period, has a whimsical charm on paper; but as a ballet, demands an unconscionable amount of marching and countermarching by the Kirov corps de ballet, dressed to represent the French and Russian armies. Except for a few energetic pas de deux, it was easily one of the most tedious ballets I have ever seen; the handsome sets and obvious brilliance of the company only made the monotonous choreography seem more uninspired. Worst of all were the touches of treacly cuteness in the sections dealing with the willful girl: instead of conveying a lively sentimentality (which I think Russians, when they do it well, do better than anyone else), these parts were embarrassingly overdone. Bearing the whole unwieldy production along was Khrennikov's music, and if one took the music as prime mover, one understood the flatness of the spectacle. It was dull music, worse than dull—the kind of leaden, pompous music that is constantly aspiring to some sort of dynamism and never achieves it, and that inspires in its listeners a very real understanding of spiritual death. It showed the influence of Brahms and Tchaikovsky as a small, barren planet might reflect the light of the stars. It was the kind of music that is often used as the background for movies—as a matter of fact, Khrennikov is well known for his movie scores. I got quite sleepy, though it was early in the morning.

When at last it was over, the female lead, with her lovely head of Napoleonic *coup de vent* curls and her rather perversely sexy hussar's costume, took curtain call after curtain call, to prolonged applause. The company also took curtain calls. Flowers were brought. Then, to a titanic wave of clapping, Khrennikov appeared onstage, bowing his big head modestly. When the lights came on, Tom and I made our way to Khrennikov's wife, who accepted our thanks for the invitation, smiled at us with entire sincerity on her beautiful faded face, and urged us to come to see her in Moscow. I wondered briefly what inner adjustments this obviously good woman had had to make in order to believe in her husband's talent. Then we worked our way over to where a crowd had gathered around Khrennikov, who stood at the front of the theatre below the big gold-embroidered curtain. We reached him in time to hear a pale young man exclaim, "You have outdone yourself, Tikhon Nikolaevich, out*done* yourself!" Everyone was embracing him, proffering programs for autographs and saying the same sort of thing. He shook our hands, and once more I felt the killing weight of his grasp. "What did you think of it?" he asked us, in a tone that showed he did not much care.

"I was astounded," said Tom politely, looking him in the eyes and smiling.

When we came out of the theatre, we were surprised to find that it was still the same gray morning with the same hidden preparations for spring. It seemed that nature should have been doing something extravagant and absurd, to echo the folly we'd seen in the theatre. But normal life went on. Trolleys ran up and down, carrying people for whom it was a working day, to whom had not been granted the opportunity of hearing the first performance of Tikhon Khrennikov's latest composition. We should have taken a trolley ourselves, but instead we walked in silence up the long canal toward Nevsky, and took a few deep breaths of the clean raw air coming in off the Finnish Gulf.

Cleopatra

On the bus these sunny mornings, I look out over the Neva—now flowing hugely, bobbing with gray ice floes—and think about the States. Of all things, I've been reading *Huckleberry Finn,* and it has made me painfully homesick, not for family and friends, but for the entire country, as if, at this far remove, it were something I could embrace with a single thought. A bit of America has in fact come to Leningrad in the form of the movie *Cleopatra,* starring Burton and Taylor; what a rich joke it is to see the big posters, with the imperial black brows of Elizabeth Taylor brooding over the streets as if she'd conquered Leningrad!

Tom and I recently went to see it at the Kinoteatr Priboi—the Surf Theatre. Tom picked up the tickets before the show; because it's so incredibly popular—it's rumored to be sexy—he had to bribe the vendor with a ruble before she even admitted that there were tickets left. As I stood in the drafty lobby, eating a hundred-gram ice cream cone (the *babushki* measure them out with a tiny scale), I wondered how dated the movie would seem. I had seen it in 1962, when I was nine and uncertain about the meaning of the romantic scenes. Russians are convinced that it is a recent movie: Tolya, for example, keeps asking if it just came out in America. In the auditorium, wedged between Tom and a strapping old man who smelled strongly of garlic and dill, I found the movie antique, and rather tragic. Instead of Egypt in circa 40 B.C., it was America in 1962. The dresses, the peekaboo sex, the stiff teased hair styles made it an early-sixties period piece, while the unquestioning arrogance of the assumption that Taylor, with her white Celtic skin intact, could rule over a country of Egyptians showed the innocence of the time, when none of our ideas about race, about sex, about leadership had been shaken, and we still rejoiced in heroes, titanic romances like Burton and Taylor's, and big, big movies.

The Russian version of *Cleopatra* was dubbed, and had the erratic jumps of most foreign films shown here after censorship, but the audience seemed to love it, murmuring appreciatively whenever Taylor appeared in a low-cut gown. I thought about the last time I'd seen it, when I'd shared as much as a child can in the boundless material self-confidence of the country—when Russia lay, a clearly articulated evil, on the other side of the world. Now here I am in Russia, and that particular innocence and arrogance have departed from me and from other Americans, probably forever. Strangely enough, it's this lost America that Russians seem most to admire, although they denounce it: the dream landscape made up of our big cars, big wasteful meals, sprawling suburbs, tough military stance.

When I tell Russian friends, especially older friends, about our pricks of conscience in the late sixties—the ideals of frugality, concern for the environment, for racial and sexual justice, for peace—they tend to sniff scornfully and suggest that we're a bunch of milquetoasts. So *Cleopatra* must be a comfort to them. As for me, I'm not particularly in love with the old or the newer vision of America. Living in Russia, however, has made me more of a patriot than I ever, ever expected to be. What I like about America is amazingly simple: that I can talk there without stopping to censor my thoughts, and that I can wander freely without passport or identification, without concern for entering a *zapretnaya zona* (forbidden zone). Minor-sounding things, but they bear on the most important liberations in life: from confinement and fear. It's impossible to imagine Huck Finn and Nigger Jim floating down the Neva, the Volga, or the Moskva—difficult to think of a great Russian work that so directly celebrates freedom. The Russian book that I find closest in spirit to *Huckleberry Finn* is Pasternak's *Doctor Zhivago*, and as everyone knows, that novel is banned in the Soviet Union.

The <u>Kronverk</u>

Aboard the *Kronverk* a few nights ago, we ate sliced cucumbers and hard-boiled eggs covered with caviar and drank several bottles of vodka and Georgian champagne while we watched the floor show. The floor show was eight pretty, hefty girls who danced artistically in a number entitled "Around the World on the *Kronverk*"; this mock cruise, which managed to avoid America and China, allowed the girls to wear snug, striped sailors' jerseys in Marseilles, and to gradually dispense with their clothes as they neared warmer climes. One of the girls was a stunner with golden hair and big slanted green eyes; she gave an excitingly paradoxical Nordic feeling to her South Seas bikini, and the dark eyes of all the Georgians in the room were fixed on her.

My two brothers are visiting us in Leningrad, and that evening we were showing them the night side of the town. Except for private parties, or the hard-currency bars that are ghettos for foreigners, there is very little to do here after ten or eleven o'clock. The *Kronverk*, a ship made into a restaurant and moored near the Peter and Paul Fortress, is a popular entertainment spot where one can eat and drink and watch a show, all for rubles. For the last reason, it is almost impossible to get reservations there. Tom managed it by going to the restaurant one morning and lying shamelessly to the effect that he was an American professor, head of a visiting delegation of radical intellectuals who were in need of a night's diversion; he finally persuaded the manager with two packs of Marlboros and a copy of *Amerika*.* When our "delegation" was

*A glossy pictorial educational/propaganda magazine published in Russian by the American Embassy.

seated at a table in the tiny hold—which, with its low ceiling and décor of nets and fishing floats and bottles, is reminiscent of an American seafood restaurant—we found ourselves surrounded by tables of handsomely dressed Georgians and Russians. Before and during the floor show, everyone in the room got very drunk. That evening, as we'd walked to the ship, the air had been still and temperate, with a hidden thrill in it, a fascinating presentiment of spring. Already the days linger quite late, the skies turning a milky lavender after sunset, and the city stretching in a handsome dark-blue silhouette along the wide river. The weather and the light make you feel giddy, almost crazy; everyone on the *Kronverk* seemed touched by it.

After the show the band crashed into a standard repertoire of Russian restaurant favorites—"Money, Money, Money . . ." originally sung by Abba; Boney M.'s "Ma Barker" (about the life of the American female gangster of the same name); a song called "Ah! Odessa!"; and several other songs that required hearty Cossack-type laughter and shouts from the lead singer, a slight man with a bulbous nose and a pneumatic pompadour of light-brown hair. Everyone got up, and soon the dance floor was a bobbing mass of plump, tipsy dancers. I danced with my brothers; I danced with Tom; we all danced together—one of the pleasant things about this country is that no one minds what odd combinations you dance in. Then I began dancing with the Georgians from the table next to ours. They were all small dark middle-aged men with wickedly handsome Mediterranean faces, and they were dressed in brand-new jeans or in impeccable suits that had clearly been made abroad. They slipped ten-ruble notes to the band, and soon the music was all Georgian, clashing with a suggestion of timbrels and psalteries.

Over the din I shouted to my partner that I had visited the Georgian capital of Tbilisi, and that I loved the vineyards there; he kissed my hand. I was doing a fake, hopping Middle-Eastern-style dance that was immediately recognizable to Tom and my brothers as a debased version of the Bristol Stomp; I heard them jeering at me from our table. The Georgians, however, were delighted. They sent a bottle of cognac over to our table, and kept calling out, "*Soyuz-Apolon!*" (Soyuz-Apollo), a reference to the Soviet-American link that our dance made. Along with Tom, my brothers—who really have entered into the spirit of things with remarkable ease—began toasting Soviet-American friendship, toasted the fertile and beautiful country of Georgia, toasted women and spring, and American blue jeans and each other. The low-ceilinged room swam with cigarette smoke. Even the waiters looked drunk, and I thought I felt waves under my feet. A fat woman in a tight pink sweater and a bulging Wrangler skirt nearly knocked me down, and as I staggered, I saw—in a dark corner near the staff quarters—someone trying to kiss the blond beauty from the floor show. It seemed to me, as the band swung into at least the tenth Boney M. song, that I saw one of my brothers climbing up onto his chair for yet another toast.

When it was over—and it was over cleanly, with the surgical precision with which Russians can end things if an official curfew is involved—we found ourselves standing on wavering legs near the Peter and Paul Fortress, looking up into a night sky as clear as a bowl of water, with faint stars shining at the very bottom. We were looking for a cab to take my brothers to the Hotel Leningrad, and Tom and me to Vasilevsky Island. It was late, and it seemed clear that we'd have to hail a private car and pay an inflated rate for our ride. (Tom and I have done this all year, sometimes paying for rides in bread trucks, electrical-repair vans, even ambulances.) Suddenly a small man appeared beside us and asked whether we needed a cab. We agreed to a rate of seven rubles for the entire trip, and climbed into a Soviet Fiat. As we took off, I looked carefully at the driver and realized that I had seen that puffy hair and bulbous nose before; it was the singer from the night club. He told us that his salary was low, and that he always moonlighted as a free-lance cabdriver after the *Kronverk* closed. "With this, I make a good living," he said. "It's strictly illegal, of course."

"We liked your singing tonight," I said.

He chuckled with pleasure, and then said, "I am a real singer—

not just a night-club singer. It was my dream to attend the Conservatory and become an opera singer, but—well, it didn't happen. Listen to this!" He threw back his head and began roaring out "Vesti la giubba" with a force that made our tipsy heads spin still more wildly. Meanwhile we were racing through the empty streets, taking corners at an alarming pace.

"Stop him, please," whispered one of my brothers.

Tom asked, "Do you know any old Russian ballads, old romances?"

He knew them, many of the melancholy old songs made famous by Nadezhdu Obukhova and Boris Gmyrya, and he sang them for us in an extravagantly sentimental voice as we headed toward the Hotel Leningrad and Vasilevsky Island. As we crossed the "Construction Workers" Bridge to the island, I rolled down my window to feel the night air, which had retained the dizzying mildness of early evening. In one glance I could see the Winter Palace, the tall rust-colored Rostral Columns, and the gleaming spires of the Peter and Paul Fortress—three rival beauties serenely facing one another across the broad river so recently freed of ice. For the first time I fully understood that for us, the coming of spring meant departure, and for me, a painful nostalgia for this strange country, by turns brutal and beautiful, but always unexpected. The driver went on singing, and I struggled with the discovery of my attachment to Russia as a woman might struggle upon finding that she is in love with a man she does not respect and of whose heart she is, in the final analysis, quite ignorant. In the muddy wasteland in front of our dormitory, we paid the driver twice what we'd agreed on. He started singing again before he reached the main street, and for a few minutes we stood in the mild air listening to the sound of his engine and "Vesti la giubba" as it faded on its way to the river.

Easter

I

We've returned from our stay in Leningrad to a Moscow transformed by the approach of spring. The skies are a limpid blue filled with strands of cloud as thin and fine as thistledown, and the sidewalks around the university are swamps of mud and grit and the odd debris left at the tide line of receding winter. Last week, three days before Easter, I went to the peasant market near the Byelorussian train station and found it thronged with people shopping for the holiday, the day the State grudgingly permits to be celebrated but does its best to suppress. Instead of durable winter vegetables—big pale cabbages, waxed turnips, giant, mud-covered carrots—the counters were heaped with the fresh spring greens that were just beginning to make their frail way into the world: sorrel, dill, dandelion leaves. A *babushka*, perhaps the oldest in the world, with earth-colored wrinkles closing in on themselves so that her tiny gleaming eyes were scarcely visible, and skinny fingers as yellow as beeswax, sold me a bunch of herbs, mumbling, "Now, this will make you a fine Easter soup!" After her trembling fingers had counted out the kopecks in change, she crossed herself.

At outdoor booths in the sunny market courtyard, vendors were selling brightly painted Easter eggs; I bought several from a short man with cheerful blue eyes and frostbite marks on his cheeks. The eggs are all exuberantly painted with naïve scenes that suggest a religious and a secular rejoicing at the fullness of new life awakening in the world: they show squat onion-domed Orthodox churches, ducklings in baskets, young suitors hurrying along with bouquets of flowers, bearded peasants clutching enormous sturgeons. All of the eggs bear the inscription XB, the Russian abbreviation for *Khristos Voskres*—Christ Is Risen. One of my most amusing eggs bears the XB inscription and, underneath it, the message: "Happy Easter, dear Comrades!" Wishful thinking. Easter and comrades in fact don't mix at all. It was pleasant to walk out into the balmy afternoon with my net bag filled with green leaves and Easter eggs, but on the subway I began to notice the people staring at the colorful paint, and I started to feel that I was openly carrying contraband. Later I heard that the market had been raided, and the Easter eggs, absurdly enough, seized by the police.

"Easter," Tom wrote recently in a letter home, "like everything else here, is a deficit good." To get into a Moscow church for the midnight Easter service, one often needs a printed invitation from the priest—something which, like every other deficit good, is easy enough for foreigners to obtain (there are, in fact, certain prominent churches to which foreigners are guided) but not easy for the average Russian. Russian friends told us that during the Easter service every church is surrounded by three rows of people: in the inner row stand policemen, checking tickets and intimidating the hesitant; in the second row, *druzhiniki* (volunteer police), wearing red arm bands, continue the intimidation; and the third row consists of hooligans and thugs ready to push around any churchgoer who happens to cross their path. Besides the physical barriers, distractions are arranged to discourage church attendance and bolster loyalty to the State. As on the eves of Christmas and "Old New Year," the New Year of the Orthodox calendar, the Party schedules a special television program on the night before Easter, a program aimed at young people, usually featuring a popular rock group like Abba or Boney M. This year, ironically enough, the day before Easter was Lenin's birthday, and so there were even greater possibilities for distraction from the religious holiday. The city just awakening to springtime was festooned with red, and the day declared a nationwide Communist *subotnik*, a day on which everyone is expected to work for free for the good of the State.

All day on Saturday, in spite of the red flags and the frantic Radio Moscow harangues about the Great Leader, there was the feeling of a vast and growing secret in the city, a gathering power that had nothing to do with Lenin. On buses and on the sidewalks, shoppers carrying bags filled with preparations for Easter feasts turned their eyes away from one another. I went into the State bread store and found there a line for *kulich*, the special tall, puffy cakes that crown an Easter dinner; yet, in all the conversations I overheard in the line, there was no mention of the holiday. The sense of some great hidden emotion increased as twilight fell—a damp, purple twilight with some of the sting of winter still in the air. At about nine-thirty Tom and I took a taxi to a small nineteenth-century church near the Sportivnoye metro station; this was a church, we had learned, where you could get in without an invitation if you came early enough. The taxi driver gave us a strange look when we told him the address, but said nothing. When we got out of the taxi, we saw at the church entrance a milling crowd that, sure enough, turned out to be made up mainly of police, *druzhiniki*, and a number of loutish-looking young men. They saw that we were foreigners, and let us through without comment. Ahead of us, a group of three old Russian women was also allowed to pass. "They know they can't keep the *babushki* away," whispered Tom. But to one side of us, a pair of teenage girls, their heads wrapped in Orenburg shawls, were being harassed by an equally young *druzhinik*. "What are you doing here, girls?" he said, cocking his cropped head to one side and grabbing one of them by the arm. "This is no place for you! Where are your invitations?"

All this was going on practically in darkness on a narrow, badly paved street, where the only light came from a few bulbs at the church door. Though the crowd of officials and churchgoers was rather large, there was only a fraction of the noise normally made by a group that size. The policemen and *druzhiniki* seemed instinctively to lower their voices, as if they felt intimidated by an invisible presence. Before we stepped into the church, I turned around to watch a broad old woman with an imperious carriage roundly berating two policemen, who, momentarily abashed, were practically shuffling their feet with embarrassment. "Why aren't you ashamed to be keeping people out of church?" she demanded in a voice that rang out above the silent crowd. "This is very un-attractive behavior!" On the balcony of an apartment across the street, where a party seemed to be going on, two or three young couples stood leaning on the rail, observing the scene below, pass-ing a bottle among them and giving an occasional catcall.

Inside, the little church was already massed with worshippers, who seemed to be made up of about three-quarters old women and a quarter young people; there were only a few people in their forties or fifties. The dim yellow lights lit up the metal covers of icons along the pillars and walls, and the room swirled with the suffocating odor of candle wax mixed with the smell of per-spiring human flesh, too tightly packed. This was, in fact, a true Russian crowd, like many of those we'd learned to fight through in the metro, or in a line for food or tickets. After we had shoved our way to a place beside a wall, I felt someone tap me on the shoulder, and turned to find an old woman thrusting thirty ko-pecks into my hand. "*Peredaite, pozhaluista.* [Please pass this on to the next person]," she said. Every day, in the crushing crowds on Moscow buses, one is constantly tapped on the shoulder, handed a few kopecks that are on their way to the ticket machine, and told, "*Peredaite.*" These particular kopecks were for candles being sold at the entrance of the church, and the candles thus purchased were making their way up to the icons in the midst of a busy buzz of directions. "Pass this candle to the Smolensk Icon." . . . "Where do you want me to send it?" . . . "Pass it on to the Kazan Icon." Fat women in kerchiefs squeezed passed us, and I marveled, as I do in every Russian crowd, at the seemingly indefinite capacity of human flesh to compress itself. Through the rippling crowd, I could see the thin brown candles burning, massed like stands of wheat in front of the icons. "There was a fire here last Easter," I heard a woman behind us say in a barely audible whisper.

"*Gospodi!* What happened?" came another woman's voice.

"An old woman fainted, and her kerchief caught on fire. But she wasn't hurt. We put it out, all of us . . ."

At that moment a church official—oddly enough, also wearing a red arm band—appeared at the front of the church to announce that no more people would be let through to the altar to kiss the Easter icon. "The passageway is closed!" he shouted. It was time for the service to begin.

The two hours we spent standing—before midnight brought the climax of the service—were a blur of candlelight, the steadily increasing heat of the airless chamber, and the voices of the crowd singing the hypnotic Old Church Slavonic phrases of the Easter service. Several times, exhausted and faint from lack of air, I felt my legs slowly giving way; each time I was buoyed up by the packed bodies around me. The first and most subtle miracle of Easter had already taken place: the crowd, which before the service had been very much like an assemblage in a marketplace, every mind intent on an individual and petty transaction, had at some point been transformed into a single body, as if the archaic words of adoration and rejoicing were a catalyst as potent as communion wine.

It had all happened as spontaneously and imperceptibly as the coming of spring itself. The priest, a man with a dwarfish body and a large head covered with greasy gray hair above his brocade robe, chanted in a high tremolo, and periodically turned upon the congregation a face whose rather heavy contours were illuminated by an expression of tender joy. The congregation replied to him in a single voice whose defining note was—as it almost always is in the Russian churches I've seen—the quavering treble of old women. I thought how different this serene yet passionate joining of spirits was from any other mass gathering I had seen in the Soviet Union. There was no feeling of compulsion, or of the carefully orchestrated hysteria that culminates in the violent cheers that seem almost torn out of the throats of the crowds gathered to celebrate Komsomol Day or the October Revolution.

Midnight approached. A quiver of activity ran through the crowd as people lit the candles they had saved for the climax of the service and hurriedly wrapped them in paper to protect their fingers. Then two churchmen somehow cleared the passageway through the congregation, and the priest advanced from the altar, surrounded by a procession of acolytes carrying icons, crosses, and candles. The congregation silently fell into line behind the procession, and soon we were outside, moving in a circle around the church. The cold night air roused me instantly from the dreamy stupor that had seized me; I looked with newly clarified vision at the moving line of candlelit figures stretching in front and back of me, and felt the keen surge of physical gladness and the sense of endless possibilities that one sometimes feels upon arising very early after a night of deep sleep.

As the procession passed the little square in front of the church, where the police and *druzhiniki* had been standing, I noticed that the hostile throng had inexplicably vanished, and that now a crowd of about fifty people—many of them young and middle-aged—stood facing the procession with candles of their own. Finally the priest stopped at the church door, and turned to call his message to the gathering: *"Khristos Voskres!"*—Christ is risen! The traditional reply came back in a glad shout from dozens of throats: *"Voistine Voskres!"*—He is truly risen! Back and forth, over and over again, went the exchange, while an expression of rapture transformed the faces of the young and old, and the deep yellow glow of candlelight lit up the square. The apartment balconies were thronged with spectators who stood silently looking down at the single mass public observance in Russia that has nothing to do with Communism.

Near the gate to the churchyard stood a group of worshippers who wanted to press forward and come inside. A deacon stood at the door and addressed them. *"Pravoslavnye,"* he called. "You may come to the door, but only if you come calmly, without making any noise." Tom and I looked at each other. We had never heard the word *"pravoslavnye"* uttered in this country, where the crowds of people are normally addressed as "Comrades," or "Citizens." *Pravoslavnye* means all orthodox Christians, all members of the flock. The group passed through the doorway, and for the first time this year I saw a crowd of Russians move without shoving: their faces, like all the faces around us, still wore the same look of rapturous rejoicing. *"Khristos Voskres!"* . . . *"Voistine Voskres!"* Candle wax was dripping on my hand, and I glanced off into the distance, where I could just make out the red stars gleaming on top of the Kremlin towers. I thought of a church I'd seen recently that had been transformed by the State into a storage facility for sinks, pipes, and toilet bowls; of the former monasteries that are now factories or institutions. It was smart of the officials, I thought, to try to stem this passionate tide of belief, for if they didn't, would there be as many voices to cheer in Red Square?

A little later the crowd began moving back through the doorway of the church to resume the service inside. It was now about one-thirty. We were expected at an Easter supper on the Sadovoye Kol'tso, so we slipped quietly into the square, leaving our candles, as the others had left them, stuck, burning, into the iron railing of the churchyard. As we walked away, I looked back once. Except for a few stragglers, the square and churchyard were almost totally deserted. Only the irregular ring of tiny flames remained as proof of the magical hour when all churches all over Moscow had been ringed with holy fire, and had regained, for the short span of the ceremony of rebirth, their ancient hold over Russian hearts.

II

We didn't see any taxis, so we walked for an hour along the boulevard toward the Sadovoye Kol'tso. The night had grown cold and still, a thick layer of clouds reflecting the grayish lights of the city. The trees and bushes we passed were still leafless, but looking closely, I could see the tips of twigs swollen with clustering buds; in this calmest hour of the night, a subtle odor of vegetation—more a phantom than an actual smell—floated lightly in the air. We were silent and elated, walking down the center of the deserted street with a buoyancy to our stride as if we were half flying, infrequently passing other night-walkers who were also returning from Easter services. We crossed Herzen Street and entered a neighborhood of beautiful old mansions, many of them embassies, the gray-uniformed Soviet guards looking out curiously at us from their tiny sentry boxes. We had turned down a side street when we heard shouts, and saw, on the corner across from us, a man and woman circling and aiming blows at each other, while two or three men stood looking on. From their features and language, they all seemed to be Tartars. The woman's long dark hair was spilling over her shoulders, and her slanted eyes and high cheekbones were clearly visible in the streetlight. She cried out again and again at the man, and in her voice there was something violent yet wailing and mournful that seemed to echo up and down the street. A child of about two stood crying unheeded a few yards away. The sight of this evil little drama gave me a chill; a *militsiya* car turned the corner and we hurriedly cut through a muddy alleyway. We emerged facing a tree-filled park immortalized in Bulgakov's *Master and Margarita* as being the site of the Devil's first appearance in Moscow; here, after encountering Lucifer in the shape of a dapper foreigner, a pompous journalist slips in a pool of sunflower-seed oil and is decapitated by a passing tram.

The first thing that happened when we arrived at Easter dinner at Lidia Borisovna's apartment is that Lidia herself, wearing a long skirt and a traditionally embroidered Russian blouse (these days, such blouses are almost impossible to obtain outside of the hard-currency stores), came up and gave us each a threefold Easter kiss, and standing back, announced quite dramatically: "*Khristos Voskres!*" Lidia is a dramatic soul, a tall, gaunt woman in her forties, with a Dutch-boy haircut and a clever, complaining, manipulative manner. She is one of the most important figures in the unofficial art world of Moscow, so flamboyant in her unortho-doxy that she probably has KGB connections; her apartment is always full of foreigners, artists, and paintings. Often she receives guests while reclining on a mattress, complaining of vague back pains and chain-smoking the cigarettes that have yellowed her beautiful hands.

"*Voistine Voskres!*" we told her dutifully, and hung up our coats. The brightly lit three-room apartment was crowded with guests; I recognized about half of them as the painters, poets, and musicians who haunt parties where foreigners are likely to appear. At the beginning of the year this had all seemed very exciting, but now the prospect of four hours of conversation about "my art—stifled in this country" seemed unbearably wearisome. I was glancing about the room for Rima, who had promised to meet us here, when I felt a small heavy hand on my arm. It was Ludmilla, a very short, fat artist who wears dresses made of long swags of embroidered material, and whose round timorous eyes in a plump pink face make her look constantly like a child about to be smacked.

"*Khristos Voskres!*" she said in a plaintive voice. "Why do you refuse to visit me? You must not like me. Next week I am giving a party, with lovely cakes. And I have some new creations." Luda makes strange little quilts and collages from scraps of hides, furs, and feathers; she tries to sell them for dollars, but to my knowl-edge, no one has ever bought anything.

"I'm sorry," I said. "We have wanted to come and visit you for a long time. Perhaps we can do it soon."

"Yes, come next week. I want to do your portrait. Come—I insist on it!" She spoke in the insinuating, nagging way in which some timid people try to exert their wills. Luda was a despised hanger-on in this artistic circle, and she knew it. I looked closely at her and realized that she was wearing a present I had given her as a joke back in the fall: a miniature Coca-Cola can hung on a necklace chain. I had chuckled about this silly present often enough, but now it seemed like a truly wicked thing to have done. I went on talking to her, and thought that my head would split with depression and fatigue. It was about three o'clock in the morning.

Two tables had been pushed together in the main room, covered with white cloths, and spread with a handsome array of *zakuski:* cold meats and cheeses, radishes and fresh coriander, cucumber and tomato sandwiches. In the middle lay two bowls of hard-boiled eggs that had been decorated with dyes, and between them lay the traditional Easter *kulich* and the sweetened raisin-filled farmer cheese that is traditionally served with it. I was approaching the table when a painter whom I vaguely knew, a balding man with purplish cheeks and a skewed eye, came up to me and tried in a vigorous whisper to convince me that I should try to smuggle a portfolio of his enormous canvases out to a dealer in New York.

"I'd get caught the same as anyone would," I protested, trying to maneuver out of the corner where he had pulled me.

"Nonsense. You could slip them right in among your luggage. Americans always have a great deal of luggage . . . You materialists!" he added, wagging his finger at me in playful admonishment. "Tell me, my beauty," he went on in the same low voice. "When are we going to meet privately? Foreign women are always drawn to Russian men, with good reason! We're real men! Once I met a French woman who was a *lesbianka*—hated men. But I convinced her differently!" He began an interminable smutty story, and I glanced around the room, whose walls were covered every few weeks with an exhibition of works by a different artist. This time there was a really wonderful set of paintings, showing Breughelesque scenes of traditional life in a Russian peasant village. Lidia Borisovna had turned off the harsh overhead light and had lit candles on the table, and the figures in the paintings—short-legged, broad-faced peasants in the marketplace, in the bathhouse, by the frozen river—seemed to take on life in the moving light. It seemed to me that they bore more relationship to the Easter service we'd just attended than did the people in the room around me.

Chairs were drawn up to the tables, and we sat down to eat pieces of Easter cake; as we ate, we chose eggs and dueled with our neighbors in a tapping game to see which shell was the strongest. Tom sat discussing Paul Robeson with a short musician with a droll winged mustache, while I played the tapping game with a young man with big glistening dark eyes and perspiring hands. Apropos of nothing, he remarked to me, "My grandfather, you know, spoke French."

"Why was that?" I asked. "Was he French?"

"No," he said, picking up a piece of shattered eggshell with the end of his moist white finger, and then, leaning earnestly toward me: "But he was, well, an officer . . . ah . . . in the Guards . . . before the Revolution, if you know what I mean . . ."

"Are you trying to hint that you have noble blood?" I asked sharply, and the frigid hauteur of my tone shocked me as much as it did the young man, who at once pretended that he had to reach for another Easter egg, and began talking briskly with the woman on his left. Far away, at the other end of the table, I heard someone say, "I disagree. It's literary mitosis!"

Then came that strange hour in a sleepless night when everything seems distorted: lights are too bright; darkness, unfathomable; conversations seem to stretch out into infinity, and the barrier between dream and observation seems to have dissolved. The hour itself seemed to last only for a minute, and suddenly it was five o'clock, the candles were drowning in pools of wax on the chaotic table, and the big square windows at the end of the room were gleaming with a pale light. From the divan in the corner came a medley of snores, and I saw the skew-eyed painter sleeping among other supine figures. My annoyance at the idiocy of the party had suddenly evaporated, and as I looked at the few people left—Lidia, our hostess, and a beautiful red-haired writer sitting whispering to each other on one hard chair, their arms around each other's necks; the short musician and a large group of others still arguing about literature, their elbows among the eggshells and empty bottles at one end of the table—I found that their voices and faces had softened, that the advent of the dawn had given a measure of dignity and humility and happiness to their manner as the Easter service had to the crowd at the church. Some kind of passion—for company, for art, for a good time—had kept them vigilant tonight as it had other nights, and any vigil makes dawn seem a blessing. Our hostess stretched, ran her fingers through her thick hair, then rose and opened the curtains to a watery sky the bluish color of skim milk. "See, friends, it's the dawn of a holy day," she said in her deep, clever voice. "*Khristos Voskres!*"

I repeated the answer with the others.

The Wedding

Rima and Vasia got married a few days ago, on a sunny morning when a green mist of budding foliage hung around the trees all over the city. We met them at a Palace of Weddings in northwest Moscow, a nineteenth-century mansion on a quiet tree-lined street; they entered with a sizable group of friends and family. Rima was wearing an embroidered gauze dress with slightly medieval lines that suited her austere beauty. Her face was waxen with excitement, and her eyes, the overvivid eyes of icons and Early Christian paintings, had a tearful glaze. She came up to me and whispered, "My dress—it's still damp! Nadia and I washed it last night, but had no way to get it dry. Does it look awful?"

"You look beautiful," I said, turning her around to tighten her sash. "And Vasia does, too."

"Oh, he's always a wonder," she said, smiling radiantly across the room to where Vasia stood talking to some friends. Vasia wore a brownish suit, the first I'd ever seen him in, and he had tied back his long hair. His handsome fair-skinned face looked absurdly ruddy and clean, as if he'd scrubbed it for hours, and this, coupled with an expression of determined solemnity, made him look far younger than his nineteen years—a bit like a Sunday School student about to give a speech. His mother hovered around him, straightening his collar, and he batted her away impatiently.

We all stood around making strained conversation in the waiting room, which was one of several in the Palace of Weddings, all of them high-ceilinged, painted in institutional pastels, and furnished, in a grisly attempt at elegance, with faded-pink banquettes, a few uncomfortable straight-backed chairs, lace curtains, and several rubber plants of alarming size and vigor. To promote a festive spirit, there was a loudspeaker playing some selections from the popular disco group Boney M.: unbelievably, the song most often repeated was "Love for Sale." Other bridal parties stood nearby, the brides dressed in white gowns and clutching bouquets of gladioli wrapped in cellophane. As people often do in restaurants here, when they are forced to double up at tables with strangers, each wedding party was politely pretending that the others didn't exist. In a corner of the big room, a buxom girl of seventeen or eighteen, wearing a wedding dress she'd obviously sewn herself and a stiff ruffle with cloth daisies pinned to her head, sat alone, clasping and unclasping her hands and peering tensely at the door. She looked as if she were about to burst into tears. All the wedding parties had been assigned a time for the brief ceremony that would take place in what must have been the central reception room of the old mansion. Even now we could hear parties entering the room; each time, a bossy female voice ordered them to line up, and when the door opened, there was the same burst of music—the first few bars of Mendelssohn's "Wedding March," played either on a recording or by a trio of live musicians. The live music cost extra, Vasia told me.

We heard the burst of Mendelssohn about five times before we lined up, and then suddenly the tall doors had opened for us, and we were entering the wedding chamber, a red-carpeted, high-ceilinged room, with ornate plaster moldings and a set of large windows overlooking a garden full of the light green of budding lilac bushes. Rima and Vasia had paid for live music, and so the trio—two glum violinists and a pianist—leaped into a sprightly rendition of the Mendelssohn, stopping abruptly at the fifth bar as if their throats had been cut. From behind an immense, ornate wooden desk, a ruddy-faced woman wearing a red shoulder sash adorned with a large metal seal beckoned to Vasia and Rima, and they advanced to stand in front of her. The ceremony was as brief and routine as any performed by an American justice of the peace. When it was finished, Vasia and Rima signed the register with a pen that for some reason had an elaborate curling plume at least three feet high. A little lame-footed official photographer took pictures of the signing, and the bridal pair with all of us. Then the long-nosed woman who had shepherded us into the room said, "Come on, comrades! Let's go, citizens!"—and we moved out through a side door into a small room where the picture-taking continued. As the door to the wedding chamber closed, I caught sight of the woman behind the desk stifling a yawn. In a minute the musicians raced once more into the Mendelssohn march.

"Well, now begins the fun part of the wedding," murmured Rima's friend Larisa as we all stood in line to embrace Rima. "At least they're not going to lay flowers on the Tomb of the Unknown Soldier." The patriotic custom of leaving a bridal bouquet at the Tomb of the Unknown Soldier in Red Square is so widespread that on any pleasant day in the fall or spring, one can see five or six brides heading in that direction, their white veils floating like foam on the wave of pedestrians passing the Kremlin. The next leg of a typical bridal journey is the classic trip to the Lenin Hills to drink champagne and be photographed against the view; this is such a standard excursion that the bridal limousines rented for the day automatically make both stops—there's no avoiding them. Rima, as a bride for the second time and an artistic free spirit, had, as far as she could, avoided this standard route. Now all of us were headed out to a party at a friend's apartment in the country, where the food and toasts and company would make up for anything the ceremony had lacked. Coming down the steps of the Palace of Weddings into the light sweet air of the April morning, I didn't feel as if I'd just witnessed the joining of two loving hearts; instead I felt melancholy and slightly foot-weary, as if I'd just finished touring a factory. I watched four more wedding parties approach the entrance, and thought what a curious country this was, that could join the socialist spirit of mass production so unbeautifully to bourgeois frills—limousines, white dresses, Mendelssohn. Rima and Vasia had looked like a young king and queen at each other's side, and I wished that they had had a worthy setting—a bower, perhaps, decked out with lilies and cloth-of-silver, with music—a triumphal march—played all the way through. As I paused on the sidewalk, Rima's beautiful friend Nadia came up to me, wearing a homemade peach-colored dress and a pair of plastic sandals so ill-fitting that they should never have been allowed on her feet. Looking at her, I thought how many lovely things in this country were destined never to receive their due. Her red lips wore a quizzical half-smile that reflected my own mixed feelings about the wedding, and the message she leaned over to whisper in my ear was not one of the usual light-hearted sentiments that people share on such festive occasions. "I'm so glad for Rima," she said. "So relieved! Now that she's married, they can't condemn her as a parasite. She's a wife now, and if she doesn't have official work, that's all right. She's respectable— she's safe."

May Day

I

Several days before the first of May, the streets of Moscow began to sprout red flags, and I had the fun, one afternoon, of watching a monstrous forty-foot poster of Lenin hoisted into place near the Kremlin with a commotion of pulleys and swarming workmen that put me in mind of the construction of the pyramids. We had had a relapse into nippy gray weather since the warmth of mid-April, and the fluttering red fabric on every statue, lamppost, and public building stood out sharply against the cloudy skies and wet streets, as if a vast, unnatural blossoming had caught the city unawares. I was impressed, as on other holidays, by the purity of tint in this festive red: it is not orange-red or blue-red, but clearly, unmistakably, red without any admixture. It is a color as power-ful and blunt as a blow from a fist, but it has the oddly repellent flatness and coldness of any unmixed color.

For May Day, we had visitors from Leningrad: Petya and his wife, Liza. During our stay in the North, we spent a number of supremely tedious evenings with them in their little apartment in the Vyborg section of the city, evenings when we would all get terribly drunk on vodka and *samagon*, and impatiently await the climax of the visit: the appearance of a huge bowl of steaming boiled potatoes that we gobbled down with entire loaves of black bread. As he filled our glasses and got more and more soused himself, Petya's small blue eyes would grow dimmer and his crooked smile would widen, showing the stumps of two teeth broken off in a fight. Our artistic and intellectual friends would probably call Petya a member of the *urla*—the working-class toughs who sometimes get kicks from beating up Russian hippies. There is no question that he is solidly working-class, and proud of it. Like his father and grandfather before him, he works as a shipbuilder at the Kirovsky Zavod, the huge factory that made armaments in tsarist times and was one of the centers of worker radicalism in 1917. "I want my son to work at the Kirovsky," he told us once.

Petya is twenty-three, short and brawny, with slightly bowed legs, a white, almost girlishly fine skin, and a nose pushed in and to one side like a boxer's. On one of his arms, near the elbow, is the crude tattoo of an anchor; he served two years in the Navy, an experience that took him to Cuba and to Canada, and provided him and Liza with a few pairs of foreign jeans. Although Petya, like the rest of his friends from the factory, wears his Wranglers and Levis proudly, he shows none of the eagerness for emigration or the fascination with Western life that characterizes many of our "middle-class" Russian friends. He is a staunch, bullheaded patriot who is clearly satisfied with his life. He told us that he wanted to come to Moscow for the May Day weekend (he has never been to the capital before) because he had always dreamed of visiting Lenin's tomb and watching the great parades. When Petya and Liza arrived to stay with us in the Moscow State dormitory, instead of trying, like most of our Russian friends, to sneak past the guard at the entrance and thus escape the stigma of fraternizing with foreigners, he strode up to the official and laid down his passport with a pugnacious take-it-or-leave-it air. "I'm a worker, and no one's going to say I'm not a loyal citizen," he declared to us later. "I don't have anything to hide. My family helped make the Revolution!"

It was appropriate, I suppose, to spend the holiday with this sturdy patriot. We spent May Day eve in a classic fashion, watching Petya's smile grow crookeder and his blue eyes smaller as we finished two bottles of Starorusskaya vodka. Liza, a small dark beauty with a mettlesome gaze and a cherry-shaped underlip, whispered to me, "All he wants to do when he gets home from work is drink, and drink. It makes me tired." She gave the exasperated sigh that Russian women seem to learn at about puberty, and Petya started a long, tipsy disquisition on Soviet-American hostilities, which had their origins, in his opinion, in the purchase of Alaska by the United States. "The U.S.A. took control of Alaska under your President Lincoln, who was a very sly man," he told us. "Lincoln foresaw that in America's future, that land would be very useful against Russia."

"I don't think that's true," said Tom. "Lincoln had no designs against Russia. Besides, we didn't just take over Alaska. We bought it fair and square."

"Even that's not right!" said Petya with a triumphant laugh. "Someone at the factory told me that in the treaty, America agreed to pay Russia for Alaska *na viek*. Now, *na viek* means two things in Russian: 'forever' and 'for a hundred years.' Russia sold that land only for a century, but Lincoln took it for good. That unfair seizure is at the bottom of all the trouble between our two nations. May the hostilities cease!"

We all grabbed our glasses and drank a last toast to brotherhood and to the speedy clarification of the Alaska controversy, and then we staggered to bed.

At six the next day, we came out of the dormitory into a gray morning with mist hanging over the trees in the university orchard. The big tower was covered with rows of red flags; flags fluttered on the two massive bronze statues of students—a youth and a maiden, both gazing ardently into the future—that flanked that particular entrance. Even the bus, when it arrived to take us to the metro, bore two tiny, jaunty red flags attached in front. It was our intention to make our way downtown before the crowds and the police had made Red Square inaccessible; we hoped to slip into the parade itself. The metro was sparsely filled with other red-eyed, shivering early risers. About half the passengers were students with scrubbed faces, wearing bright orange, blue, or green jumpsuits which indicated that they were going to march with some special division of athletes in the parade. Their expressions were alternately excited and embarrassed, and I found myself thinking of cheerleaders before a big American football game. Liza yawned and asked me whether we celebrated the first of May in the United States. "Some American Communists celebrate it," I said. "But there's of course no official celebration. All of us think of May Day, though, as the first real day of spring. It's an ancient holiday."

"Yes, but we made it something better," said Liza.

The metro car had gotten more and more crowded with spectators and parade participants, and at the Gorky Park stop, a voice over a loudspeaker announced that anyone going to the parade must get off here. We walked out of the metro onto the broad Sadovoye Kol'tso, ordinarily crowded with traffic but now empty except for groups of pedestrians walking up past Smolensk Square. Almost everyone who wasn't in uniform had a red ribbon pinned over his heart. We went along the very middle of the huge thoroughfare, feeling wildly exhilarated, as if we'd taken possession of the whole city. The clouds had thickened, and a thin drizzle was falling over the gleaming streets; up ahead, the banners stretched in two red lines, the brightly dressed groups of people had joined into a true crowd, and from somewhere—perhaps from someone's radio, since the parade had not begun—drifted the music of a band, compelling and slightly sad. At Smolensk Square, a thirty-foot red-and-yellow poster had been erected that showed a titanic steelworker brandishing a rivet, and an equally enormous female tractor driver holding up a sheaf of wheat that could have nourished the entire city of Moscow; they announced to the world: "We will carry out the decisions of the Twenty-fifth Congress of the Communist Party of the Soviet Union!" The people walking about in the shadow of that piece of inspirational art looked shrunken and out of place. It was an impression I was to have all day: of humanity dwarfed by monumental art and ideas.

Soon we came upon people preparing floats and banners at the sides of the street; most of the floats were posters attached to small red carts about ten feet long that ran on rubber tires. These floats were intended to be propelled by groups of people, and like the banners, they mostly bore informative or hortatory messages:

> THE SOVIET PEOPLE HEARTFULLY SUPPORT THE PEACE-LOVING LENINIST FOREIGN POLICY OF THE SOVIET UNION!
>
> THE KRASNOPRESINSKY REGION HAS CONSTRUCTED 5000 NEW HOUSING UNITS AND 16 NEW FACTORY COMPLEXES IN FULFILLING THE LAST FIVE-YEAR PLAN!
>
> LET US RAISE EFFICIENCY AND QUALITY!

A particularly impressive float was made in the shape of two huge red books that held a gold-lettered poster between them. The books represented volumes I and II of Brezhnev's *Real Issues of Communist Work of the Communist Party of the Soviet Union,* and the poster read: THE BOOKS OF L. I. BREZHNEV—A MAJOR CONTRIBUTION IN THE THEORY AND PRACTICE OF IDEOLOGICAL WORK!

In the midst of all these lofty sentiments, as in the setting-up stage for any parade or amateur theatrical event, people were balancing themselves precariously to hammer in last-minute nails, while others waved their arms about and shouted things like "Higher on the left! The left! Can't you see that it's crooked?" From somewhere appeared big posters bearing representations of important Politburo members like Suslov, Kirilenko, and Andropov, head of the KGB, their painted features cast in the same heroic mold as the giant steelworker. The crowd grew thicker, and more and more red flags and multicolored balloons appeared. Parents carrying small children on their shoulders stood back against the buildings, and on the faces of the children watching the birth of the parade was an expression of frantic delight.

We breakfasted on pale boiled sausage in a little café near the Arbat, then walked with the crowd down Kropotkin Street, past the Tolstoy Museum. It was somewhat startling to see this mass of humanity and red flags moving through that former aristocratic neighborhood of white-columned Palladian mansions, as if the Revolution were taking place all over again. It was ironic, I thought, that many of these mansions had survived the devastating fire of 1812, only to be nationalized into museums and administrative buildings after 1917. At Marx Prospekt, we reached the ornate white Rumyantsev Palace, now part of the Lenin Library, and found there a long line of police; they were sorting out those with the right to participate in the parade and preventing everyone else from entering Red Square. The four of us immediately gave up hope of joining the parade. Suddenly, however, we caught sight of a huge red sign bearing a quotation from Lenin on the value of science and the words MOSCOW STATE. "The university contingent!" shouted Tom; we all pushed our way toward the sign, and by flashing an identification card at a harried parade marshal, found ourselves somehow in the ranks of the History Faculty, and headed toward Red Square.

For some reason, the History Faculty were all carrying big branches of fake cherry blossoms; walking in the procession was like being in a moving orchard. Somewhere a band struck up a deafening march, and an official in a leather jacket darted up and handed Tom a red flag. As we marched toward the Manege, I could see the Stalinist façade of the Gos-Plan building covered with red bunting, and beyond that, two more immense streams of humanity flowing into one at the entrance to Red Square. Now last-minute preparations began. The Chemical Faculty of the university inflated a huge red hot-air balloon printed with the words ALL HAIL TO THE COMMUNIST PARTY OF THE SOVIET UNION. The GTO contingent, a group of male and female students who make up the civilian defense squadron for the university, began practicing drills with the rifles they carried. From somewhere appeared another impressive float: a giant blue globe with the slogan LABOR AND SOCIALISM in red across the continents. Far ahead, a Moldavian group (their sign said: 600,000 BUSHELS OF WHEAT IN THE LAST FIVE-YEAR PLAN) brandished immense papier-mâché stalks of wheat, while a sports contingent in tight blue jumpsuits practiced some kind of mass acrobatics. I was suddenly seized with a wild, childish excitement, the kind I hadn't felt since exhibition days for parents at school; I only wished that our

The current of the procession, swifter now, swept us toward St. Basil's, and as we prepared to leave the square, banners drooped. "Now the fun begins for everyone," said Petya, and he snapped the side of his neck with his fingers in the Russian gesture that means "to get drunk." "But remember," he said, and with a mock-ferocious look on his pugnacious face, turned and read to us the words on a passing banner: *"Kommunizm Pobedit!"*—Communism Will Triumph! Up ahead of us, the big balloon was slowly collapsing. I turned and looked back over the crowd at the comical and gorgeous domes of St. Basil's, which had been outdone all morning by a more extravagant spectacle; as I watched, the square was flooded by more masses, as the incomprehensible tribute continued.

II

Around six o'clock that evening the skies cleared into sultry sunlight, and by eight, we were climbing a path from the river up into the Lenin Hills. Since noon, when we'd handed in our flags and cherry blossoms, we'd been wandering on foot around the city, occasionally eating buns or chocolates from stands on the street. Now, in the dreamy, slightly nauseous state of exhaustion that for me since childhood has accompanied holidays or trips to the circus, we were on our way to watch the May Day fireworks. The muddy concrete steps led steeply uphill through piebald spring woods where maples already showed curled new leaves the size of a baby's fist, but where most other trees remained stubbornly bare. All around us were families with small children on their way to the fireworks; the damp air rang with childish squeals of excitement, and with parental admonitions: "Sashenka, come this way! No, don't run, don't run!" One immensely plump toddler wearing a tunic, a miniature Pioneer cap, ribbed stockings, and tiny rubber boots fell squarely into a patch of mud and lay wailing miserably until his indulgent mother came to rescue him. "This seems to be a good place to watch the display," said Petya. "In

Leningrad, there are no hills like this, of course. We'll find ourselves a nice place to stand . . ." The sky was dimming into twilight.

When we reached the top of the ridge, however, the first thing we saw was a line of soldiers. "To the fireworks?" one of them said to the group ahead of us. "That way. To the right. Not to the left. It's forbidden."

"But the best view might be to the left," I said to Petya.

"Never mind," he said. "We have to go right."

To the right, the road—the pleasant, broad thoroughfare that runs along the top of the Lenin Hills—was lined, strangely enough, with army trucks as far up as I could see; on either side of the trucks—that is, on the street and on the sidewalk—stretched two lines of soldiers, shoulder to shoulder. They were not there, I realized, as a continuation of the parade, but for crowd control; they stared sternly and impersonally ahead as the parents and children and other spectators going to the fireworks walked quickly past them in the gathering dusk. When we reached the scenic overlook directly in front of the university, we saw that the intention of the authorities was to contain the crowd within this rather small square, behind its concrete balustrade. There was to be no idle wandering in the woods or haphazard finding of seats on the hillside. Although the fireworks were all at a safe remove, and there were miles of lovely open hilltop that looked out over the city, the crowd had to stand pent up in this tiny enclosure, encircled by troops. It was already crowded; children were crying, and parents lifted them up onto their shoulders as much to breathe as to see.

Somehow we shoved our way through to the balustrade, and stood there with the crowd pressing at our backs. Across the dark river curving below us lay Moscow, a grid of lights under a placid evening sky, with a single dark bar of cloud lying across it like a distant shore. A whiff of damp earth and last winter's dead leaves came rising out of the woods, and over it, like a counterpoint, was the fresh indefinable scent of new growth. Deep in the woods, I could hear a few broken strains of birdsong. I felt tired, and squeezing myself around in the crowd, I found an awkward seat on the edge of the balustrade. Almost instantly I heard a sharp voice saying, "Young woman, that's forbidden!"— and I looked to see a soldier motioning me to stand up. Tom got angry, and pushed his way over to the soldier.

"What's the matter?" he asked, and I could see the Russian spectators around them shifting and turning their heads away uneasily. "Why do you need troops for a fireworks display? No one's here to do any harm."

The soldier coughed uncertainly, and through the dusk, I saw that he was very young, probably eighteen or nineteen, with blond hair and a guileless plump face. "We have orders," he said. "It's a crowd with many children in it, and they need protection and supervision."

So along with the rest of the crowd, crammed, toward the end, almost unbearably into the little square, we watched the fireworks bursting over the Lenin Hills and over the different neighborhoods of Moscow. All of the explosions, through some masterful feat of Russian ingenuity, were perfectly synchronized. *"Urá!"* screamed all the little children in the crowd as the fiery blue, green, red, and golden blossoms opened on the sky. I, however, was filled with a sour anger at the authorities who had seen fit to pervert an innocent spectacle into a monument to needless caution and repressive fear. If children, as the soldier had said, needed troops for supervision while watching May Day fireworks, it was only, I thought, because this country treats its citizens like children it can't trust with any independent judgment or activity. When the fireworks were over, the troops rearranged themselves to allow the spectators to disperse in two directions instead of the single one by which they'd been allowed to enter, and the four of us walked back toward the university. For a while we walked silently. Then Petya shook his head and said, "It embarrasses me to have you see that. Our government is awfully afraid of riots, you see. People gathered together make revolutions, and we can't have another one of those."

Nightingales

The sun comes up at about five these mornings, and after a night spent under only one light blanket, we jump out of bed, feeling so lively that the blood in our veins seems to have been replaced with something thinner and more volatile—vodka or Georgian wine. Salads of tender green lettuce leaves have recently appeared in the university cafeteria, and the musty little booths and dark corners where the old women sit knitting and regulating student life have been brightened by jars of drooping lilacs. A freshly worded warning against drunkenness has been pinned up on the bulletin board down the hall, and next to it is a poster for a Komsomol "Spring Ball," with pasted-on pictures of balloons and dancers. Our days are filled with preparations for our departure at the end of the month, and with farewells to friends.

On these short spring nights the woods on the Lenin Hills are alive with nightingales. One night last week we went out to listen to them with our *stukach* friend Grigorii. It was about nine o'clock, and we'd been drinking beer and pitching the bottles out of the window since seven. We came out of the tower into the cool, sweet-scented air, and walked past the reflecting pool toward the bluff that runs down to the river. There were groups of people strolling all around us: student friends, young lovers, adult couples, some of them carrying *magnitophoni* (tape recorders), which, naturally, were playing Abba or Boney M. "Money, money, money . . . It's a rich man's world!" came the soft disco refrain over the night air. It struck me that as they grow more prosperous, Russians are slowly becoming "box people," the kind that drive you mad with their portable music on New York subways. I caught sight of a group of "sportsmen" from our sector of the dormitory—big blond soccer players with alarmingly ruddy faces, who used their formidable size to cut ahead in all cafeteria lines. They were calling out to three girls going by with linked arms. "Girls! Why are you out so late? Don't you need someone to walk you back to your rooms?" The girls giggled and slowed down.

"Hooligans!" said Grigorii, regarding them wistfully. That night he was wearing his spring outfit, which is the same as his fall and winter outfits except that he wears a short-sleeved polyester shirt with the suit jacket and pants. His hair is still close-cropped and he stands with the same near-military erectness, but the nose-piece of his glasses has been broken and mended with yellow tape, which gives him a rakish and decidedly unorthodox look. Even though I have never trusted him, I still feel a little leap of affection when I see his insubstantial figure, his bony, small-featured face that wears the unwaveringly tranquil expression of a spirit that has never permitted itself any interesting ideas. Over the last nine months Tom and I have managed to fence off our perception of the fact that he has been assigned to spy on us, and we have grown close to him through shared experiences. On this particular expedition Grigorii was flushed and a little giggly; though Russian beer is weak, we'd drunk a lot.

We walked to the balcony overlooking Moscow, and stared out for a minute at the lights of the city, spread out across the river under a thin moon curled like an eyelash. Suddenly Grigorii tensed and said, "Listen!" From the wooded hillside to our right came a faint phrase of birdsong. "That's the one I was telling you about!" said Grigorii excitedly. "He sings in the same thicket every night. Let's go!" He pulled us over to a small dirt path, and we stumbled downhill, into the trees. The woods were full of blooming bird-cherry and wild crabapple, and as soon as we were away from the lit walkway, the music, and the voices, I felt a stealthy enchantment fall over me; I could imagine these woods as an inlet of the vast Russian taiga, alive with birdsong and clouds of blossom in the spring night.

Grigorii crept along the path ahead of us, with a spidery limber gait that was exactly how I'd imagined him walking in the woods. Once he slid down a muddy incline, exclaiming *"Chyort!"*—The Devil!—and spent a long time wiping the mud off his suit. All the time we were coming closer to the nightingale, which sang on steadily. We finally found it in an alder bush about five feet tall, in a small clearing. As I made my way cautiously through the underbrush, remembering the Indian games of my childhood when I'd learned to avoid snapping twigs by exerting a gradual steady pressure, I suddenly stepped on a human leg and nearly screamed. "Excuse me, excuse me!" I said, as the other person, a young man, swore angrily, and Grigorii turned and whispered, "Quiet!" Whispers of "Quiet!" came from another side of the clearing, and I realized all at once that there were four or five people besides us sitting, standing, or crouching among the bushes to listen to the nightingale. We sat down on the damp ground, and for almost an hour lingered there in a state between sleeping and waking. This was the first nightingale I had ever heard; listening to it was, I reflected, not the experience of an American in Russia, but the experience of an American in the Old World that has woven poetry and folklore around this powerful night-singer. But in what other country, I wondered, would seven or eight people be grouped around a tree, attending as carefully to the song of a bird as Americans do to their stereos? I thought of Turgenev's essay "About Nightingales," which in the matter-of-fact words of an old huntsman (one of Turgenev's house serfs, who actually narrated much of it to the writer) celebrates the national passion for the bird; it describes the delicate craft of the nightingale hunters, seasoned woodsmen who showed a meticulous, emotional appreciation of birdsong—and the extravagant market for the birds they captured, some great singers going for as much as a thousand rubles apiece.

The song I heard was harsher than I'd expected, full of sharp clicks and near-guttural whirring sounds that broke abruptly into a repeated liquid phrase, like a rough landscape tumbling down to a thread of a stream. It was not sweet; it was loud and disturbingly wild, a fierce incantation that gave a curiously uncanny quality to the mild blossoming woods. I remembered that Turgenev's huntsman said that nightingale hunters occasionally used black magic to help ensure capture of their birds.

"Listen," breathed Grigorii after a while. "That's a cuckoo he's imitating! And there's a phrase that sounds like a robin . . . Wait, I'll tell you. This is a good nightingale, a powerful one." Edging forward on hands and knees, he pointed out the tiny silhouette of the bird among the twigs. His angular dark figure in his bureaucrat's suit looked entirely absurd there in the starlit clearing, but his voice was reverent, almost ecstatic. It occurred to me that this was the most human we'd ever seen him—on his knees in front of a nightingale.

Later, when we'd left the clearing and crept up the muddy path to the lit walkway, Grigorii removed his comical taped glasses and unashamedly wiped his eyes. As we turned back to the pointed dark tower of the dormitory, with its blinking red star, we could hear, in the woods along the river, the faraway voices of what sounded like a dozen nightingales. The crowd of strollers had vanished, and we could see only a few couples keeping to the shadows. The thin moon had vanished, and the stars above us resembled drops of mercury—very moist and bright and heavy. "What a night, what a night!" said Grigorii with a noisy sigh. "Ever since I was small, my parents and I have gone out wandering to hear the nightingales. My dear sister, too. You won't believe it, but I have a short recording of nightingale song that I can play on my tape player. I listen to it when I'm alone, after I've finished my studies. It makes me think of spring and the forest."

At the Dacha

The young movie actress was neither as vulgar nor as unattractive as Seryozha had described her. In fact, there was something so taking about her as she sat on the shady front porch of the dacha, threading raw mutton onto a shashlik skewer, that it was possible to see that Seryozha's unflattering description had been on the order of a preventive charm, a device to halt the development of an attraction he already felt. The actress, whose name was Lyubov Alekseyevna, was very popular—a star who wore rococo wigs in the lavish costume melodramas cranked out by Mosfilm. Her own hair was straight brown, deliciously plain. She had a narrow, slightly feral face, with the luminous fair skin of youthful Russian women, and she displayed, on introduction, a surprising reticence, broken only by a vivid, eager laugh. Snobbish Seryozha had described her as a *plebka*—a little plebeian wench—but I was aware only of an absence of the clumsy affectations that spoil so many Russian girls of "good" family. Twenty-six and divorced, she was said to be very rich. She was the only Russian woman I have ever met who owned and drove a sports car. Whenever she laughed, the men in the group turned their heads toward her in an almost invisible tropism, and Seryozha's thin cheeks flushed angrily.

This was about a week ago. Twelve were there that afternoon, a number of us strangers to one another. I dwell on the actress because any congregation of people has its central, defining point, and she was ours. The dacha was a big green wooden house sprawled among pine trees, lilacs, and red-currant bushes in the town of M., outside Moscow. Seryozha and Tom and I had come here at the invitation of Anya, Seryozha's dear friend. Anya had told us that there would be interesting people here—"actors, artists." Seryozha had smiled at this, an annoying smile of doubt, and he had also been acting obnoxious since we met him that morning at the Moscow train station. Anya privately told me the reason. A few months earlier Lyubov Alekseyevna had met Seryozha through a friend and had immediately conceived a romantic interest in him—a fact that in Moscow artistic society, with its dense network of gossip, had not remained secret for long. Skittish as usual, and sensitive because of his recent divorce, Seryozha had reacted with horror. Now he balked at visiting the dacha, since he feared the actress might be there.

We finally had to push him onto the train. All during the long trip through the Moscow suburbs, he sat sulking on the hard wooden seat next to Anya. Rarely have two friends seemed more unsuited: Seryozha, the dilettante descendant of aristocratic intellectuals, with his elfin features, his dandyish black-market clothes, his long, pale, morbidly nervous hands; Anya, part Polish Jew, frequenter of peasant markets, breathless reader of romantic stories in cheap magazines, with her black bangs, her glowering glance, her round body, and her shrill, warm, tumultuous voice. The two of them long ago passed the stage of being lovers; now they share a friendship "of the bosom"—an alliance, for Russians, much more passionate, jealous, and binding than simple romance.

We got off the train at one of the small concrete rural stations where there is usually an ice cream kiosk, a postcard stand, and a tiny old woman selling sunflower seeds from a sack. We walked toward the dacha settlement through a rough green field where several goats were tethered. It was one of those fantastically lush May days that the devious Russian spring looses suddenly upon the countryside. The sun was strong, and the air—raw and stinging through April—felt like a new element: superbuoyant, caressing. The fields that just a few weeks earlier had been seas of mud dotted with gray heaps of melting ice were now shaggy with buttercups; far off we could see bluish pinewoods checkered with the light green of young birch foliage. All around us walked families bound for the settlement, their newly bared arms already reddening in the sun. Everyone was lugging big bundles of gardening tools, provisions, and tomato seedlings. A tall stoop-shouldered youth passed us, carrying a wicker basket from which chicks peeped feebly; from time to time he lifted the cover and peered inside with such an expression of dull-witted solicitude that Seryozha began to giggle. "Village idiot, village idiot!" he whispered, poking Anya. "Look at his ears!" An old woman, still wearing a winter head shawl and bowed beneath the weight of a huge green rucksack, stared hard at me and at Seryozha's black-market clothes. "Look at the foreigners," she said to her companions.

At the dacha, everyone was very fashionable, with foreign jeans and American catch phrases like "Okay" and "Forget it." The woman who owned the place was rumored—like half the people in Moscow—to be part Jewish and to be planning to emigrate to New York. Her name was Svetlana; she was an anxious-looking, fresh-faced brunette of thirty, faintly stout, who used cosmetics with the skill of an American secretary. With considerable pride she motioned us to a table on which stood several bottles of Chianti and a few cans of California almonds. "Darling Aldo brought these to me from the diplomatic store," she said. Aldo was an Italian businessman, short and bald, with a shy grin and a pair of enormous sinewy arms. Svetlana was obviously thrilled at being able to achieve what for a Moscow hostess is the utmost in chic: to display several foreigners at a private gathering. Besides Aldo and Lyubov Alekseyevna, there was a thin, surly artist named Volodya; a plump Ukrainian poet with protruding cheeks that nearly hid his tiny gray eyes; a plain girl who was a friend of Lyubov Alekseyevna and whom she addressed as Olya; and two villainous-looking old women, painted, penciled, and dyed, who worked for Mosfilm.

As soon as he could, Seryozha dragged me out into the side yard. "I won't stay," he whispered frantically. "Let's leave, please! My second cousin has a dacha around here. We could catch a bus right down the road."

"That would be rude," I said. "There's a meal prepared for us."

"They're vulgar people. It wouldn't matter." He was in a state. He has been in various nervous states since his particularly nasty divorce and the resulting traumatic encounter with the KGB.

Just then Anya came down the dacha steps and wandered over to us, lifting her feet high in the moist grass to avoid staining her Spanish espadrilles. (She had spent ten minutes on the train explaining her black-market maneuverings to get them.) She slipped her arm around Seryozha and tickled him. "Don't worry, Seryozhenka!" she said. "If Lyubov Alekseyevna attacks you, we can always say we're engaged."

Seryozha gave her a furious glare and abandoned his efforts to get away. He put on a bright, false smile and began to chatter about Mick Jagger. Was it true that Mick and Bianca had split up? Who was the other woman? What did Western magazines have to say about the split?

Anya whispered to me, "He's such an infant. I don't know why I love him so much. Igor thinks I'm crazy." Anya's husband, Igor, is a tall balding artist who treats Seryozha lovingly and patiently. He had always remained so much in the background that it wasn't until well after I'd met her that I realized she was married.

The three of us walked through the yard—past a nettle patch, an outhouse whose open door revealed an interior papered with British and American cigarette ads, a rusted bicycle, an ancient wooden arbor, and a caved-in greenhouse—to a small, weedy pond. The banks of the pond were thick with buttercups, and a strong swampy smell rose from the water. "Careful," said Seryozha, taking a finicky step backward. Anya squealed as her new shoes got wet. Over the back fence, which was just beyond the pond, we could see into the yards of other dachas—all big, flimsy wooden houses like the one behind us, most with the same herringbone pattern of boards, painted gray or blue or dark green. In some gardens, stunted apple trees still held a few white blossoms; in the fall, I knew, they would produce the small, gnarled, half-wild apples that friends are always pressing upon you, fruit which is always unexpectedly sweet and juicy. There were people in all the yards: children playing, men and women gardening or drawing water from wells. In the yard directly in front of us, two middle-aged men and a woman were sunbathing comfortably in their underwear on newspapers spread out on the grass. Dragonflies and water striders zigzagged across the pond and the sky slowly turned hazy. I dreamily watched the teeming life in the back yards and the pond, and thought about the long, slow, cold months that had gone before. How suddenly everything had changed! My shoulders were still compensating for the weight of a sheepskin coat.

Anya said, "My uncle had a dacha near here. The same kind of place: big, creaky, buried in pines. We had a good time there when we were little. But he sold it. Most dachas are a nuisance— no plumbing, no insulation. And it gets boring, summer after summer, with nothing to do but eat raspberries and gossip."

I went inside again, through the back door. In the kitchen, the two painted old women were washing bunches of Georgian herbs in a bucket. Their excessive makeup seemed even more ridiculous and exaggerated in that long room of raw wooden slats with its tiny single-burner iron stove and the bunches of camomile hung up to dry near the ceiling. The old women's wrinkled hands, however, moved with the skill common to all *babushki*, wringing off stems, breaking leaves into big chipped enamel basins. And their voices were traditional—gossipy, mumbling. I wandered through the two main rooms, which were high-ceilinged and unevenly lined with woodgrain paper. As in other dachas I'd seen, there were only the bare essentials of furniture—an ancient couch-bed covered in rubbed velvet, a case of mildewed books, a modern television set, and an enormous square dining table with a ring of mismatched chairs.

On the porch, Aldo and Volodya were cooking shashlik over a short-legged iron brazier. Seated on a battered divan in a corner, with our hostess and the plain-faced Olya, was Lyubov Alekseyevna. I went over and sat with them. The actress reached out and touched my blouse. "It's so pretty," she said in English.

I felt flattered, and very happy to be near her. One of the most pleasant things about Russian women is the unfeigned delight they take in other women's appearances. "I like your dress," I said.

"My dress—oh, it's American!" she exclaimed, lapsing back into Russian. She got up and started to twirl around and model the dress with unself-conscious vanity, like a little girl parading before a circle of adults. The dress was gathered white cotton in the so-called peasant style, and her tiny red slippers had laces that tied around her ankles. "I have trouble when I wear it in town. You know. People are so backward. All the old *babushki* say 'My God!' whenever I wear anything the slightest bit stylish. What business of theirs is it what I wear?"

The other women murmured sympathetically. They knew what it was like to try to wear Western styles—especially a peasant look—in a city where real peasants still clump through the streets in felt boots.

"Lyubochka, your hair!" our hostess exclaimed admiringly.

The actress smiled and patted her sleek locks. I noticed that her hands were small and childlike and that her red fingernails were bitten down to the quick. "They do it at the studio," she said, walking over to peer at herself in a tarnished mirror. "They have everything you could think of there: makeup, permanents—nice, modern, American, or French . . ."

In her voice now I could hear just a trace of the coarseness that Seryozha had accused her of; it gave her speech a not unpleasant edge, like nap on a fabric, and her pirouetting vanity was oddly charming: it became her, like the red shoes.

Anya came along and drew me out onto the steps. "She's really exquisite, isn't she? Perfect for Seryozha—the fool! And she's got that car and a wonderful big apartment off Kutuzovsky Prospekt."

"You really want this for him?" I said.

"Of course," said Anya. "He needs someone to take care of him."

It occurred to me that the possessiveness of her friendship with Seryozha was so complete that there was not even any question of competition. Anya grinned at me, and her eyes sparkled. She brought her lips close to my ear, and I smelled her Eau de rochas. (All Moscow women who have access to foreign-currency stores are wearing it this year.) A Western scent, but her thrilled whisper was that of the countless peasant women I overheard on the tram each day. "Do you know why Lyubov Alekseyevna divorced her first husband? My dear, he used to beat her terribly, just terribly . . ."

By the time the shashlik was ready, the day had grown very hot. A solid, moist, pine-scented heat seemed to be pressing the walls of the dacha, and the hard blue sky of the morning had turned white. It was two o'clock. The twelve of us sat around the enormous table, which held plates heaped with shashlik. The spiced charcoal scent of the roast meat was very strong. I sat between Anya and Volodya. Through the screen I could see into the back yard of another dacha, where a sunburned fat man wearing a small white cotton hat was very slowly and carefully washing a car. Through some wizardry of seating, Seryozha had been placed next to Lyubov Alekseyevna; on the other side of the actress sat Aldo. Lyubov Alekseyevna chatted gaily with the Italian, and he paid her ponderous compliments in his excellent Russian. She had grease on her chin. We were all a bit greasy from the shashlik, which we ate with the sharp dark-green herb the Georgians call *kindzi*. The hostess apologized for the lack of napkins and passed around a roll of toilet paper instead; this was the occasion of jokes and several toasts. We emptied our ill-matched glasses of Chianti and Armenian cognac, and perspired happily. After three toasts the morose Volodya suddenly brightened and began to talk in a swift, monotonous undertone. I learned with some surprise that he was engaged to marry our hostess.

"Congratulations!" I said.

His face darkened. "Shut up, shut up!" he said rapidly in English. "There are people here who shouldn't know about this yet."

I sank back abashed in my chair, reflecting with some irritation on the scope of feud and intrigue within the smallest Russian group. While we were outside, Seryozha had told me a convoluted story about one of the painted old women, whom he despised and distrusted because she had been the mistress of . . . and then of . . . but had really been suspected of . . .

Anya, Lyubov Alekseyevna, and Olya were teasing Aldo about his ignorance of Russian women. "You'll never understand us, never!" they were saying shrilly. "Not even if you live here for twenty years!"

I looked at Seryozha, who was wincing at the tone and subject of this conversation as if he were being dragged over hot coals. Unlike the Italian, who had bloomed perceptibly with the oily meal and the strident feminine surroundings, Seryozha looked half destroyed with discomfort. His feline face was pale and wore the same annoying false smile he had adopted in the yard. I had a momentary mental glimpse of Seryozha's curly head framed in the high white stock of one of Pushkin's heroes, and sighed to myself. He would never fit in anywhere, least of all in the brash land-scapes of fashionable Soviet society. And what a shame, I thought, that he resisted Lyubov Alekseyevna, who could pay for the dream world he loved to live in. He sat beside her, ignoring her, with a constraint in the muscles of his left side as if a concrete wall had been erected there. Lyubov Alekseyevna, with an actress' facility, managed to divide her behavior down the middle, so that half of her was the delicious hoyden who stuck parsley in Aldo's hair and half was a delicate girl of sudden blushes, full of care for her white dress. At one point she asked Seryozha to cut her meat, speaking with a piteous timidity that must have sent a chasten-ing pang through him, for whom discourtesy heads the list of cardinal sins. He cut the meat for her graciously enough.

"Why did you ask him to do it, and not me?" Aldo asked plaintively.

Lyubov Alekseyevna shook back her pretty hair and gave a strange shriek of laughter, which made Seryozha wince. "Because he's a Russian man and understands what a Russian woman wants!" she answered.

After we had carried our dishes out to the kitchen, the hostess went to draw a few buckets of water from the well. The two old women were busy unwrapping some jam tarts in the pantry, and Volodya was feeding twigs into a samovar by the back steps. I sat on a little bench with Anya and Seryozha and watched him stuff the twigs into the angled copper pipe. The samovar sputtered pleasantly, and Volodya, grown unexpectedly cheerful, chuckled to himself as he tended it. The weather had turned cloudy and very humid, and the blue smoke pouring from the pipe stayed low, creeping over the currant bushes. The smoke made Seryozha sneeze. He rubbed his eyes and turned to Anya. "This is unpleasant. We've stayed here long enough," he said. "May we please leave now?"

Anya gave him a hard look. "Not until after the tea is served. How can you not be ashamed, Seryozhenka, to be so rude?"

"Why can't we leave?" Seryozha persisted.

"Because." Anya threw a pebble at the samovar.

"Why, my little piglet?" Seryozha leaned his elbow on Anya's shoulder and batted his eyes amorously. "Piglet" is his favorite name for Anya.

"Because of our hostess! Think of how offended you would be if guests came and stayed only three or four hours. You know, at times I can't believe in this blue blood you're supposed to have. I'm half peasant, and I have better manners than you have."

I walked over to Lyubov Alekseyevna's friend Olya, who was sitting on a battered wooden garden chair. She had done little all afternoon but form part of the chorus of admiration that surrounded her brilliant friend. She was a tall, gawky girl with a gap-toothed smile and unexpectedly fat legs, which protruded from her short print dress like two pink poles. Like Anya, she wore Spanish espadrilles, which she regarded complacently and caressed often, on the pretext of adjusting the strings. I picked a buttercup and showed her how American children hold the blossom under a companion's chin: "Do you like butter?" It was getting too dark for the game. A slate-colored wall of cloud had sprung up from somewhere, and a hard wind suddenly blew through the dacha grove, scattering the pile of sticks that Volodya had set up by the samovar and sending a newspaper flapping across the bushes. We all dashed for the house. Volodya picked up the samovar and hurried up the steps as the first big raindrops came down. From the front porch, I could see underwear-clad sunbathers running up the dirt road from the field. From far away came a bleat from one of the tethered goats. There was a rumble of thunder, a slight pause, and then the rain, coming down in a solid whitish sheet. We guests stood clustered by the windows in the darkened house, stunned into silence by the suddenness and ferocity of the storm. Outside, the pine branches bobbed in the downpour like the necks of restless horses. In a corner of the room, a TV performance of the ballet *The Sleeping Beauty* was interrupted by crackling static as lightning flickered over the sky. Someone murmured, "Capricious weather. A real Russian storm."

When we sat down to tea, one thing was obvious that had been in the back of all our minds since the first drops of rain. This was that Lyubov Alekseyevna and Aldo were trapped somewhere outside together. We all avoided one another's eyes. Olya said in a low voice that they had taken a walk to the river. One of the old women cackled, and said, "That sly Italian! He probably arranged this storm!" At this, Seryozha blushed still more furiously than he had when the actress filled the room with her laughter.

The rain continued. We sat around the table and ate pieces of jam tart with glasses of tea. The wall of rain and leaves outside made the air stifling. I found myself staring at the samovar—domesticated now, with the crooked, smoking pipe removed and a fat blue teapot nestled in its place. With the actress gone, things seemed flat. All afternoon the little group had arranged its physical and mental attitudes around Lyubov Alekseyevna, as a crystal blossoms around some center point; now, so late, we had to find different affinities, different ways of arranging ourselves. It was depressing, too, to find the filaments of romantic possibility which had enlivened the afternoon knotted so abruptly. Most of us were silent, picking moodily at our jam tarts. The hostess' small son (from a previous marriage) came running into the room, begging his mother to eat a piece of tart with him in the kitchen. "Only with you, Mama, only you!" She gave him a kiss and left the room with him. Only Seryozha seemed perversely enlivened by the situation. He took helping after helping of tart and chattered with an irresponsible gaiety about Mick and Bianca. Looking at his mobile face, which needed only powder to turn him into a Pierrot, I thought what a complicated mechanism his frail soul was. Who would ever understand him? I glanced over at Anya and shook my head. She shrugged.

The storm was over by the time we had to start back to the station at M. It is hard to describe the odor that met us when we walked down the rain-soaked wooden steps of the dacha: the entire spirit of the vegetable world—that bushy mass that Russians call, reverently, "the green"—seemed to hang distilled and dizzying in the wet air. The path we had followed through the field was now a shallow brown stream; we took off our shoes and made our way cautiously through sopping ankle-high grass that was full of the smell of wild onions. The dacha community was coming back to life. At one gate an old woman in a newspaper hat stood calling "Alyo-sha! Alyo-sha!" By the side of the road a man in shorts wiped raindrops off a new Russian Fiat. A pinkish rift had appeared in the dark clouds in the west, and the woods seemed to smoke with moisture in the new light. We caught sight of two figures walking across the field toward us. "No, it's not, it can't be, this is too good," said Anya. It was indeed Lyubov Alekseyevna and the Italian. They waved, and came toward us.

The Italian looked damp and uncomfortable, with his shirt clinging to his shoulders and his hair in strings, but Lyubov Alekseyevna looked sprightly and fresh. Watching her come across the field with her little red shoes dangling from one hand, I understood for the first time her formidable popularity in the films that I had never seen. "What a beauty!" Anya breathed into my ear.

When the two of them had reached us, Aldo began to say something, but Lyubov Alekseyevna coolly interrupted him and turned her clear greenish gaze on Seryozha. "Are you going already?" she asked softly.

Seryozha flushed and looked down at his feet. "It's quite late and I have things to do," he answered in a gruff voice. I had never seen the adroit Seryozha so churlish. It was evident that he realized the impression he was making and that it angered him, for he raised his eyes suddenly and gave her a haughty glare that would have quelled a less confident young woman. But Lyubov

Alekseyevna looked at him calmly and said, in the same soft voice, "It's very unusual, you know, to leave so early on a Sunday. I'm afraid you didn't enjoy our company very much."

"Not at all true, not at all," Seryozha said smoothly and angrily, his voice under control but his face twitching a bit. "I merely have an urgent project under way at home."

They looked oddly similar as they argued—the actress who so often played noble roles, and Seryozha, with theatricality evident in every gesture of his slender body. I saw clearly that each of them, in some mysterious way, compelled the other, and that there would be other meetings, other dialogues. A little later we all said goodbye, and I turned to watch Lyubov Alekseyevna's white American dress grow small and disappear into the dacha grove. Seryozha was raging as we walked toward the station. "That *plebka!* How dare she reprimand me for bad manners when she herself is an exercise in bad taste! Imagine her sitting out the storm with that comic-opera Italian! I bet her foreign passport is all nicely arranged by now!"

We reached the station platform and started down the slippery iron steps. All around us, a crowd with sunburned faces and muddy shoes carrying big, damp bunches of lilac and newspaper parcels of early lettuce. It was about seven o'clock. Anya took Seryozha's arm and said, "You *were* rude, Seryozhenka. I think it was terrible. And to such interesting people, such a beautiful girl. Any other man would be overjoyed to have her in love with him. Why did you act that way?"

Seryozha gave her a squeeze. "Because you are more beautiful," he said frivolously. "My piglet. My wooden egg."

Anya pushed his hand away. "What am I going to do with you, fool?" she said—flashing him, however, her swift, glowing smile from under her bangs.

"Drown me. I'm hopeless," said Seryozha, inspecting a damp spot on the side of his jeans. "What a terrible day! We should have gone to my cousin's place. They really know how to receive guests. What vulgar people there were at this place! And, especially, what horrible food!"

The Moscow train arrived. We climbed on and were carried

through wet fields, through pine and birch woods, past quarries and factories where red-lettered banners urged us to "bring to life" the decisions of the Twenty-fifth Party Congress. The train passed a few fishermen standing beside muddy ponds and streams; it stopped in industrial towns full of shoddy high rises; it skirted collective farms and decaying wooden villages with names like Daisy Spot and Muddy Place, where one or two old men were likely to be braving the hot weather in worn-out fur hats. Over the broad, mild landscape, with its modest hills and flatlands and its occasional shallow ravine, hung a stupendous archipelago of sunset clouds; through the window, in a sharp, fresh stream, blew the intoxicating scent of the countryside. We passed innumerable dacha communities: some brand-new, mere collections of varnished boxes set close on a field; some older, larger, set in weedy yards within pine groves, like the dacha we had visited. I stared at these places and wondered about the inhabitants. What atmosphere of feud and flirtation were they imbibing along with tea and vodka? And was there anywhere another girl like Lyubov Alekseyevna? I glanced at Seryozha, who had leaned his cheek against the window; he gave me a sweet, enigmatic grin. A little later we started an argument about Bulgakov, and kept at it until the bright evening faded over the woods and the train pulled up under the lights of Moscow.

Boston

The entries, notes, and fragments of my journal come to an end with the description of the afternoon at the dacha. It would be pointless to describe our last few weeks in Russia, filled as they were with packing and dismal trips to small offices where we conducted ritual breast-pounding arguments with bureaucrats about procuring visas and train tickets to Warsaw, our first stop after Moscow. These weeks were also filled with the smoky fragrance of the lilacs our friends brought us, as over and over, like lovers who draw out their farewells, we met to drink a last glass together, take one more stroll in the woods. On the eve of our departure, we sat with Valerii by the duck pond in front of the deserted Chinese Embassy, and he showed me how to weave an old-fashioned garland of meadow grass. I hung it on the wall of our bedroom in the dormitory; the last image I have of that room, which had come to seem so curiously dear, is of the hanging green garland, the window open to a soft current of spring air, the bronze flag outside.

Our departure had the correct note of absurdity: there were suddenly no taxis to take us to the train station, so we caught a ride with a lumbering off-duty cement truck, whose driver was eager enough to make a few extra rubles. Rima and Vasia were waiting for us at the station, but there was no time for the traditional farewell drink, no time for anything except a few hurried kisses and photographs. I have one of those pictures now: the two beautiful bony faces look somehow washed out in the vaporous sunlight of that June afternoon, as if they were dream images already starting to disperse. Rima—to whom I'd given nearly all my clothes—was wearing a dress of mine; for a moment it seemed that I had left myself in Russia.

Through the afternoon and evening, as the train rolled away from Moscow toward the Polish border at Brest-Litovsk, Tom and I felt a gradual lightening of mood, a sense of celebration that by nightfall seemed almost unbearable; we found ourselves laughing and rolling around the compartment as if we were drunk. Both of us had a crazy sense of freedom; we felt released from a subtle and deadly confinement, which, we only now realized, had sapped our spirits for ten months.

The next morning we arrived in a Warsaw mobbed with tourists and filled with a holiday rejoicing incomprehensible to us until we learned something that Russian newspapers had neglected to mention: Pope John Paul II had that day begun his historic visit to Poland. For us to emerge from Russia at this hour of mad festivity seemed an almost miraculous conjunction of events. I am afraid that we took the Polish holiday to be entirely our own—ignoring the pontiff, acting as if the streamers and confetti in spring colors of yellow and white, the cheering, the music over loudspeakers, the ecstatic gladness on the faces of the tall, fair-haired people had all been arranged for us.

In a few days we traveled south to the Aegean, to awaken further from Russia in the purest, most logical light in the world. It was only months later that we looked back, to discover how much we missed life in the tower.

As for the people described in this journal, many of them have kept up a tenuous contact with Tom and me through the channels that every American with Russian friends knows well: hearsay from recent Soviet émigrés; second-hand greetings delivered by strangers who have visited the Soviet Union; the rare letter that like an elusive bird manages to find its way through the barriers. I have learned that Rima and Vasia have received permission to emigrate, may, in fact, already be on their way to the America we discussed so often in Vasia's dark kitchen. Valerii, the friend we took with us to the Marine Bar one night, wrote in a note filled with cryptic English slang that he was surviving. Anna and Volodya are apparently still eating well, even through the shortages that followed the Olympics. Grigorii is completing a journalism internship in Siberia—a post for which he, naturally, volunteered; he writes pleasant articles about wildlife, and is moving ever higher in the *apparat*.

Other friends are unwilling or unable to communicate. An American student who tried to locate Seryozha found that he has disappeared. This book is meant in part as a greeting to Seryozha and other silent ones. Their faces, instead of fading in my memory, have only gotten clearer.

About the Author

ANDREA LEE was born in Philadelphia, and received her bachelor's and master's degrees in English from Harvard University. In 1978 she and her husband spent a year in Russia, where Ms. Lee began writing *Russian Journal*. In 1980 she received the Front Page Award for Distinguished Journalism by the Newswomen's Club of New York. Ms. Lee and her husband live in Rome, Italy.

VINTAGE BIOGRAPHY AND AUTOBIOGRAPHY